Mediated Images of the South

Mediated Images of the South

The Portrayal of Dixie in Popular Culture

Edited by Alison Slade, Dedria Givens-Carroll, Amber Narro

LEXINGTON BOOKS
Lanham • Boulder • New York • Toronto • Plymouth, UK

Published by Lexington Books
A wholly owned subsidiary of The Rowman & Littlefield Publishing Group, Inc.
4501 Forbes Boulevard, Suite 200, Lanham, Maryland 20706
http://www.lexingtonbooks.com

Estover Road, Plymouth PL6 7PY, United Kingdom

Copyright © 2012 by Lexington Books

All rights reserved. No part of this book may be reproduced in any form or by any electronic or mechanical means, including information storage and retrieval systems, without written permission from the publisher, except by a reviewer who may quote passages in a review.

British Library Cataloguing in Publication Information Available

Library of Congress Cataloging-in-Publication Data

Mediated images of the South : the portrayal of Dixie in popular culture / edited by Alison Slade, Dedria Givens-Carroll, Amber Narro.
  p. cm.
  Summary: "Mediated Images of the South : The Portrayal of Dixie in Popular Culture, edited by Alison Slade, Dedria Givens-Carroll, and Amber Narro, seeks to explore and understand the impact of the image of the Southerner within mass communication and popular culture by looking at images in politics, film, television, public relations, advertising, sports and social media. While there is a long list of successful southern politicians, historical figures, businessmen and women, actors and actresses, sports figures and other national and world leaders, this edited collection finds that there is still work to be done to present southerners as capable and educated"—Provided by publisher.
  Includes bibliographical references and index.
  ISBN 978-0-7391-6715-1 (hardback)—ISBN 978-0-7391-7265-0 (electronic)
  1. Southern States—In popular culture. 2. Southern States—Civilization. I. Slade, Alison, 1977– II. Givens-Carroll, Dedria, 1960– III. Narro, Amber J.
F209.M43 2011
975—dc23
                                                                            2011038578

∞™ The paper used in this publication meets the minimum requirements of American National Standard for Information Sciences—Permanence of Paper for Printed Library Materials, ANSI/NISO Z39.48-1992.

Printed in the United States of America

I do not see plays, because I can nap at *home* for *free*. And I don't see movies 'cause they're trash, and they got nothin' but naked *people* in 'em! And I don't *read* books, 'cause if they're any good, they're gonna *make* 'em into a miniseries.

—Ouiser Boudreaux, Steel Magnolias

Contents

Introduction: Southern Images in Popular Culture   1
Alison Slade

Chapter 1: An Acceptable Stereotype: The Southern Image in Television Programming   5
Alison Slade and Amber J. Narro

Chapter 2: An Ethical Inquiry of the Blue Collar Comedy Tour's Appropriation and Commodification of Redneck Culture   21
Mark Glantz

Chapter 3: Hip Hop, Commerce, and the "Death" of Southern Black Manhood   41
Franklin E. Forts Jr.

Chapter 4: The Rise, Fall, and Rise of the Kingfish—How Southern Politicians Are Successful in the Face of Overwhelming Stereotypes   57
Kevin Unter, John Sutherlin, and Joshua Stockley

Chapter 5: Magnolias and Manufacturing: Southern Imagery in Mississippi's Promotional Publications, 1945-1955   89
Burt Buchanan

Chapter 6: Recognizing the Past, Celebrating Change: The "Mississippi Believe It!" Campaign Redefines the South   107
Wendy Atkins-Sayre

Chapter 7: Poor as Job's Turkey: Back to the Land as a Rhetoric of   123
Authenticity in Foxfire's Appalachia
Jason Waite

Chapter 8: The Trivialization of Traditional Southern   147
Religion in the Film *The Grass Harp*
Michael P. Graves

Chapter 9: College Football Fanaticism and Online Communities: 159
A Reflection of Football as a Religious Experience in
the South
Dedria Givens-Carroll and Alison Slade

Bibliography   177

Index   195

About the Contributors   199

Southern Images in Popular Culture

Poor white trash. Racecar drivers. Drunkards. Racists. The South has heard all the stereotypes. Often perpetuated in popular media, these classifications also are known to the world. In a Google search of "southern celebrities," the first two topics were "Stupid Celebrity Gossip: 10 Hottest Southern Celebrity Babes" and "Redneck—Wikipedia, the free encyclopedia." Television shows such as *Reba* and *My Name Is Earl* often show Southerners in the stereotypical slow-talking, slow-moving fashion of people who care little about moving up the corporate ladder or progressive lifestyles. Characters are often shown living in modest homes or below modest homes, and these characters have reflective attitudes. Most notable of these programs include *The Andy Griffith Show, The Beverly Hillbillies, Gomer Pyle, U.S.M.C., Green Acres, Petticoat Junction, The Real McCoys* and *Mayberry RFD*. However, within the last decade, new programs reflecting the Southern image have arrived, such as *My Big Redneck Wedding, Country Fried Home Videos, Real Beverly Hillbillies, Paula Dean, Down Home with the Neelys* and *Reba*. Are the new programs featuring Southerners truly a far cry from the Southern image that began on television in the 1960s? The answer is perhaps both yes and no. These "new and improved" images are not limited to television programming, but also appear in film, advertising, books, public relations campaigns and political discourse and image. Notably, the division of race, class and gender are still portrayed unequally and negatively in the South. Therefore, this anthology seeks to explore and understand the impact of the image of the Southerner within mass communication and popular culture.

The first part of the book will examine television programming and stereotypical characters in the South. In chapter 1, Alison Slade and Amber Narro explore the stereotyped images of the Southerner within television programming in general. This chapter explores how these stereotyped images are still in place today and, by placing the television programs of the past against more recent programs depicting Southerners, argues these portrayals are one of the last remaining acceptable stereotypes in modern mainstream media. In chapter 2, Mark Glantz offers a critical inquiry examining the processes of appropriation and commodification at work in the rhetoric of the *Blue Collar Comedy Tour* film series. Glantz takes the reader through the *Blue Collar Comedy Tour*'s stereotypical "real" cast and those who are the punchlines of their comedic routines.

In chapter 3, Franklin Forts further explores popular culture through an examination of the development of Southern Hip Hop music within the larger post-civil rights phenomenon of Southern blacks claiming a distinctive identity that is both African American and Southern. This is done through an investigation of the discourse used to mediate representations of black Southern masculinity within Southern Hip Hop.

The anthology looks through a more historical lens in chapters 4 through 7. The image of the Southerner in politics is the focus of chapter 4, as Kevin Unter, John Sutherlin and Joshua Stockley seek to answer the question of bias regarding Southern politicians. Through language analysis, the authors take an in-depth look into the Southern "culture" and how the media itself (in all its forms) has inadvertently made the South a dominant player in national politics, oftentimes allowing these politicians to actually have character development— hero to villain and back again.

Traditional history and political science aren't the only avenues of historical analysis for the Southern image. Authors also examine advertising and public relations campaigns as well, answering how Southerners attract tourists and present themselves. In chapter 5, Burt Buchanan takes a look at the Mississippi manufacturing publications of the 1950s and their use of Southern imagery. Wendy Atkins-Sayre also delves into the history and current issues in Mississippi public relations in chapter 6, with an in-depth analysis of the "Mississippi Believe It!" campaign, created in 2006 to counterbalance negative images of the state. The chapter argues that in attempting to redefine Southern identity (both in Southerners and in popular images of the South), the "Mississippi Believe It!" campaign effectively pulls from multiple strands of identity, and articulates a new identity that acknowledges cultural pride and recognizes change.

In chapter 7, Jason Waite explores the 1960s Foxfire project of Southern Appalachia and argues the Foxfire project rhetorically constructed an alternative to mainstream representations of Appalachia and then deployed that alternative as the "authentic" Appalachia. Southern Appalachia, and the South in general, has a long history of being marginalized, of subjugation to alterity.

Chapter 8 turns the focus to ideas surrounding Southern religion, as Michael Graves analyzes Charles Matthau's artfully crafted motion picture taken from Truman Capote's short novel, *The Grass Harp*. This chapter illustrates how the film valorizes nature-religion and trivializes two strains of Southern Protestant Christianity: (1) the traditional small town congregational culture, and (2) the "tent revival" tradition. The chapter also raises questions about the differing capacities of written and filmic narrative to present religious expression fairly. Finally, chapter 9 explores the unique relationship between college football and fans in the Southern United States. It traces the literature comparing these relationships to religious experiences, and argues social media have become the new houses of worship and deification of the key figures in college football in the South.

While there is a long list of successful Southern politicians, historical figures, businessmen and women, actors and actresses, sports figures and other national and world leaders, this edited volume finds there is still work to be done to present Southerners, overall, as capable and educated. Stereotypical images are not only being used by outsiders, but some of the South's most famous and notable individuals are using these stereotypes to promote themselves as being "real" Southerners. While there are proud traditions in the South, not all of them involve slow-talking arguments about Friday night football and carefree Sunday dinners at grandma's dirt-road mobile home positioned on cinder blocks. It will be interesting to see how and if these pictures change over time or if these images will continue to define and monetize the South within the media.

Chapter One
An Acceptable Stereotype: The Southern Image in Television Programming
Alison Slade and Amber J. Narro

The South has a peculiar place in American history. Its (mythologized) heritage, and the enduring socio-economic patterns set by the aftermath of Reconstruction, has generated prominent ideological templates through which race and class relations in the United States have been mapped and contested. Over the course of the twentieth century, the South has been recurrently portrayed in the broader national media as a benighted and backward region that mirrored the presumed prejudices and character flaws of its poor white rural inhabitants.[1]

Images of Southerners on television programming remain a constant figure of popular culture. The portrayal of Southerners as slow or dumb due to accent and dialect, or the depiction of the assumed living conditions in the Southern region as humorous, is historically grounded in the assumption this stereotype is accurate and acceptable. Scholars and media critics have long been concerned with the media's portrayal of stereotypes in general. A program offering Southern humor, no matter how debasing or degrading to the Southern image, is hardly met with a grimace. Yet programs featuring stereotypes of gender, race or class are likely to anger and threaten societal groups. Why does the negative Southern image continue to be accepted in our culture? Organizations such as Monitor South, developed in the early 1950s, is an attempt to combat these negative images. Though these groups were short-lived and ineffective, as historically these depictions have remained a part of the visual media fabric, they call attention to the problems inherent with placing Southerners in a negative light. This chapter explores how these stereotyped images are still in place today and, by placing the television programs of the past against morerecent programs depicting Southerners, argues these portrayals are one of the last remaining acceptable stereotypes in modern mainstream media.

Ideology, Myth and Stereotypes

In order to understand the pervasive nature of stereotypes, one must first explore how television programming utilizes myth and narrative to perpetuate these images to the viewing audience. According to Barker,[2] Barthes[3] notes "myth naturalizes that which is historically contingent making particular world-views appear unchangeable and God-given." Kellner[4] stated myths are simplistic stories, which "explain, instruct, and justify practices and institutions." Kaminsky[5] stated mythology most likely came from the dominant ideology, which "controls how we look at reality." The dominant ideology, the ideas and belief systems presented by the dominant elite, are relatively conservative, "identifying and perpetuating a narrow range of 'correct' choices in the political, economic, sexual, familial, and other spheres of life," as well as expressing certain myths concerning "the veneration of industrial capitalism, individualism, the traditional nuclear family, [and] heterosexual romance."[6]

Further, the functional aspect of ideology is stability for the people, but also deception, as the dominant class ideology fools the masses into believing certain ideas about their reality, situations, and interests.[7] Further, myths are linked with the hegemonic ideology found within society, as myths can help to illustrate or resolve conflicts. Kellner[8] offers an example of this hegemonic relationship by examining the police drama *Starksy and Hutch*, noting the program dealt with the conflict between social conformity and individuality. Finally, myths act as a unifying agent in what often appears to be diverse narratives. For example, Nachbar and Lause conducted an analysis of the myth-narratives found within the 1960s sitcom *The Beverly Hillbillies*, and found the myth of material success interwoven with the myth of rural simplicity, noting: "On its most basic level the series contrasts the 'good' Clampetts and the 'bad' Drysdales as a means of pinpointing the form of material success that should be believed and valued."[9] Additionally, Nachbar and Lause assert a majority of the episodes from *The Beverly Hillbillies* present a variety of complex myth narratives, including technology, fame, fortune, and childhood, presenting to the viewer beliefs and values regarding these ideas as "drastic simplifications of reality."[10]

The beliefs and values associated with myth and mythic narratives provide the cultural frameworks for stereotypes. The term stereotype initially referred to a printing stamp, which was used to make multiple copies from a single model or mold. Lippmann adopted the term in the 1922 publication *Public Opinion* and defined stereotypes as a standardized mental picture held in common by members of groups and that represents an oversimplified opinion, prejudiced attitude or uncritical judgment. Lippmann further argued stereotypes are simple, acquired second-hand, erroneous and durable.[11] Through the distortions of myth narratives in television programming, Southern stereotypes have long been presented to the viewer in a variety of formats, and these stereotypes of Southerners in television programming are perpetuated through myth-narratives, which conform to the dominant ideology. Before analyzing the Southerner on television, one must first examine the development of Southern stereotypes in Western society.

Southern Stereotypes

There is a history to stereotypes held about the South. Portwood-Stacer dates poor white inferiority stereotypes to the late nineteenth and early twentieth centuries, during which whites were already superior and furthered segregation from other races, including poor whites to "justify the exclusivity of dominant whiteness."[12] People who were not like the dominant white and powerful were looked upon as unfit to partake in the role anyway. Often referred to when considering the history of the South and the stereotypes within are the Civil War and Civil Rights movement, just prior and following the timeline in the study by Portwood-Stacer. Shimp, Dunn, and Klein say the roots of Southern animosity were staged at the onset of the Civil War. Resulting from landowners' perceived right to own slaves and conflicts involving the interpretation of the U.S. Constitution, the Civil War was fought for four years and, of course, resulted in the South's loss. The North then asserted authority over the South by occupying the South to oversee Reconstruction. In addition, news coverage of the Civil Rights movement in the 1960s "led many Northerners to form vivid images of ugly events in southern cities."[13]

Such activity as consumerism, education, and simple respect come into play when considering stereotypes in any form. Negative stereotypes associated with the South will be explored in this section.

As Slow-Talking and Inferior

Fridland and Bartlett said, "Southern dialects have long been viewed as less prestigious dialects of American English, and stereotypes of the dumb-but-sweet Southerner abound in the media."[14] Mainstream entertainment enjoys the inclusion of Southern stars such as Harry Connick, Jr., Matthew McConaughey, Reese Witherspoon, and Oprah Winfrey, as well as several athletes such as Brett

Favre, Shaquille O'Neal, Charles Barkley, and the Manning *family* of athletes. While some of these stars certainly talk slow, they are far from inferior. On the other hand, the shocking actions of Britney Spears often put the South in a negative light. From the small town of Kentwood, Louisiana, Spears has portrayed the "white trash" inferiority Portwood-Stacer examines—marketing herself "with a kind of trashy sexuality, enacted in a celebrity culture of high fashion and unfathomable wealth."[15] In the study, Portwood-Stacer notes in her short and cataclysmic show with Kevin Federline that depicted their lives as a young, famous and married couple, Spears often falls from her "cutesy Southern accent into a twangy Louisiana drawl."[16] Cute? Twangy? Would successful professionals like their speech labeled as cute or twangy? It is not often that the Southern accent is considered professional or proper. Even Southerners question their speech as being accepted. Fridland and Bartlett said, "at some level, speakers must find the use of these shifted vowel variants rewarding, even if they consider them uneducated and unpleasant compared to non-shifted variants.[17] The researcher found that although Memphians feel their speech is inferior to that of other regions of the country, many still hold on to the drawl, which defines them. Perhaps it is tradition, and perhaps while Southerners do enjoy and participate in the progressive lifestyle often associated with the North, they want to hold on to their identity as Southerners who *sound Southern.* While it possibly isn't a "cute twang" that bonds them to the rest of the nation, it may bind them together as a nation in and of themselves. Fridland and Bartlett said, "Even in the face of long-standing and often pejorative stereotypes, this speech region's continued distinctiveness clearly attests to the remarkable power of social and historical solidarity in the face of external language pressure."[18]

Language may cause emotional response on stereotypical views. In a study of speakers of the three main languages of the Eastern Cape, De Klerk and Bosch reveals "discrimination against people may well be linked to the sort of language they use."[19] De Klerk and Bosch used language for surveyors to predict attributes such as reliability, education, confidence, and even attractiveness for different languages and accents. It already has been found that teachers rate videotaped samples of children's speech to what they expect from those ethnic populations.[20] Whitehead and Miller report, "It appears that the stereotype may act as an anchorpoint about which the teacher-subject differentiates the individual child when presented via the videotape stimulus. Thus, ratings of the actual child may be a combination of stereotype ratings and the differentiation of the actual child relative to the stereotype."[21] Could the difference in languages and accent and the attitudes toward children who represent them also spill over to the Southern versus Northern accent?

As Racist

Although it is simple for researchers to point to historical events such as the Civil War and Civil Rights movement as proof that Southern racism was widespread and alive during those times, Wilson's study revealed:

> For the most part, stereotype findings are similar. Both in the South and elsewhere, post-World War II cohorts born during 1945-60 less often stereotype minorities than prewar cohorts do, especially the oldest prewar cohorts. In the South, however, cohorts born between 1961 and 1972 show no general tendency toward further reduction in stereotyping (stereotyping of Hispanics is the single exception). But outside of the South, findings differ sharply: Most-recent cohorts born between 1960 and 1972 are actually more likely to adversely stereotype minorities (Hispanics, Asians, Jews, though not blacks) than their immediate predecessors born between 1946 and 1960.[22]

Of course, the study lists other findings about the small details of the survey, which asked questions concerning the social distance desired between self and minorities and stereotypical beliefs of other races (i.e., unintelligent, violent, lazy), but an astounding finding in this study is that it seems there is an increase in the stereotypical beliefs outside of the South. Wilson found "among earlier cohorts, southerners tend to be more prejudiced than non-southerners, but that there is little regional difference in prejudice among most-recent cohorts. These findings imply that as a result of cohort succession, prejudice levels both in the South and outside of the South can be expected to continue to converge."[23] Additionally, Wilson's study "has found that in the south, most-recent cohorts are, if anything, less prejudiced than the earliest cohorts, while outside of the South, most-recent cohorts are no less prejudiced than the earliest cohorts (at least toward Hispanics, Asians, and Jews) and, if anything, tend to be more prejudiced (at least toward Jews)."[24] The researcher says over time and resulting from cohort succession, "regional convergence may come about not as it has in the past, because prejudice is declining faster in the South than it is outside of the South, but because in the future prejudice will decline only in the South while it remains stable and perhaps even increases elsewhere."[25]

Portwood-Stacer notes, like all racist attributions, these negative traits were perceived to pervade the whole population of poor whites, particularly in the South. The attraction of such biological explanations for socially undesirable characteristics is the people who are not implicated (i.e., middle-class whites) are reassured they are not in danger of acquiring the traits (Nicole Hahn Rafter). Of course, that depends on their not polluting their genes with those of the inferior ilk—a neat mechanism for ensuring social castes do not mix.[26]

Shimp, Dunn, and Klein found regional animosity exists (preference for the geographic in-group and animosity toward those living in geographic regions outside of the in-group). In this study, the researchers supported that people preferred products from their own region and were at times willing to pay top dollar for those products.[27] Although it buttresses Fridland and Bartlett's findings that Memphians felt the Southern regions are less correct than others,[28] regional animosity does give reason as to why Northerners may reject the Southern "drawl" or what they perceive is the Southern way of life. Babin, Boles, and Darden suggest "stereotypes influence consumer emotions, and these emotions then mediate the relationship between stereotypes."[29]

We are far past the years of the Civil War. We are almost fifty years out from the events that took place during the Civil Rights movement. And of course, we are over a century past the height of immigration at the turn of the twentieth century. Still, we are looking for answers on how to dismiss the stereotypes that are still associated with the South and believed to have begun and been magnified with these events. Do Southerners embrace some of these stereotypes? Do they like having a "twang"? Are we okay with racial desegregation, but not with North/South desegregation? Most importantly, how does television programming reflect, both historically and in the present, these accepted stereotypes?

A Long History of Southerners in the Media

Images of Southerners on television programming are not a new phenomenon. When Newton Minow referred to the vast wasteland in 1961,[30] the idea was to remove the rampant violence found on the tiny tube. However, one of the lasting effects of this speech was the broadcasting industry response to produce an array of mindless comedies. Historically speaking, the 1960s was the richest period in television programming for what has been deemed the "Southern," a variation on the Western in which the genre features mainly rural settings and characters.[31] Most notable of these programs include: *The Andy Griffith Show; The Beverly Hillbillies; Gomer Pyle, U.S.M.C.; Green Acres; Petticoat Junction; The Real McCoy; and Mayberry RFD.* McGee notes "the rural situation comedy became *the* way to portray the South and Southerners in the 1960s."[32] Blake said by 1967, an average of six Southern themed shows aired per season on the major networks.[33] As more networks relied on the Southern comedy for ratings and shares, some programmers, such as CBS, became concerned with their primarily rural image and scaled back on the situation comedies focused on Southern ideology. For example, when CBS cancelled *Gomer Pyle, U.S.M.C.* in 1969, the program was in second place in the ratings. Though the rural program disappeared for a few seasons to make way for the more socially conscious programming of the early 1970s (e.g., *All in the Family*), new programming featuring the Southerners appeared in the late 1970s in the forms of *The Dukes of Hazard* and *Dallas*, while *Designing Women* arrived on the scene in the late

1980s.

Programming of the previous four decades relied on the characters themselves (although stereotypes) and the myth-narratives to explain or illustrate the dominant ideology. The importance of characters in transferring cultural knowledge has been well documented. Abelman notes characters serve as "metaphors for sociopolitical values and issues, and conflicts between characters are enactments of conflicts over ideologies between social groups."[34] In addition, Himmelstein suggests several real-world ideological constructs, which pervade our television programming through the use of characters, including: the sanctity of the ordinary American family, the celebration of celebrity, personal initiative triumphs over bureaucratic control, one's gain at another's expense and personalizing and dismissing social ills.[35]

Early programming relied on a simpler stereotype of the Southerner. For example, Lichter, Lichter, and Rothman noted, "Gomer Pyle relied on the stereotype of the good hearted foul-up whose naïveté both charms and frustrates his superiors."[36] This is directly related to the dominant perception of Southerners as ignorant or dumb. Brown identifies the stereotypes of *The Beverly Hillbillies* characters as following a "time honored theme of the innocent country bumpkin."[37]

The appearance of the characters can also be examined. One rarely sees Aunt Bea of Mayberry outside the kitchen without her apron or warm apple pie. Further, characters on programs set outside the South never seem to fit into their new surroundings. For example, the Clampetts of *The Beverly Hillbillies* never dressed any differently from the backwoods attire they wore in their home state of Tennessee, yet Mr. Drysdale often assumed the country dress to fit in with his meal ticket at the bank. On the contrary, the characters on *Green Acres* never altered their dress from the city slicker image; though longing for "fresh air," they could not undo the "Times Square" influence on their appearance.

Two of the most prominent myth-narratives found in the early Southern programming were the myth of rural simplicity and the myth of the nuclear family. The myth of rural simplicity is the idea that American virtue and happiness can be achieved by escaping the hectic atmosphere of life and getting back to the basics, usually indicated by living in the country or on a farm.[38] In early Southern programming, the rural setting often ignored the current events of the day, where country life was immune from the oft-traumatic world events of the time. For example, Vaughan notes the purity of *The Andy Griffith Show* was reflected in the program's ability to ignore the tumultuous events of the 1960s (e.g., the Civil Rights movement, Vietnam, Kennedy's assassination), and focus on providing an "avenue of escape from life's vicissitudes by depicting the simple life with small, solvable problems."[39]

The myth of the nuclear family holds the most desirable family unit is two parents (a mother and a father), two children, and a pet. Though the face of the typical family unit has shifted over generations, the myth of family values and togetherness remains strong. Research suggests parents within the family unit strive to continually offer their children bigger and better life experiences over time.[40] Both Magoc, and Vaughan recognized the importance of the narrative of family and family values in the older Southern programming, noting one of the main themes within these shows was the interaction between the characters depicting wholesome family values and family togetherness.[41]

Another myth-narrative found within early Southern programming was the myth of justice. Nachbar and Lause identify the myth of justice as "the Law is made by powerful figures who . . . create a legal web which protects the status quo, punishes the innocent," noting justice outside the law is also an acceptable practice.[42] The myth-narrative of justice in older programming featuring the Southern image usually coincides with the stereotype of the backwoods Southern lawman, such as blundering Barney Fife. "The inept lawman, particularly the bumbling small-town sheriff, has been a common stereotype over the years. Don Knotts won an Emmy as the stammering deputy Barney Fife on *The Andy Griffith Show*. Fife was so inept he had to carry his single bullet in his shirt pocket, lest he shoot himself in the foot."[43] *The Dukes of Hazard* followed this same pattern with the bumbling lawman Boss Hogg, who was continually foiled by Bo and Luke Duke.

The Southern-based programs of today are more likely to feature one or more of three related white identity myths that have been prevalent in commercial representations of Southern culture:

> The myth of the Lost Cause: the Confederacy viewed as a legion of gallant Christian Knights serving a divine cause, which serves to release white Southerners from guilt by reshaping their memories of the brutal conditions of the slaves. Moonlight and Magnolias represents Southern womanhood as a vulnerable vessel of virtue. The Celtic myth stereotypes poor Southern whites as lazy, drunk, uneducated hillbillies, due to their Celtic bloodline, which projects blame for societal problems on the racist Southern redneck.[44]

However, according to Nachbar and Lause, viewers must take in these myth narratives with caution, as they say "the mere acceptance of these myths puts us at some personal risk . . . what if what we believe is not obviously what is out there?"[45] Thus, this is the inherent problem with the more recent programming depicting Southern stereotypes. Gone are the good ol' days and rural simplicity. Whereas older programming relied on a gentler version of the Southern stereotypes, these new television programs mock Southerners at all costs for a laugh and the almighty dollar.

Southerners on Television Today

Situation Comedy

The situation comedies of more recent times include *Reba* and *My Name Is Earl*. *Reba*, the only successful sitcom produced by the WB cable network, focused on the life and family of single mother Reba (played by country music star Reba McIntyre). Set in Texas, the sitcom breaks the mold of the good ol' days and escapist plot lines by focusing on the harsher realities in life. The show opens with Reba in the middle of a divorce from Brock, her husband of twenty years. Brock, a dentist, left Reba to marry his pregnant dental hygienist, Barbara Jean, a similar situation to Reba's pregnant seventeen-year-old daughter, Cheyenne marrying her boyfriend Van, star of the high school football team. The characters and myth-narratives illustrate Southern stereotypes in a variety of ways, all more elaborate and boisterous from prior Southern programming. For example, on the episode "The Steaks Are High," the myth-narrative of football as religion in the South is played out for the viewer. When Reba offers to host the pre-game dinner for the high school football team, she refuses to follow what Brock refers to as the "pre-game Bible." Reba serves the wrong potato salad, and when the team finds out, they are convinced they will lose game, and in fact, cannot overcome their superstitions to play together as a team. The myth of family togetherness still exists; however, the situations faced by the family are more realistic (e.g., teen pregnancy). The character of Barbara Jean best illustrates the stereotype of the Southern woman: the loud, neurotic, overweight, former beauty queen who speaks with a drawl and is a little slow.

A second, more recent sitcom focusing on the Southerner is NBC's *My Name Is Earl*, which debuted in 2005. The program features two brothers, Earl (Jason Lee) and Randy, as Earl journeys on a karmic quest to undo all the bad things he did to people over the years. Set in a location only referred to as Camden County, this sitcom is rife with Southern stereotypes. For example, Randy, often portrayed as Earl's bumbling sidekick, holds the Camden County record for staring at the sun. In addition, Earl's Southern-talking, beautician ex-wife left him for the short order cook at the local diner, but Earl was allowed to stay in the family trailer. Finally, in the first season episode, explaining how Joy and Earl's first child was named Dodge, the viewer learns Joy was not sure who the real father of the boy was, but that he drove a Ford pickup, so they named the baby Dodge after the competition.

Humor on Cable

Several comedians have made a living making fun of Southern stereotypes. The same can be said of several minority comedians as well. Often the media portrays "southerners as race-car driving, gun-toting, liquor-swilling, hood-wearing, and cross-burning intemperate fools."[46] While the racism issue isn't necessarily a part of the redneck humor, certainly the racecar driving, gun-toting, liquor-swilling part is well submerged in the comedy acts. *Blue Collar TV*, hosted by Jeff Foxworthy, Bill Engvall, and Larry the Cable Guy, looks to the stereotypes of the South to brand itself—and makes millions doing so. The program, airing on Comedy Central, pokes fun at the South and Southerners through a variety of short skits and stand-up routines. One of the most common stereotypes featured in the program is one of white trash, or the Southern redneck. Portwood-Stacer defines white trash as "an American subculture, whose members are thought to be characterized by poverty, violence, shame, racism, criminality, immorality, laziness, ignorance, poor health and hygiene, and of course, whiteness."[47] Most of these attributes are evident in the Blue Collar comedy routines.

Animated Humor

Episodes of animated programs also feature Southern stereotypes. The problem with this programming is although these programs are written for an older audience, younger audiences are exposed to these stereotypes. A 2001 episode of *Family Guy* titled "To Live or Die in Dixie" featured the Griffin family placed in the witness protection program in the Southern United States. The episode made reference to the film *Deliverance*. Chris Griffin, the oldest child of the family, witnessed a robbery in Quahog, and the Griffin clan was sent to the South to hide from the death threats. During their stay in the rural area, the family adopted a new way of life rich with Southern stereotypes. Stewie, the baby, is seen wearing a diaper and playing a banjo in a bluegrass band with the neighbors, playing "Dueling Banjos" in a scene reminiscent of the film, *Deliverance*. Peter, the family patriarch, spends time turning the family car into a replica of the General Lee (from *The Dukes of Hazard*). Chris falls in love with Sam, a local teenager presented as a male, who was later determined to be a girl, reflecting the stereotype Southern girls can be seen as transgendered.[48]

The Simpsons also featured an episode in which Lisa feared becoming a failure like all the Simpson men. Her nightmare of failure featured an older Lisa living in a trailer, with a new Southern accent, overweight, with twenty kids, and married to a man dressed in a "wife-beater."[49]

The animated program *King of the Hill* is set entirely in the South, in Texas, with Hank Hill as a propane gas salesman. His niece aspires to be nothing more than a local beautician, and his friends stand around and drink beer in their undershirts all day. Boomauer, Hank's buddy, speaks such garbled English the viewer cannot understand him, but his friends can, because they speak "Southern."

Finally, older cartoons featuring Southern stereotypes can still be seen on the Cartoon Network owned cable channel *Boomerang*, including shows *Huckleberry Hound* and Warner Brothers Looney Tunes shorts *Foghorn Leghorn*. Ironically, when Ted Turner acquired the rights to the Looney Tunes shorts in 1999, he chose to discontinue animated shorts featuring Speedy Gonzalez, citing the political incorrectness of a cartoon portraying Mexicans as "lazy, irresponsible, and drunk."[50] Though public outcry forced Turner to return Speedy Gonzalez to the lineup in 2002, albeit only during the early morning hours between 2 a.m. and 5 a.m., Foghorn Leghorn and Huckleberry Hound have remained feature players in the Looney Tunes shorts at all hours.

Distorted Reality?

As reality television programming continues to grow to higher volume, networks continually strive to up the bar for the bigger and better reality program. Reality programs consistently utilize stereotypes to increase not only viewing audience, but also to create better and more interesting narratives. For example, Haralovich and Trosset note *Survivor* contestants are grilled mercilessly before selection and are chosen from a generated form of character types, such as "the entertainer, leader, flirt, determined victim (i.e., the underdog), professor, zealot, mom, athlete, wild and crazy guy or girl, quiet one, everybody's friend, feral child, introvert, redneck, slacker, or snake."[51] These character types have both positive and negative attributes, which the producers hope will make for a more interesting program. Reality television programming focused on Southerners follows the same pattern of searching for the typical Southerner to feature.

In 2002, CBS developed a short-lived reality program entitled *Real Beverly Hillbillies*, in which "genuine rednecks transplanted to a mansion in Beverly Hills, California, where they will show what fools they are while trying to live it up Hollywood style."[52] This was the beginning of a new trend in reality programming, where the Southerner became the focus of the show.

Cable network CMT offers viewers Southern programming such as *My Big Redneck Wedding*, where Southerners flaunt their rural weddings for the cameras. In one episode, set in Louisiana, the wedding party dressed entirely in camouflage, and the bride's wedding gift from the groom the day before the wedding was a custom designed pink shotgun, complete with an engraved handle declaring their love.[53]

American Idol's new venture the 2008 season was to create a more personal relationship with viewers by offering a more in-depth look at the lives of the contestants. One contestant, a Southerner, was seen sitting on a tractor and chewing tobacco. His family sounded unintelligent, and host Ryan Seacrest poked fun at this. Other contestants from other regions did not get the same treatment.

The Simple Life, starring Paris Hilton and Nicole Ritchie, also featured episodes in season one where the women traveled through the South on their way from Miami Beach to Los Angeles. On the episode "Louisiana," Paris and Nicole stay with a Louisiana family on the bayou and spend a majority of their time mocking the Southern way of life in the swamp.[54] The episode "Texas" found the girls on a Texas ranch, learning how to handle horses and spending time with the family. Paris and Nicole take the teenage daughter shopping, and convince the girl to spend a large sum of money on clothing. When the girl's mother forces her daughter to return the clothing, the stercotype of the poor Southerner comes to light in the myth-narrative.

The latest reality programming features students from the University of Mississippi. Cable giant MTV traveled to Oxford, Mississippi in the fall of 2007 to scout for participants for the program *True Life*. Archer notes the program came looking for a Southern belle and chose Ole Miss for its reputation throughout the nation as "a school with traditions deeply rooted in Southern culture and manners, and this stereotype has not been overlooked by reality TV show producers."[55] Archer also interviewed Dunbar Flinn, a former cast member on *The Real World,* who arrived on the Ole Miss campus to screen potential participants. Archer quoted Flinn as saying MTV was looking specifically for "a self-contradicting Southern belle who was a good Christian lady in front of her parents and sorority, but who acts differently around others, a Scarlett O'Hara with panties around her ankles."[56]

Y'All Come Back Now, Ya Hear?

Poor white trash. Racecar drivers. Drunkards. Racists. The South has heard them all. Often perpetuated in popular media, it's also what is shown to the world. In a Google search of "southern celebrities," the first two topics were "Stupid Celebrities Gossip: 10 Hottest Southern Celebrity Babes" and "Redneck—Wikipedia, the free encyclopedia." Television shows such as *Reba* and *My Name Is Earl* often show Southerners in the stereotypical slow-talking, slow-moving fashion of people who care little about moving up the corporate ladder or progressive lifestyles. Characters are often shown living in modest homes or below modest homes with reflective attitudes.

The future of the Southern stereotype is one of continued success for the networks and producers, but one of continued depression for the Southerner. With new forays of reality television into the Southern stereotype, the likelihood of breaking the stereotype mold seems impossible. Lichter, Lichter, and Rothman argue the days of the idiot sitcom are over, and the future of television programming will see "no more flying nuns, talking horses, or millionaire hillbillies," with the new face of programming including more divorce courts, reality television, businesses, hospitals, and "eccentric small towns a far cry from Mayberry RFD."[57] But the critical media consumer must question the viability of this statement. Are the new programs featuring Southerners truly a "far cry" from the Southern image that began on television in the 1960s? The answer is perhaps both yes and no. Though Elvin quotes columnist Kathleen Parker as saying "we enlightened 21st-century Americans would never permit such a blatant denigration of any other group,"[58] the fact remains the Southern stereotype is alive and well, prospering on both network and cable. New shows featuring the Southerner utilize myth narrative steeped in the dominant ideology of "Southerners are stupid, lazy, and ignorant" to attract and maintain viewers. This research further argues the new versions of the Southern stereotype(s) on television rely on a more debased cultural attitude toward the South. When networks executives have attempted to remarket the Southern image, those attempts have failed, most notably with the failure of cable network Turner South in 2006.

Turner South was launched in 1999, with the following marketing campaign: "Turner South brings you wholesome programming that's uniquely Southern. From lifestyle and self-improvement, to home improvement and cooking, Turner South is award-winning television programming for everyone, not just Southerners."[59] With a motto of "Your South," Ted Turner spent millions on advertising and production, as well as promotional tours of Turner South's six state viewing area (including Alabama, Georgia, Mississippi, Tennessee, South Carolina, and North Carolina). Interestingly, the remarketing of the Southern image only touched the Southern states, and ironically, the first program to run on the "remarketed Southern image" network was *The Rick and Bubba Show*, a program that featured two Alabama morning radio personalities bringing their skits to television.

A plethora of organizations exists today to combat negative stereotypes of a variety of groups across race, class, and gender, yet few groups exist today calling for a halt to the negative Southern image within mainstream media. This research has only scratched the surface of the lingering Southern stereotype in television. What about film, radio, and advertising? Networks do not need to rebrand or remarket the South to the Southerners, but rather the negative Southern stereotypes should be eliminated from these broadcasts.

Notes

1. Craig Thomson and Kelly Tian, "Marketing the South: Commercial Mythmaking and Reshaping of Popular Memories," *Journal of Consumer Research* (February 2008),

accessed October 26, 2011, http://www.eurekalert.org/pub_releases/2008-01/uocp-mts010808.php.
    2. Chris Barker, *Television, Globalization, and Cultural Identities* (Buckingham: University Press, 1999), 108.
    3. Roland Barthes, *Mythologies* (London: Cape, 1972).
    4. Douglas Kellner, "TV, Ideology, and Emancipatory Popular Culture," in *Television: The Critical View*, ed. Horace Newcomb (New York: Oxford University Press, 1987), 480.
    5. Stuart Kaminsky, *American Television Genres* (Chicago: Nelson-Hall, 1985), 167.
    6. Laura Stempel Mumford, *Love and Ideology in the Afternoon: Soap Opera, Women, and Television Genre* (Bloomington: Indiana University Press, 1995), 11.
    7. Arthur A. Berger, *Media and Society: A Critical Perspective* (Lanham, Md.: Rowman & Littlefield Publishers, 2003).
    8. Kellner, "TV, Ideology, and Emancipatory Popular Culture."
    9. Jack Nachbar and Kevin Lause, *Popular Culture: An Introductory Text* (Bowling Green, Oh.: Bowling Green State University Press, 1992), 196.
    10. Nachbar and Lause, *Popular Culture*, 197.
    11. Walter Lippman, *Public Opinion* (New York: The Free Press, 1922).
    12. Laura Portwood-Stacer, "Consuming 'Thrash': Representations of Poor Whites in U.S. Popular Culture" (paper presented at the annual meeting for the International Communication Association, San Francisco, California, May 24-28, 2010).
    13. Terence A. Shimp, Tracy H. Dunn and Jill G. Klein, "Remnants of the U.S. Civil War and Modern Consumer Behavior," *Psychology & Marketing* 21(2004): 80.
    14. Valerie Fridland and Kathryn Bartlett, "Correctness, Pleasantness, and Degree of Difference Ratings Across Regions, *American Speech* 81(2006): 358.
    15. Portwood-Stacer, "Consuming 'Thrash'," 10.
    16. Portwood-Stacer, "Consuming 'Thrash'," 10.
    17. Fridland and Bartlett, "Correctness," 360.
    18. Fridland and Bartlett, "Correctness," 358.
    19. Vivian De Klerk and Barbara Bosch, "Linguistic Stereotypes: Nice Accent—Nice Person?" *International Journal of Sociology of Language* 116(1995): 17.
    20. De Klerk and Bosch, "Linguistic Stereotypes."
    21. Jade L. Whitehead and Leslie M. Miller, "Correspondence Between Evaluations of Children's Speech and Speech Anticipated upon the Basis of Stereotype," *Southern Speech Communication Journal* 37(1972),: 385.
    22. Thomas Wilson, "Cohort and Prejudice: Whites' Attitudes toward Blacks, Hispanics, Jews, and Asians," *Public Opinion Quarterly* 60(1996): 269.
    23. Wilson, "Cohort and Prejudice," 272.
    24. Wilson, "Cohort and Prejudice," 272.
    25. Wilson, "Cohort and Prejudice," 272.
    26. Portwood-Stacer, "Consuming 'Thrash.'"
    27. Shimp, Dunn and Klein, "Remnants."
    28. Fridland and Bartlett, "Correctness."
    29. Barry Babin, James Boles and William Darden, "Salesperson Stereotypes, Consumer Emotions, and Their Impact on Information Processing," *Journal of the Academy of Marketing Science* 23(1995), 94.
    30. Newton N. Minow, "Television and the Public Interest," address to the National

An Acceptable Stereotype: The Southern Image in Television Programming   19

Association of Broadcasters, Washington, D.C., May 9, 1961.
    31. Lester Brown, *Encyclopedia of Television* (New York: Zoetrope, 1982).
    32. Marsha G. McGee, "Prime Time Dixie: Television's View of a 'Simple' South," *Journal of American Culture* 6(1983): 101.
    33. "The Dukes of Hazard and Television's Simple South," Ted Blake, accessed March 28, 2008, http://xraods.virginia.edu/~ug97/blake/part1.html.
    34. Robert Abelman, *Reaching a Critical Mass: A Critical Analysis of Television Entertainment* (Mahwah, N.J.: Lawrence Erlbaum Associates, 1998), 67.
    35. Hal Himmelstein, *Television Myth and the American Mind* (London: Sage Publications, 1994).
    36. S. Robert Lichter, Linda S. Lichter and Stanley Rothman, *Primetime: How Television Portrays American Culture* (Washington, D.C.: Regnery Publishing, 1994), 383.
    37. Brown, *Encyclopedia of Television*, 159.
    38. Nachbar and Lause, *Popular Culture*; Himmelstein, *Television Myth*.
    39. Don Rodney Vaughan, "Why *The Andy Griffith Show* Is Important to Popular Culture Studies," *Journal of Popular Culture* 38(2004): 398.
    40. Himmelstein, *Television Myth*.
    41. Chris J. Magoc, "The Machine in the Wasteland, *Journal of Popular Film and Television* 19(1991): 25-35; Vaughan, "Why *The Andy Griffith Show* Is Important."
    42. Nachbar and Lause, *Popular Culture*, 98.
    43. Lichter, Lichter and Rothman, *Primetime*, 322.
    44. Thompson and Tian, "Marketing the South," *2008*.
    45. Nachbar and Lause, *Popular Culture,* 107.
    46. Shimp, Dunn and Klein, "Remnants," 80.
    47. Portwood-Stacer, "Consuming 'Thrash'," 2.
    48. *Family Guy*. Episode 40, first broadcast 15 November 2001 by FOX. Directed by Dan Povenmire and written by Steve Callaghan.
    49. *The Simpsons*. Episode 195, first broadcast 8 March 1998 by FOX. Directed by Susie Dietter and written by Ned Goldreyer.
    50. Jon Cooke, "Ted Turner Bans Speedy Gonzalez from Cartoon Network," Freerepublic.com, accessed March 26, 2008, http://www.freerepublic.com/forum/a3a36c3ed264d.htm.
    51. Mary Beth Haralovich and Michael W. Trosset, "Expect the Unexpected: Narrative Pleasure and Uncertainty due to Chance in Survivor," in *Reality TV: Remaking Television Culture,* ed. Susan Murray and Laurie Ouellette (New York: New York University Press, 2004), 89.
    52. John Elvin, "Redneck Television Scores Low Rating from Critics," Insight on theNews,accessed December 29, 2010, http://findarticles.com/p/articles/mi_m1571/is_37_18/ai_92589569/.
    53. *My Big Redneck Wedding*, Episode 17, first broadcast 9 January 2009 by CMT. Directed by Mark Therrien.
    54. *The Simple Life,* Episode 14, first broadcast 7 July 2004 by FOX. Directed by Claudia Frank.
    55. M. Archer, "Reality TV Seeks Modern-Day Scarlett O'Hara with a Twist," *The Daily Mississippian,* November 14, 2007, A1.
    56. M. Archer, "Reality TV Seeks Modern-Day Scarlett O'Hara," A1.

57. Lichter, Lichter and Rothman, *Primetime,* 27.
58. Elvin, "Redneck Television."
59. "Turner South to Launch Friday, October 1, to Nearly One Million Subscribers," September 29, 1999, www.timewarner.com/pressrelease

Chapter Two
An Ethical Inquiry of the Blue Collar Comedy Tour's Appropriation and Commodification of Redneck Culture
Mark Glantz

The processes of cultural appropriation and cultural commodification are central to popular representations of the South. In order for any representation of the South to reach its intended audience, it must be taken, adapted, mirrored after, or transformed from, some space of cultural practice or performance—in other words, it must be *appropriated*. Next, the South must be marketed, packaged, advertised, or otherwise made fit for participation in capitalist symbol systems—it must be *commodified*.

The popular Blue Collar Comedy Tour (BCCT) franchise, because of its rather knotty portrayal of Southern culture, provides a unique context with which to study cultural appropriation. There has been very little critical discussion of appropriation as it manifests itself in stand-up comedy, or humor in general. The case of the BCCT is particularly interesting because Southern culture is being appropriated and commodified intra-nationally. For the mass American audiences that enjoy the BCCT, the Southerner is a not-so-distant "other." This initial lack of distance or difference has led to a reliance on the image of the "redneck"; an ignorant, unsophisticated, country-bred bumpkin, similar enough to the audience to invite identification but different enough to tempt ridicule.

For the purposes of this analysis, I will rely primarily on the BCCT's own definition of the term "redneck." Jeff Foxworthy, the group's leader enthusiastically claims that to be redneck is to exhibit a "glorious lack of sophistication."[1] Foxworthy provides a useful starting point, but this analysis will reveal that there is much more to construction of the concept than Foxworthy would care to explicitly acknowledge.

Because the participants in the BCCT films demonstrate an awareness of the cultural activities in which they are engaged and present arguments in defense of those activities, these artifacts offer critics an excellent opportunity to study the way texts can resist easy interpretation and operate differently among diverse audiences.[2] James Clifford has argued that such critical/cultural projects ought to focus on "the complex historical processes of appropriation, compromise, submersion, masking, invention, and revival."[3] In other words, those who engage in analyzing and/or criticizing cultural appropriation are charged with a tall task; it is a difficult endeavor to understand the complex interactions between cultures, texts, audiences, and critics. Of course, such pursuits are surely valuable if, as Claire Sponsler has argued, the study of cultural appropriation can aid us in understanding history as it is being written.[4] Such arguments, in the context of representations of the South, remind us that it is not just the history of images that is at stake here—it's the history of the South.

Understood as the taking, borrowing, or transforming of a culture other than one's own, cultural appropriation research often makes either implicit or explicit judgments about the ethical nature of the acts and artifacts it studies. This focus is likely due to an interest in the ways that indigenous cultures from America, Canada, and Australia have been managed, controlled, bastardized, celebrated, and mimicked by more dominant cultural forces.[5] A closely related body of research deals with commodification, which focuses on the way elements of certain cultures are packaged for economic gain, thus transforming the meaning of a culture's symbols.[6] Almost all of these studies advance either implicit or explicit judgments regarding the ethical problems associated with appropriation and commodification of particular cultures.

In this essay, I aim to keep ethical and ideological considerations in the foreground of my analysis. To meet this end, I use James O. Young's work on the ethics of cultural appropriation[7] to understand the discourse produced by the BCCT and its performers. First, I examine the specific processes by which members of the BCCT appropriate and commodify the image of the authentic Southerner. The way in which the Blue Collar comedians obfuscate the ethical issues that surround their cultural appropriation by problematizing group membership is a major concern of this section, as is their use of meta-discursive techniques for justifying their rhetorical acts. Second, I consider the ways in which the BCCT may generate what James O. Young termed "profound offense."[8] More specifically, it is argued here that the racist, sexist, and homophobic rhetoric, purportedly advanced from the perspective of authentic Southerners, is offensive to multiple audiences on multiple levels. Finally, I apply Young's criteria for evaluating the ethicality of cultural appropriation to the BCCT and its audiences. This final step serves as an excellent means for verifying my own evaluations in some instances, and tempering them in others. Before embarking on the tasks plotted above, I will describe the artifacts being evaluated.

The Blue Collar Comedy Tour

In 2000, with the aid of his management company, Parallel Entertainment, comedian Jeff Foxworthy began the Blue Collar Comedy Tour.[9] Foxworthy, who had already sold more recordings than any other comedian in history,[10] recruited his friends Bill Engvall, Larry the Cable Guy, and Ron White, to join him as part of a package stand-up comedy tour and film that would appeal to America's heartland. In an interview with the *New Yorker*, Parallel Entertainment CEO J. P. Williams discussed the name of the tour, and by extension, the tour's guiding *ethos*: "'Blue Collar' is everywhere and resonates of hard work, of mines, and mills. It has more universal appeal than 'redneck,' which is more southern, more hillbilly, more negative."[11] Thus, Williams confirms that although the package was to benefit from the "redneck" shtick of each of its major players, the show was given a more palatable, less contentious title in order to appeal to more people.

The original tour was very popular and *The Blue Collar Comedy: The Movie* was an enormous success for all parties involved, earning 38 million dollars in DVD sales[12] and inspiring a pair of sequels (*The Blue Collar Comedy Tour Rides Again* and *The Blue Collar Comedy Tour: One for the Road*). Although no longer traveling as a unit, the group still reaches audiences through their television program, *Blue Collar TV*, as well as with merchandise such as talking dolls, keychains, bumper stickers, and t-shirts. Because the project is the creative outcome of each of the four members of the tour, it is worth briefly exploring the nature of each man's humor, as well as some of the career opportunities they have been afforded due to the BCCT's success.

Foxworthy, who was the star of the short-lived 1990s sitcom, the *Jeff Foxworthy Show*, rose to fame on the success of a collection of jokes punctuated by the phrase, "You might be a redneck," in which Foxworthy, in his Southern twang, kids about the peculiar characteristics of "rednecks." Some popular quips, published in the mass market paperback, *You Might Be a Redneck If . . .* , include, "You might be a redneck if your richest relative buys a new house and you have to help take the wheels off of it,"[13] and "You might be a redneck if you own more than three shirts with the sleeves cut off."[14] Foxworthy's manner of speech and dress mark him as a redneck, but he also explicitly identifies as such in his stand-up routine. He is fond of saying, "'I always thought you couldn't talk about rednecks unless you are one, and I are one."[15] The Georgia-born comedian assumes the persona of a Southern family man and journalists are fond of noting that when not on the road, Foxworthy attends Bible studies in the back room of a barbeque restaurant.[16] Such media commentary speaks to his authenticity by verifying that he is the same big-hearted redneck off the stage as he is on.

Bill Engvall is often labeled "the nice guy" of the BCCT by entertainment critics.[17] Raised the son of a doctor in Texas, Engvall has told the press that he believes himself to the be the least "Blue Collar" or "redneck" of those on the

BCCT.[18] His comedy, like Foxworthy's, tends to focus on marriage and family issues. His most popular comedic theme is one in which he suggests that people who ask stupid questions ought to wear a sign that says, "I'm stupid." For instance, he says, "We were having a small earthquake the other day, and my wife asked, 'Is this an earthquake? I said, 'Nope. I just put a quarter in the vibrating house machine.'"[19] Engvall has also become the star of the TBS sitcom, *The Bill Engvall Show*, written a best-selling book (*Just a Guy: Notes from a Blue Collar Life*), recorded a number one record (*15 Degrees Off Cool*), and produced a popular line of merchandise that include "Here's Your Sign" license plates.

If Engvall is the least redneck of the characters on the BCCT, Larry the Cable Guy is probably the most. Larry the Cable Guy assumes the role of the stereotypical, ignorant, unsophisticated, Southern redneck, complete with a flannel shirt torn at the sleeves and a camouflage cap that sports an image of the Confederate flag. "The Cable Guy" is a character created and performed by former theatre major Dan Whitney, who grew up in both Nebraska and Florida.[20] He has come under fire numerous times for the offensiveness of his comedic material, drawing criticism from fellow comedians Doug Stanhope, David Cross, and Steve Hofstetter for his often racist, homophobic, and misogynist remarks. That said, he may also be the most popular entertainer in the group. In 2006, he made $21.5 million in tour revenue, the most for a comedian in that year.[21] His solo stand-up comedy DVD titled Git-R-Done after his most popular catchphrase, went platinum twelve times, and his line of such items as compact discs, hats, and t-shirts are prized by fans.

Ron White, who has tagged himself with the farcical nickname "Tater Salad," is a veteran of both the Vietnam War and the professional bull-riding circuit.[22] Both on the stage and off, White embodies the redneck success story, wearing expensive suits, sipping Johnny Walker Black, and smoking fine cigars. His narrative humor, which typically employs foul language and explicit sexual references is toned down when he is part of the Blue Collar Comedy tour.[23] He was nominated for a Grammy for his solo album, *You Can't Fix Stupid*, made guest appearances in numerous television and film projects, and wrote a book titled, *I Had the Right to Remain Silent . . . But I Didn't Have the Ability*.

The trilogy of stand-up comedy films produced by the Blue Collar Comedy franchise will serve as the texts for analysis here. Each of the films was recorded in front of live audiences and released to movie theatres. All three of them were later packaged as DVDs for retail store shelves. Each movie features fifteen to twenty minute comedy routines by each of the four performers. At the end of every film, the comedians appear together as an ensemble to tell more jokes and give their audience a climactic conclusion. The first film, *Blue Collar Comedy Tour*, is interspersed with "behind the scenes" video clips of the comedians horsing around in a variety of different contexts. The two later films, *Blue Collar Comedy Tour Rides Again* and *Blue Collar Comedy: One for the Road* did not include such footage. I argue here that the brand of redneck humor executed by the members of the BCCT constitutes a form of unethical cultural appropriation that is problematized by the comedians' rhetorical construction of group membership. The degree to which the discourse presented by these "redneck" performers possesses the potential to generate "profound offense," as described by James O. Young is also explored. Young's criteria for exploring the ethical dimensions of cultural appropriation are then applied to the artifacts in an attempt to understand the ways in which the Blue Collar discourse fails to meet some of these criteria and eludes others.

Cultural Appropriation

James O. Young defined cultural appropriation as the "taking of something produced by members of one culture by members of another."[24] As straightforward as this definition seems, it can still be difficult to apply critically. There are instances in which group membership is not so easy to identify and understand. The BCCT is an example of this. Perhaps in anticipation of objections to their treatment of redneck culture, the members of the BCCT have developed a rather complicated construction of cultural membership. First, they move rhetorically to avoid charges of cultural appropriation by staking their own claim to redneck culture. If the members of the BCCT are authentic members of Southern culture, then they have merely expressed the true nature of their being, rather than appropriate another culture for their own artistic and economic advantage. Simply put, you can't take what's already yours.

Second, they have constructed the redneck identity as one in which just about all Americans could be included. Indeed the tagline to their first film is, "Like it or not, they're just like you."[25] Not only are the BCCT boys authentic rednecks, but so is each viewer, particularly those who might relate to the material by means of laughter. Such constructions of cultural group membership make it difficult to apply Young's lens for analyzing acts of cultural appropriation because "the concept of cultural appropriation has no application unless insiders and outsiders, members, and non-members of a culture can be distinguished."[26] In other words, if the BCCT performers had it their way, they have not engaged in cultural appropriation.

"We're Rednecks"

A combination of overt identification with redneck culture and a diligent performance of authenticity identifies the BCCT players as genuine rednecks. Jeff

Foxworthy, who has utilized this redneck shtick throughout his entire career, claims on *Blue Collar Comedy Tour: The Movie*, "Not only am I a redneck, I married into them too."[27] Statements such as this clearly label Foxworthy (and by extension, his tour mates) a redneck. His rhetoric demonstrates an awareness of the problems inherent to the type of comedy that centers on a particular group of people and customs. He claims, "I always thought you couldn't talk about rednecks unless you are one, and I are one."[28] This disclaimer appeals to the idea that members of an in-group have special license to criticize other members of the same group. This is a popular notion among comedians and their audiences, and is often invoked by Hispanic and African-American performers. For instance, Chris Rock is able to criticize and speak about his own African-American community in a manner that white performers are not permitted. However, any analogy between Rock and Foxworthy is not entirely valid. If we understand the African-American community as having a long history of marginalization, Rock's work and the reactions it encourages can be seen as a form of cultural resistance. It would be difficult to argue that the heterosexual white male represented in the BCCT is a similarly persecuted or marginalized individual in the United States. The BCCT's discourse does not bear the mark of a marginalized group attempting to unite, find a voice, and claim its rightful place in world affairs. Instead, it reads more like a backlash, orchestrated by white men, for the purpose of rejecting any contemporary movements that threaten their long-standing sociopolitical dominance.

Like Foxworthy, BCCT member Ron White makes overt statements about his identity and experiences in an effort to establish his redneck credentials and define himself as a member of the Southern culture he too jokes about in his act. He tells the audience, "I'm from Texas. I'm a cowboy. A real cowboy. I was a bronc' rider for six years of my life."[29] By establishing their redneck authenticity and invoking their right to make fun of themselves, this sort of disclosure attempts to reduce the offensiveness of their negative representations of Southern or rural culture.

The BCCT's identification with redneck culture is also apparent in the topics the comedians choose to discuss. Humorous narratives about NASCAR and hunting paint the performers as genuine members of redneck culture. This authenticity is performed throughout the BCCT films and manifests itself in the way the performers dress (denim jeans and cowboy boots are popular), and perhaps much more importantly, in the way the comedians speak. Each performer speaks in a distinct regional (Southern) dialect, and with an obvious twang in his voice.

The BCCT comedians often speak about their own consumerist ideals. In doing so, they manage to encourage and celebrate their audience's consumer appetites as well. All the while, their message advances the popular capitalist myth that what you buy (and where you buy it) says a lot (maybe everything) about who you are. For instance, Jeff Foxworthy reminds audiences that rednecks shop at Wal-Mart.

I did a five-hour book signing at a Wal-Mart one Saturday afternoon. And during that five hours, I had a revelation. And that is there's not a whole lot of supermodels shopping at Wal-Mart. [laughter]. It's pretty much just us rednecks. [laughter].[30]

Not coincidentally, the BCCT offers an extensive line of merchandise that helps audiences express their allegiance to redneck culture. These items are often sold at the same retail settings they mention in their acts. Hats, t-shirts, and license plate holders emblazoned with redneck slogans serve as excellent means by which BCCT fans can conspicuously announce their redneck-ness. Thus, the BCCT encourages a climate of consumerism and provides a means by which loyal audiences can satisfy that appetite.

A series of semi-scripted, "behind-the-scenes" video clips of the four comedians goofing around together on tour is included between each stand-up comedy performance on the first BCCT film. These skits work to extend the illusion of authenticity that the BCCT tries so hard to construct. Because the clips show the performers acting and speaking like rednecks off the stage, they strengthen the notion that Foxworthy, Engvall, White, and the Cable Guy are actual members of Southern or rural culture. During a fishing trip, a visit to the mall, a day at the spa, and a shopping jaunt to the fishing-hunting-camping retailer Outdoor World, the comedians demonstrate the precise lack of sophistication that their on-stage discourse posits as the primary criterion for qualifying as a redneck. Such sequences suggest these men are legitimate rednecks and are therefore free to ridicule the culture of which they are a part. Importantly, this ridicule is as much a celebration of redneck culture as it is a condemnation of it. However, such complex symbolic constructions have been interpreted by others as "the ultimate violence . . . appropriation in the guise of embrace."[31]

Another marker of authenticity within the BCCT discourse is the narrative style with which the comedians address their audiences. The conversational tone of these narratives presents the impression of truth and fidelity. Occasionally, the truthfulness of the BCCT's stories is made explicit. For instance, Bill Engvall finishes his humorous tales with comments such as "that's real, my friend," and Jeff Foxworthy tells his audience "the best stuff is not stuff you make up, it's true stuff."[32] Ultimately, this creates the impression that if these stories—which include redneck characters in redneck situations—are true, then the comedians themselves must be actual rednecks.

According to Young, cultural appropriation is ethical when the appropriation of a cultural product is "freely sanctioned by a competent authority within the culture that produced it."[33] If we are to accept the redneck credentials offered by the performers in their own discourse, then their appropriation is entirely ethical (if it constitutes appropriation at all). For many audiences, these men probably do represent "true" rednecks with the authority to reproduce and poke fun at their own culture. Some of these men have college degrees and are from relatively wealthy families. For instance, Larry the Cable Guy is college-educated, having once majored in theatre at a small Baptist college.[34] The Southern drawl, mode of dress, and feigned ignorance/unintelligence were all appropriated in Dan Whitney's creation of the "Larry the Cable Guy" character. Similarly, Bill Engvall grew up the son of a doctor and probably did not experience the sort of socioeconomic hardships that lead to the lack of sophistication necessary for being a true Southern redneck.

Even if these men were raised in the redneck tradition, there would be reason to question just how authentic their shtick could be after having achieved their level of success. There is reason to question whether, upon becoming multimillionaires, the BCCT performers experience the socioeconomic constraints that encourage the "glorious lack of sophistication" said to define redneck culture. On the other hand, this may actually expand the appeal of what it means to be redneck. Audiences that recognize socioeconomic differences between themselves and their comedic heroes may actually find it all the more endearing that these characters have retained their lack of sophistication. In other words, the BCCT's construction of redneck-dom attempts transcends economic boundaries.

Still, there are numerous reasons for sharp critics to doubt whether the BCCT entertainers are the competent authorities on Southern culture that they have presented themselves as. In the case of the BCCT films, Young's criteria for ethical appropriation are not fulfilled. Young reminds us how difficult questions of proper authority can be, writing, "no one, neither an individual nor a culture has the right to control a general idea. Only particular workings-out of general ideas are protected by a legal or moral copyright."[35] I argue in a later section of this essay that the particular workings-out of Southern redneck *ethos* are performed in a profoundly offensive manner. But first, I turn to another means by which the BCCT entertainers attempt to obfuscate questions of group membership and deflect criticism for their appropriation of rural American culture.

"You're Rednecks, Too"

Not only do these rhetors construct themselves as rednecks, but they construct everyone else as rednecks too. The term itself, which typically bears a pejorative meaning, is reclaimed in the BCCT's rhetoric as something to be celebrated. In glorifying the term and all its related concepts, the actors have defined a redneck so broadly as to include the Southerner, an inhabitant of any rural location, and indeed, just about every American. With the construction of a universal redneck identity, the BCCT further obfuscates the issue of group membership, erecting an *a priori* defense against charges of cultural appropriation or negatively portraying Southern culture.

As part of his standup routine, Foxworthy advances the premise, "You can be part of a group and not even know you're part of a group until you read about it or see it on TV."[36] In this instance, Foxworthy is actually speaking about how his wife watches television shows about people with rare diseases and then becomes convinced that she too suffers from these ailments. However, by analogy, BCCT audiences may have always been rednecks, but never really known it until Foxworthy and company brought it to their attention. Such understandings of group membership exemplify the way in which the BCCT attempts to obfuscate and eradicate common notions about cultural belonging.

When Jeff Foxworthy discusses being a redneck in *Blue Collar Comedy Tour: The Movie*, he says being a redneck can be "full time or part time" and stresses even if one is not a redneck, their friends and family may be. This broad construction of what constitutes a redneck changes the rhetoric's focus from a particular culture or region of the country, to a far-reaching set of behaviors that large segments of the American populace would be able to recognize in themselves or those they know. Interestingly, the very ability to understand and appreciate a "redneck" joke by responding with laughter could be loosely construed as evidence that an audience has related to, or identified with, the material. Of course, if the BCCT comics are representing everybody and making fun of everybody, then nobody has a right to get upset. If they make fun of themselves, they can make fun of everyone else. Such constructions of group membership serve to reduce culpability for their potentially destructive characterization of Southern culture. The precise ways in which the BCCT's discourse may be destructive are detailed in the next section.

Profound Offense

According to Young, an act may be labeled profoundly offensive when it strikes at one's moral sensibilities" and "core values or sense of self."[37] I contend that the rhetorical and artistic acts performed by the BCCT do just that by relying on racist and sexist material to achieve their communication goals. Indeed there are numerous audiences for whom the BCCT may be profoundly offensive.

To begin, any member of one or more of the many marginalized groups the BCCT ridicules may take offense to this brand of comedy. This includes women, members of the LGBT community, African-Americans, Asian-Americans, Inuit people, people of Middle Eastern ancestry, and others. Each of these groups is the object of derision at some point in the discourse of the BCCT. Importantly, group membership is not a necessary criterion for taking offense at such sexist and racist speech. Any individual concerned with equality and justice for all persons, regardless of sex, gender, race, culture, etc., may fault the BCCT for its abhorrent communication.

In addition to those targeted by the discriminatory rhetoric of the BCCT, anybody who identifies as a Southerner, a blue collar worker, resident of rural America, or even a redneck, may find the BCCT offensive. These mediated representations of the South perpetuate such an objectionable portrait of the Southerner, that it may strike at the self-identity of any individual who would otherwise identify with Southern or rural culture. The same is true for those who would call themselves blue collar because every bigoted rhetorical act is technically performed in their name. Individuals who see themselves as part of any one of these groups might very well view the BCCT as a misrepresentation of their culture and object to the idea that such hate and bigotry is a part of their way of being.

Finally, the degree to which the image of the Southerner is appropriated and commodified for the sake of profits renders it potentially offensive to both fervent Marxists and ethically minded capitalists. That the image and identity of the Southerner is (mis)appropriated for the purposes of personal monetary gain may make the BCCT's rhetoric even more upsetting for some. The authentic Southerner after whom much of this comedy is modeled must sit passively by as his image is perverted for someone else's profit. This, of course, is where the concept of commodification becomes so relevant to the present study. The actors in the BCCT films are savvy marketers, turning rural American ways of life into exchangeable goods. Having discussed the groups that may be profoundly offended by the BCCT's humor, I now turn to a more specific discussion of the sexism and racism promoted by the BCCT.

Sexism

In the opening sequence of *Blue Collar Comedy Tour*, the film's key players, Jeff Foxworthy, Bill Engvall, Larry the Cable Guy, and Ron White are fishing on a small lake while talking about women and sex. Just seconds into this first scene, Ron White asks the question, "Who do you think has been with the ugliest woman here?" Foxworthy plays along with White's set-up by asking, "Have you ever been with an ugly woman?" To this, White boasts, "The ugliest woman I've ever been with, I was with last week, and uh, I'm starting to miss her."[38] Of course, White's joke relies on the audience's realization that he is almost certainly speaking about a woman with whom he has been romantically involved for a long period of time. Notably, the sexist and disparaging tone of this exchange, which is also the audience's initial introduction to the Blue Collar gang, is echoed throughout the rest of the BCCT's discourse. The all-male ensemble consistently focuses their discourse on the deficiencies and deformities of women (physical, emotional, and psychological).

The BCCT comedians often challenge the competence and intelligence of women. When women are presented as characters in the narratives that Foxworthy, Engvall, the Cable Guy, and White share, those women are consistently the butt of the joke. Women are commonly accused of nagging or otherwise behaving irrationally in the stories told by the four performers. For instance, Bill Engvall makes fun of his wife because she collects twist-ties from loaves of bread. She is portrayed as an annoying female who is fixated on trivial affairs and unable to see what is really important in life. This theme resonates through a pair of stories, one told by Engvall, the other by Foxworthy, about times when their wives accompanied them on hunting trips. In both narratives, the women were represented as chatty, impatient, unintelligent obstacles to men's happiness. Because the women were excessively concerned with frivolous matters such as fashion and hygiene, they were unable to attend to the serious business of killing animals for sport.

In prescribing stereotypical gender roles, the BCCT sets up a familiar dichotomy regarding what it means to be a man and what it means to be a woman. In one segment, Engvall boasts he has finally figured out the difference between men and women:

> I think the biggest difference between men and women is this. Men are basic. Just basic. There is not a whole lot of frills. That's why, ladies, when you ask a fella a question, a lot of times the answer you get is, "I don't know." [laughter]. My friend Joey and I were working out the gym the other day. Joey says to me, hey man, I'm getting a divorce. And I said, oh that sucks, can you spot me? [laughter]. That was our whole conversation. I understood it. He understood it. [laughter].[39]

On one side of the dichotomy Engvall constructs, there are men, who are intelligent, rational, patient, skilled, calm, and emotionally uninterested. On the other side are women, who are finicky, irrational, intuitive, and lacking any applicable skills or knowledge. The BCCT's humor works by exploiting perceived differences and creating differences where they might not otherwise exist. Importantly, the two stations of this gender dichotomy are never purported to be equal. The men of the BCCT are proud of reminding the audience that men's way of being and knowing are superior and correct.

In addition to insulting women's character, the BCCT also attacks women's physical characteristics. Larry the Cable Guy is perhaps the worst offender in this respect, as he consistently associates women with physical deformity. Rarely does a female character appear in his stories without suffering a grotesque physical ailment. In one joke, the Cable Guy flippantly asserts, "I used to date this girl, [she] had one boob bigger than the other. [laughter]. She got in a wet t-shirt contest and took first and third place out there in the contest. [laughter]."[40] Other prominent characters are described as being extremely overweight or being covered from head to toe with moles. Many of these characters do not need to be women for the joke to work (nor are these physical descriptions always essential to the humor), but the Cable Guy and his audience appear to derive extra pleasure from ridiculing female bodies.

Jeff Foxworthy's comedy demonstrates the same misogynist trend when he performs an extended comedic bit on the topic of redneck fashion tips. The premise of these jokes is certain articles of clothing should not be made in certain sizes. While he does comment on a few men's garments, he focuses almost exclusively on the hideous bodies of women he claims to have seen out in public. He ridicules large women who wear spandex, belly shirts, and pants with words on the backside. He also makes fun of women who have had children but do not wear a bra: " . . . that cleavage line is like three feet long and it's got these little wrinkles coming off of it. [laughter]. Looks like you're looking down into the Grand Canyon out an airplane window."[41] Another example of Foxworthy objectifying and ridiculing women and their alleged physical flaws is presented when he describes some women's breasts as "something that looks like those long balloons four days after the birthday party. And they ain't floating up to the ceiling, they are on the floor. Hell, you could step on them and they wouldn't pop."[42] This violent image comes part and parcel with the notion that there is something inherently disgusting and vile about women's bodies. Such deformities are particularly repugnant in the eyes of these performers because if we are to trust their rhetoric, they believe that women's value comes from their appearance. Thus, women are to be looked at, with little regard ever being paid to the actual use-value or biological functions for which bodies and their parts are intended.

In addition to belittling femininity, these performers also glorify masculinity. They portray themselves as beer drinking, sex-seeking, car-loving, ass-scratching hunters and buffoons. They consistently celebrate the myth of the emotionally illiterate male who feels nothing and remains equally oblivious to the feelings of others. When Larry the Cable Guy rouses an audience by saying, "I went in there to Victoria Secrets (sic). You ever been in there? Yeah. Git-R-Done! That's like a grown feller Chuck-E-Cheese in there. I like that,"[43] he simultaneously establishes his own sexual preferences and reminds audiences of what interests and behaviors are acceptable and normal for "fellers."

Another prevalent means by which BCCT comics perform their heterosexuality is by attacking homosexuality as something disgusting and laughable. For instance, in the following excerpt, Ron White demonstrates a willful ignorance and abhorrence for any individual with a different sexual orientation than he has:

> My wife's been in Europe for three weeks. She left two days after Valentine's Day. And for Valentine's Day I was going to take her to see *Brokeback Mountain*. It was sold out so we're gonna go see it tomorrow. And uh, Heath Ledger and Jake Gyllenhaal are both amazing actors. And if you've seen the movie,

don't ruin it for me. I don't want to know which one plays the sheep. [laughter].[44]

With reference to a popular film about a romance between two grown men, White manages to equate homosexuality with bestiality, degrading not just a couple of fictional characters, but an entire LGBT community. Such rhetoric asserts a mainstream hegemonic masculinity that tolerates a very narrow range of orientations and behaviors.[45]

Racism

Women are not the only marginalized group these performers disparage. The discourse is punctuated by an often blatant xenophobia. The performers consistently point out differences between themselves and others by insulting the character and competence of racial minority groups. For instance, upon recalling an encounter with an ugly woman, Larry the Cable Guy says he "disappeared like a set of rims at a Puff Daddy concert."[46] Here, he insults the black recording artist and his presumably African-American audience, by perpetuating the racist notion that African-Americans are criminals. That this joke was understood so immediately and generates such laughter is evidence of the manner in which such statements reflect and perpetuate taken-for-granted racist sentiments that contribute to the oppression of marginalized groups.

The racist attitudes embedded in comments such as those made by Larry the Cable Guy are particularly interesting when one considers the BCCT's inclusion of African-American comedian David Alan Greer. Greer acts as a sort of host or team manager in the first BCCT film. So if the BCCT is so racist, why does it include a well-known African-American comedian in its film? The answer is twofold. First, much of the BCCT's racism is rather covert. This is a stand-up comedy event, not a Klan rally. Therefore, racist sentiments, which may not even be understood as racist by those who utter them, are made palatable for mainstream mass consumption. Second, we must seriously consider the possibility of tokenism, whereby a solitary member of a minority group is included in an event, organization, text, etc., in a way that obscures the reality of the situation: Minorities are not included or worse yet, not welcome.[47]

Ron White advanced a series of particularly offensive jokes about the Inuit people of Alaska on *Blue Collar Comedy: One for the Road*. He set up these comments by remarking on how his airplane flight out of Fairbank, Alaska, was delayed for three days.

> Stranded there, with the Eskimo people. Not a great looking group of folks. [laughter]. And I mentioned that on stage, and they got pissed off. [laughter].

And I didn't see why they got so mad. I didn't insinuate that they had no character. I mentioned that they weren't attractive. I thought they knew. Apparently I let some big cat out of the bag. [laughter]. Have you seen their teeth? They could make keys. [laughter]. You don't have to be in Fairbank very long before you figure out what that nose-rubbing deal is all about. [Mimes nose-rubbing]. "No, I'm good." [laughter]. Anyway, I got this scathing letter from the head Eskimo, frosty, or whatever his name was. [laughter]. And uh, halfway through the letter, he said he would have me know that the Inuit tribe is one of the purest races on the planet. [laughter]. And I'm like, that's kind of what I'm talking about. Nobody will have sex with these people. [laughter]. And then later in the letter, it said that there are less Inuits every year, which I guess means it's getting to where they won't even have sex with each other. [laughter].[48]

In a very short period of time, White uses a pejorative term (Eskimo) to refer to the group, disparages their appearance as though each member of the group looked exactly like the others, mocked the group's culture, and attempted to defend his own racism by insisting the group had overreacted to his destructive comments. Under the guise of the "I call it like I see it," straight-shooting comedian, White exploits racial and cultural difference, marking one errant group as "other" while confirming the superior identity of the white, Anglo-Saxon, Protestant, audiences with whom he is presumed to identify. This blatant ethnocentrism is used to comic effect in order to advance White's communication and economic goals.

Other blatant examples of the group's perpetuation of racist stereotypes can be seen when Bill Engvall attempts to imitate his acupuncturist, an Asian man, by contorting his own face and speaking in a ridiculous voice. Like the other comedians on the tour, Engvall relies here on the exploitation of differences in order to get laughs. Similarly, Jeff Foxworthy jokes about attacking airplanes with a leaf blower and in doing so uses the voice of an Middle Eastern man, thus perpetuating the idea all terrorists are Middle Eastern, and for that matter, all Middle Eastern people are terrorists. Ron White expresses this same sentiment in *Blue Collar Comedy: One for the Road* when he argues,

If I'm standing in line to get on a plane and the guy in line ahead of me needs two loads of phlegm to pronounce his name, I'm checking his shoes for fuses. [laughter]. And I don't care who knows it either. And it's not being racist . . . it's . . . it's profiling.[49]

From White's perspective, different names, dialects, and voices are to be feared. Such people variations are wrong and dangerous. When featured as part of a comedy routine, these racist ideas begin to earn the status of "common knowledge" that "everyone gets," and then risk becoming the sort of taken-for-granted belief that perpetuates and justifies discrimination against marginalized groups who these rhetors, because of their own ignorance, fear and actively misunderstand.

The rhetoric employed by the comedians who comprise the BCCT can be considered profoundly offensive in several different ways and to many different audiences. The misogyny expressed here could be construed as offensive to women, the racism could offend any individuals of the different ethnicities or cultures targeted in these films, and those who identify as Southerners or blue collar workers could contest the (mis)representation of their kind by the four BCCT comedians. Importantly, group membership is not a prerequisite for taking offense to sexist/homophobic/racist language. Individuals who are concerned about the well-being and equality of various demographic groups could also object to the discourse presented by the three BCCT films. Additionally, it is possible even if group members had encountered few or none of the offensive speech acts on the films, a simple knowledge of their existence could prove to be profoundly offensive.[50] Having argued that the BCCT appropriates and commodifies Southern culture in a manner that is profoundly offensive, I now consider additional criteria for evaluating the ethicality of specific instances of cultural appropriation.

Supplementary Considerations

There are numerous critical criteria, adapted from the work of Joel Feinberg[51] that problematize and complicate evaluations about the ethicality of particular instances of cultural appropriation.[52] These include the social value of the artifacts, concerns over freedom of speech, consideration of time and place, the extent to which the act is tolerated by a culture, and the degree to which offense may be considered reasonable or unreasonable. Each of these issues must be confronted if one is to fairly assess an artifact that is accused of unethical cultural appropriation.

First, I consider the social value of the BCCT films. Laughter and entertainment are certainly worthy goals. The ability to generate either is a skill to be admired. Of course, comedy is not always just for fun and deserves to be taken seriously. Historically, comedians have been in unique positions to critique our society and culture. However, this is generally not the primary aim of the BCCT's discourse. Rather than attempt to right social ills, much of the films' rhetoric actually reinforces them. Even if we were to accept the idea that the BCCT has observed and expressed some indispensable cultural current that no other source had yet identified or described, the social value of the project is questionable.

It must be conceded that just about any work of art has some social merit. However, because the BCCT films seem to produce as many potentially harmful dialogues as they do socially valuable ones, Young's social value criterion fails to redeem the BCCT's unjust appropriation of Southern, rural, American culture.

Freedom of expression is also important to consider when criticizing some rhetorical artifact for being unethical. Although the BCCT's speech is profoundly offensive, that speech is also legally protected. It is important to note that neither I, nor Young, have advocated the censoring of any particular acts. Young writes, "Artists do not act wrongly when, in good faith and in response to a compelling imperative, they produce artworks in pursuit of self-realization and disinterested inquiry."[53] While their acts are certainly protected as free expression, they cannot be said to qualify as "disinterested" because of their role in acquiring massive profits for the comedians.

Artists certainly deserve to be justly compensated for their creative acts. The problem with the BCCT is not the ends they have ultimately achieved, but the means by which they achieved them. Plenty of stand-up comedians have managed to achieve great financial success without resorting to the exploitation and ridicule of group differences, and without appropriating another culture. Furthermore, the degree to which the Blue Collar franchise encourages consumerism is problematic here. For instance, after the performers tell a joke, it is not uncommon for the camera to focus on an audience member who is holding a piece of that performer's merchandise. Such blatant advertising creates the impression that the jokes are simply the means by which the BCCT comedians can profit from the sale of t-shirts, license plate holders, and bumper stickers. The artistic pursuit is very much complicated here by the performers' hyper-consumerist tendencies. In short, the free speech criterion does little to reduce the responsibility or guilt of the offending actors.

Young's third criterion for evaluating acts of cultural appropriation deals with issues of time and place. Certainly, particular works of art may be more acceptable in certain times and places than others. Importantly, the rhetoric of the BCCT is not forced on anybody. It is up to consumers to determine the time and place at which they decide to experience the discourse. Those who do not wish to expose themselves to the tour's appropriation of culture are not required to watch the films (further reason that censorship would be unnecessary and unjust). Such an observation is particularly important for understanding why this material, however objectionable, should not be censored. Upon considering the standard of time and place, the BCCT's discourse may be judged as less egregious. Although the ideas the entertainers espouse may spill out to others who never sought those messages in the first place, one must stop and consider the point at which a rhetor's responsibility ends. To what extent are the progenitors of mediated representations of the South responsible for what their audience does with their messages? Ultimately, such a question may have as many different answers as it does answerers.

Another measure by which cultural appropriation can be assessed relates to whether the group being appropriated tolerates the act. The BCCT films are tolerated by a large segment of the very population that the film's actors choose to (mis)represent and ridicule. Americans from low-income, rural backgrounds enjoy the films as much as—if not more than—any other portion of the American populace. For some audiences, the BCCT likely offers a fresh perspective with which it can identify. Some audiences may even see their own perspectives and cultural preferences reflected in the rhetoric of BCCT films. It is even plausible that for some, the BCCT's main performers actually model admirable redneck behaviors to be imitated and perpetuated. The question then becomes, if the appropriated culture doesn't oppose a discourse, why should anyone else? Importantly, while this criterion can absolve the comedy troupe of its negative portrayal of "rednecks," it still does not account for attacks on people of different races, gender, or sexual orientations.

Where consent is concerned, the potential role of ideology and hegemony in relationships between large media corporations and ordinary audience members must be considered. The power wielded by media and entertainment can manipulate groups into consenting to their own oppression, exploitation, and ridicule. Theories of false consciousness remind us that it is plausible for masses of people to be misled into acting against their best interest.[54] Unfortunately, the possibility that cultural appropriation can have an oppressive, colonizing influence has gone relatively unnoticed by Young. In fact, this was one of the primary objections of his work raised by Jennifer Epp and Steven Burns. Epp and Burns generally offer stricter criteria than Young for what constitutes ethical appropriation.[55]

Finally, Young encourages the critic to consider whether one's taking offense to an act is reasonable or unreasonable. He writes, that something is reasonably offensive if it "violates appropriate norms of conduct."[56] Moreover, an act's perceived offensiveness may be increased if it that offense is foreseeable. It is unlikely that any artist could be so naïve as to believe that the sort of blatant sexism, racism, and homophobia present in the rhetoric of the BCCT would not rightly offend particular individuals and groups. Young explicitly describes situations that deal with a "history of unequal treatment" or "racial slurs," as instances of reasonable offense. Simply put, any offense taken to the BCCT is likely valid, thus this criterion fails to reduce the apparent offensiveness or harmfulness of the BCCT's rhetoric.

Conclusion

I have argued here that the complementary concepts of cultural appropriation and cultural commodification are central to any and all mediated images of the South. Because ethical dilemmas are common to instances of cultural appropriation and cultural commodification, I critically analyzed the rhetoric of the BCCT's films to reveal how these artifacts unethically appropriate rural, Southern, redneck culture. Young never stated his concerns more simply than when he wrote, "in adjudicating cases of cultural appropriation, a crucial factor is the good of humanity as a whole."[57] As harsh as this criticism may seem, the BCCT's rhetoric does little or nothing for the good of humanity as a whole.

In order to justify their acts of cultural appropriation, the BCCT's performers attempt to problematize common notions of group membership. First, they claim that because they are rednecks, they have license to say whatever they like about rednecks. Next, they define the notion of "redneck" broadly enough to include any and all potential listeners. Thus they are not unfairly targeting a specific group, but indiscriminately making fun of everybody.

The ways in which the BCCT's discourse may generate profound offense on behalf of women and racial minorities is also discussed here. The BCCT perpetuates blatant sexism by associating femininity with deformity and propagates racist sentiments by exploiting difference for the sake of humor. Of course, because these offensive discourses are advanced from the perspective of so-called rednecks, any self-respecting Southerner or resident of rural American may also take offense at the misrepresentation of his or her culture.

Finally, a host of supplementary criteria for evaluating the offensiveness of an act of cultural appropriation were applied. Some of these criteria, such as time and place, and toleration for an act, severely complicate some of the negative evaluations of the BCCT I have made here.

Notes

1. *Blue Collar Comedy Tour: The Movie*, DVD, Directed by C.B. Harding (Burbank, CA: Warner Bros. Entertainment, 2003).
2. Doris Sommer, "Resistant Texts and Incompetent Readers," *Poetics Today* 15, no. 4 (1994), 524.
3. James Clifford, *The Predicament of Culture: Twentieth Century Ethnography, Literature, and Art* (Cambridge, MA: Harvard University Press, 1988), 336.
4. Claire Sponsler, "In Transit: Theorizing Cultural Appropriation in Medieval Europe," *Journal of Medieval and Early Modern Studies* 32, no. 1 (2002), 36.
5. See Thomas Heyd, "Rock Art Aesthetics and Cultural Appropriation," *Journal of Aesthetics and Art Criticism* 61, no. 1 (2003), 37-46; Christian Moraru, "Dancing to the Typewriter: Rewriting cultural Appropriation in 'Flight to Canada,'" *Critique: Studies in Contemporary Fiction* 41, no. 2 (2000), 99-113; Janice Stewart, "Cultural Appropriations and Identificatory Practices in Emily Carr's 'Indian Stories,'" *Frontiers: A Journal of Women Studies* 26, no. 2 (2005), 59-72.
6. See Kent A. Ono and Derek T. Buescher, "Deciphering Pocahontas: Unpackaging the Commodification of a Native American Woman," *Critical Studies in Media Communication* 18, no. 1 (2001), 23-43; Lisa Penazola, "Commodification of the American West: Marketers' Production of Cultural Meanings at the Trade Show," *Journal of Marketing* 64, no. 4 (2000), 82-109; H. Leslie Steeves, "Commodifying Africa on U.S. Network Reality

Television," *Communication, Culture, & Critique* 1, no. 4 (2008), 416-446; Mary E. Stuckey and Richard Morris, "Pocahontas and Beyond: Commodification and Cultural Hegemony," *World Communication* 28, no. 2 (1999), 45-77.
7. See James O. Young, "The Ethics of Cultural Appropriation," *Dalhousie Review* 80, no. 3 (2000), 301-316; James O. Young, "Cultural Appropriation Revisited: A Rejoinder to Epp and Burns," *Dalhousie Review* 80, no. 3 (2000), 320-322.
8. James O. Young, "Profound Offense and Cultural Appropriation," *Journal of Aesthetics and Art Criticism* 63, no. 2 (2005), 136.
9. Tad Friend, "Blue-Collar Gold: Comedy between the Coasts," *The New Yorker*, July 10, 2006, www.lexisnexis.com.
10. *USA Today*, "Blue Collar Comedians Bring in the Green," June 25, 2007, www.lexisnexis.com.
11. Tad Friend, "Blue-Collar Gold: Comedy between the Coasts."
12. Tad Friend, "Blue-Collar Gold: Comedy between the Coasts."
13. Jeff Foxworthy, *You Might be a Redneck If . . .* (Athens, Ga.: Longstreet Press, 1989), 1.
14. Jeff Foxworthy, *You Might be a Redneck If . . .* (Athens, Ga.: Longstreet Press, 1989), 2.
15. *Blue Collar Comedy Tour: The Movie*.
16. Tad Friend, "Blue-collar gold: Comedy between the coasts."
17. Michael D. Schaeffer, "Heartland Humor: Nice-guy Comic Bill Engvall Found His Niche on the Blue Collar Comedy Tour," *Philadelphia Inquirer*, July 17, 2004, www.lexisnexis.com.
18. Bill Keveney, "Engvall's Sign Says It's His Show," *USA Today*, July 13, 2007, www.lexisnexis.com.
19. Bill Engvall, *Here's Your Sign*. (Nashville, Tenn.: Thomas Nelson Inc., 2005), p. 11.
20. Neely Tucker, "Potbelly Laughs for the Cable Guy: Blue Collar Comic Smacks Suburbia on the Funny Bone," *Washington Post*, March 17, 2006, www.lexisnexis.com.
21. *USA Today*, "Blue Collar Comedians Bring in the Green."
22. Phil Roura, "White Hot Stand Up: The Comic They Call Tater Salad Is Ready to Mix It Up at Mohegan Sun," *New York Daily News*, March 18, 2007, www.lexisnexis.com.
23. Tad Friend, "Blue-Collar Gold: Comedy between the Coasts."
24. James O. Young "Profound Offense and Cultural Appropriation," 136.
25. *Blue Collar Comedy Tour: The Movie*.
26. James O. Young "Profound Offense and Cultural Appropriation," 136.
27. *Blue Collar Comedy Tour: The Movie*.
28. *Blue Collar Comedy Tour: The Movie*.
29. *Blue Collar Comedy Tour Rides Again*, DVD, Directed by C.B. Harding (Burbank, CA: Warner Bros. Entertainment, 2004).
30. *Blue Collar Comedy Tour: One for the Road*, DVD, Directed by C.B. Harding (Burbank, CA: Warner Bros. Entertainment, 2006).
31. Doris Sommer, "Resistant Texts and Incompetent Readers," 543.
32. *Blue Collar Comedy Tour: The Movie*.
33. James O. Young, "The Ethics of Cultural Appropriation," 303.

34. Neely Tucker, "Potbelly Laughs for the Cable Guy."
35. James O. Young, "The Ethics of Cultural Appropriation," 307.
36. *Blue Collar Comedy Tour Rides Again.*
37. James O. Young, "Profound Offense and Cultural Appropriation," 136.
38. *Blue Collar Comedy Tour: The Movie.*
39. *Blue Collar Comedy Tour Rides Again.*
40. *Blue Collar Comedy Tour: The Movie.*
41. *Blue Collar Comedy Tour: One for the Road.*
42. *Blue Collar Comedy Tour: One for the Road.*
43. *Blue Collar Comedy Tour: One for the Road.*
44. *Blue Collar Comedy Tour: One for the Road.*
45. Nick Trujillo, "Hegemonic Masculinity on the Mound: Media Representations of Nolan Ryan and American Sports Culture," *Critical Studies in Mass Communication* 7, no. 3 (1991): 231-248.
46. *Blue Collar Comedy Tour: The Movie.*
47. See Dana Cloud, "Hegemony or Concordance? The Rhetoric of Tokenism in "Oprah" Winfrey's Rags-to-Riches Biography," *Critical Studies in Mass Communication*, 13, no. 2 (1996), 115-137; Judith L. Laws, "The Psychology of Tokenism," *Sex Roles* 1, no. 1 (1975): 51-67.
48. *Blue Collar Comedy Tour: One for the Road.*
49. *Blue Collar Comedy Tour: One for the Road.*
50. James O. Young, "Profound Offense and Cultural Appropriation."
51. Joel Feinberg, *The Moral Limits of Criminal Law, Volume 1: Harm to Others* (New York: Oxford University Press, 1985); Joel Feinberg, *The Moral Limits of Criminal Law, Volume 2: Offense to Others* (New York: Oxford University Press, 1985).
52. James O. Young, "The Ethics of Cultural Appropriation."
53. James O. Young, "Profound Offense and Cultural Appropriation," 141.
54. Frederick Engels, "Letter to Mehring," (1893), www.marxist.org; Ron Eyerman. "False Consciousness and Ideology in Marxist Theory," *Acta Sociologica* 24, no. 1 (1981): 43-56.
55. Jennifer Epp and Steven Burns, "Cultural (Mis-)Appropriation: A Reply to James O. Young. *Dalhousie Review* 80, no. 3 (2000): 317-319.
56. James O. Young, "Profound Offense and Cultural Appropriation," 144.
57. James O. Young, "Cultural Appropriation Revisited: A Rejoinder to Epp and Burns," 321.

Chapter Three
Hip Hop, Commerce, and the "Death" of Southern Black Manhood
Franklin E. Forts Jr.

"It is in popular culture that the pedagogy of race, class, and gender takes place."
—bell hooks, *Cultural Criticism and Transformation*

"Hip Hop is a man's game."
—Marion "Suge" Knight (former Hip Hop record producer),
Beyond Beats and Rhymes

"We the kings! We the kings man! We be the kings of this."
—Fat Joe, Hip Hop artist, *Beyond Beats and Rhymes*

One of the defining elements of American social and cultural history since the civil rights movement has been the movement of large numbers of African Americans back to the American South. This development reverses a trend that began over a century ago with the Great Migration—that series of migratory waves occurring between 1915 and 1975 that saw approximately seven million black Americans move from the rural south to the urban centers of the North and coastal West. Many of these black Southerners were pulled out of the South by economic opportunities offered in the growing smoke-stack industries of cities such as Philadelphia; Detroit; Gary, Indiana; and later Oakland, California, to name a few. And yet, they were also pushed out of the South by racial subordination and the violence that enforced it. This Great Migration aided in changing America from a rural nation to an urban one. Some of the repercussions of this population shift would be seen in the African Americas contributed to the development of the America urban music scene. This influence was first seen in the development of Jazz, then later the Big Band sound, and a generation or so later in soul, rhythm and blues, and continuing on to today in Hip Hop. In politics, blacks in Northern urban centers would become an important constituent in the coming Democratic juggernaut that would dominate the White House from 1933 to 1952. Yet, in the closing decades of the twentieth century we have witnessed a seismic shift in this demographic trend. By the late 1980s, large numbers of African Americans were moving back to the land from which their grandparents or parents left behind decades before.

In the first decade of this new century, this trend continues. The U.S. Census bureau reported in 2006 that among the counties with more than 100,000 residents, those that gained the greatest numbers of blacks from 2000 to 2006 are in Georgia, Florida, Texas, North Carolina, Maryland, and Virginia. No matter where one looks in the South of the Old Confederacy, Southern blacks are laying claim to a region and a culture which their ancestors helped create and for which many are proud. This "call to home" has not gone unnoticed by Southern historians.[1] Past presidents of the Southern Historical Society such as Jimmie Franklin, Jim Cobb, and Nell Painter, among others, have written and spoken on the freedom that desegregation has brought to the South in the form of "new thoughts, new associations and new identities." Whether it is the call of a shared material culture centered in food and speech, or the comforts of a shared evangelical Protestant heritage, blacks and whites in the Old Confederacy are taking joint pride in a place and region where both groups of Southerners continue to negotiate and work out Southern identity for the twenty-first century.[2] Commenting on the effects of this "reverse" migration Peter Applebome notes:

> In a logical extension of the civil rights battles of the past, [southern blacks], are staking claim to their vision of the South—not as background figures on the mythic landscape of moonlight and magnolias, not as victims of oppression dragged here from Africa, but as Southerners, with as much stake in the region as any Mississippi planter or Virginia farmer.[3]

We can see black Southerners staking a claim to the region in two important elements that compose popular culture: film and popular music.

In the film industry—maybe the most powerful and therefore most influential genre in popular culture—the "coming home" scenario is a major plot device used to demonstrate how black Southerners are reclaiming their Southern heritage. These films usually center on a Southerner who moved away from the region, or whose parents or grandparents once lived in the Dixie. These one-time Southerners, or descendants of Southerners, have become cynical and jaded about modern life. Our protagonist has entered into some existential crisis and is therefore adrift in the urban landscape of the North or some emotionally vacuous West Coast city. As the plot advances, these alienated misplaced Southerners find their way back to the South and of course go through a metamorphosis. Once back home, our central character (re)discovers—either through contact with family, religion, romantic interest, or all three—the values that have laid dormant as he has attempted to live in the pre-fabricated materialist societies on the West coast, or in the hurried and emotionally cold environments above the Mason-

Dixon Line. Some of the more notable films of this genre have been *Passion Fish* (1992); *Sweet Home Alabama* (2002); *The Fighting Temptations* (2003); and the entire cottage industry of films and television shows developed by the Atlanta-based director and producer Tyler Perry.[4] Save for the 1992 *Passion Fish*, set in the Bayou country of Louisiana and an exceptionally good piece of filmmaking, viewers are not missing much. Yet even a cursory viewing of these movies reveals that this "coming home" motif always set in a rural South, is the latest example of an older and longstanding American tradition of anti-urbanism, anti-intellectualism, and the romantic notion of American rural life as redemptive.[5] In addition to film, the desire of African Americans to lay claim to their Southern heritage is also seen in the youth driven world of Hip Hop. Just as the first "Great Migration" saw the transfer of certain Southern art forms and black Southern culture to the North, so this latest "reverse" migration has witnessed the movement to the South of certain urban art forms and its accompanying urban aesthetic. One of the most powerful, if not most powerful, cultural transfers has been that of Hip Hop and its primary form of musical expression, Rap.

One of the unique features of Rap music is that it is one of the few American popular music genres not to originate in the American South. Certainly one finds historical connections between Rap and earlier forms of African American musical expressions: the African American storytelling tradition, slave field hollers, and the blues are a few of the antecedents. Yet, unlike these older forms, Rap's birthplace was in the Northern ghettos of New York City, not the slave quarters and cotton fields of the Old South, or the juke joints or churches of the Jim Crow South.

Since its emergence in the South Bronx during the early to mid-1970s, Hip Hop has developed into a powerful cultural and artistic phenomenon affecting youth cultures around the world. For many people, Hip Hop reflects the social, economic, political, and cultural realities and conditions of their lives, speaking to them in a language and manner they understand. In the summer of 2005, the editorial board for the *Journal of African American History* dedicated an entire issue to Hip Hop, giving as their reasoning:

> As a result of both its longevity and its cogent message for many youth worldwide, Hip Hop cannot be dismissed as merely a passing fad or as a youth movement that will soon run its course. Instead, Hip Hop must be taken seriously as a cultural, political, economic, and intellectual phenomenon deserving of scholarly study, similar to previous African American artistic and cultural movements such as the Blues, Jazz, the New Negro Renaissance, and the Civil Rights, Black Power, and Black Arts Movement.[6]

Many Americans mistakenly equate Hip Hop with Rap music. Rap is a constituent part of Hip Hop, but the two are not the same. As rapper KRS-One once said, "Rap is something you do. Hip Hop is something you live." Hip Hop is composed of four fundamental elements: disc jockeying (DJing), break dancing, graffiti art, and rapping (emceeing). Along with these elemental components, Hip

Hop has also come to encompass a style of dress, dialect, language, a worldview, and an "aesthetic that reflects the sensibilities of a worldwide population of young people born since the American Civil Rights Movement."[7] Not since the advent of swing jazz in the 1930s has an American music form exploded across the world with such overwhelming force. Hip Hop's defiant culture of song, graffiti, and dance has ripped popular music from its mooring in every society it has permeated. In Brazil, Rap rivals Samba in popularity. In China, teens spraypaint graffiti on the Great Wall. In France, it has been blamed for the worst civil unrest that county has seen in decades. No matter where in the world Hip Hop has found followers, it has shaped notions of personal and collective identity.[8] In fact, Hip Hop influence is so pervasive in this nation that it is aiding the erasure the few remaining differences in regional identity in this country. This can be seen by examining the confluence of three major currents of American historical development: traditional ideas associated with American manhood; the historical development of African American masculinity; and the commercialization of Hip Hop.

The long-established ideas shaping the construction of American manhood were born in the cultural imagination of this nation during its violent westward continental expansion. Cultural critic Michael Eric Dyson gives a succinct description of these ideas:

> The notion of violent masculinity is at the heart of American identity. So the preoccupation with Jesse James, the outlaw, the rebel, much of this is associated in the American mindset, in the nation's collective imagination with the expansion of the frontier. And in the history of the American social imagination, the violent man using the gun to defend his family, his kit and kin, becomes the suitable metaphor for [American] manhood.[9]

Whether one is white, or black, a rural resident or city dweller, this violent masculinity is the DNA of American masculine performativity. When one adds to this idea the transgressive element connected to American popular music, we get a rough view of the forces at work shaping black manhood within the world of Hip Hop. A look at the gender dynamics in the African American experience since emancipation demonstrate the powerful and pervasive influence of this ideal of manhood.[10]

In the years since the end of slavery, black men have sought to attain the privileges and prerogatives of maleness within America's patriarchal society. For some, these privileges were the Holy Grail of racial justice. One need only remember the signs carried by the Memphis City sanitation workers during their strike in the late winter and early spring of 1968, which loudly proclaimed, "I am a Man." Whether it was the grass roots organizing done by the these sanitation workers, or the Southern self-defense group Deacons for the Defense, or the brash boldness of the Black Panthers, and even the anti-heroes of the Blaxploitation films, black men for much of this nation's history have struggled to live out patriarchal expectations connected with manhood and violence. But as

American racial history reveals, black men have not always been successful living out these patriarchal expectations. Writing in *A Question of Manhood*, Darlene Clark Hines and Earnestine Jenkins claim a compensatory/resistive performative framework for African American masculinity.[11] They persuasively argue that during the approximate one hundred years between emancipation and the civil rights and black power eras, black men sought ways to compensate and resist their second-class status as men. Yet, with the collapse of de jure segregation and the opening of American society to minorities and women, we have seen a decline in this compensatory/resistive framework, but it has not entirely disappeared. The image of manhood in Hip Hop culture gives an excellent example of the continued existence of this binary framework. The explosive growth and commercial success of a Hip Hop musical subculture called Gangsta rap—a genre whose contents focus on gang violence, a willingness to kill, and the glories of being a thug—has been accompanied by the rise of bodily muscularity as the physical ideal of manhood. The body becomes an instrument of intimidation, a symbol of personal power and vigor, which sends the message "be wary of me." In a 2007 interview, anti-violence educator Jonathan Katz commented on the rise of muscularity as a feature of manhood in Hip Hop:

> If you are a young man growing up in this culture and the culture is telling you that being a man means being powerful, being dominate, being in control, having the respect of your peers, but you don't have any real power . . . what do you have power over? You have access to your body [which sends the signal] that you are someone deserving of respect.[12]

Many black youths—especially those from low income families and tough neighborhoods—find themselves cut-off from access to traditional forms of symbolic power: a college education, a promising job, or professional and familial connections. Yet our patriarchal society tells all men that you are not fully men unless you exercise some form of power. Therefore, cut-off from symbolic power, many black men resort to the visible "power" of intimidation gained through a muscular body.[13]

The present-day emphasis on muscularity is also heavily influenced by the role of the "bad nigger" tradition in the discursive framework shaping black masculine performativity. As Jerry Bryant writes:

> The bad nigger was the white man's worst nightmare: the slave or (after emancipation) the laborer who refused to knuckle under, who repeatedly ran away, who deliberately slowed down work. . . . He was the out-of-control negro, the surly slacker, the belligerent troublemaker, and occasionally the killer of whites.[14]

This "heroic" type of the bad nigger refused to accept the subordinate position white society sought for blacks. He rebelled against the indignities and slights directed toward all African Americans. Yet, because of his refusal to "knuckle under," he often did not live a long happy life. The power of the bad nigger tradition has always laid in this man's rejection of the values of white society, a society that had ignored its values for equality and justice for hundreds of years.

If we were to look in our present-day society for a place where the values of mainstream American appear to have failed, one need look no further than America's inner cities, the ghetto. And this brings us to another key discursive element used in constructing black masculinity in the eyes of generation Hip Hop. Since the political victories of the civil rights movement in the mid-1960s, we have seen the development of a fascination with the ideal of "ghetto" as the authenticator of true black identity.

The rise of the "mythical ghetto" as the authenticator of true black identity began with the politicization of the black working class in the 1960s. Groups such as the Black Panther party, or Ron Krenga's U.S. organization turned their backs on the civil rights movement goals of racial integration and mainstream political participation. Rather, the Panthers and other Black Nationalist groups turned toward a celebration of black America's African heritage and a worldwide solidarity with other peoples of color. The black nationalism of the Panthers or the cultural nationalism of the U.S. organization saw as its goals the rejection of mainstream American political and cultural institutions. This difference, of course, had an effect on how gender identity was perceived and constructed within civil rights organizations and the black power/black nationalism groups. Writing on this shift from a dominant cultural mode of black masculinity connected to the idealized middle-class-identified men of the early civil rights movement, to one now connected to the ghetto Michael Eric Dyson comments:

> Rap developed as a relatively independent expression of black male artistic rebellion against the black bourgeois weltanschauung, tapping instead into the cultural virtues and vices of the so-called underclass, romanticizing the ghetto as the fecund root of cultural identity and authenticity, the Rorschach of legitimate masculinity and racial unity.[15]

Dyson goes on to support this observation through an examination of what he calls the rise of the "ghetto aesthetic" in a series of films from the early 1990s. Unlike the Blaxploitation films of the early and mid-1970s, with their complex characters and often positive images of strong black male and female heroes, the films of the Hip Hop era "probe the unhealthy and disenabling consequences of black manhood within African American life, particularly as it takes shape in the black ghetto and often in relation to black female identity."[16] Part and parcel of the "ghetto aesthetic" is the prominence of prison life as a signifier of true black manliness, and as a badge of honor. Beginning with the rise of the crack cocaine epidemic within the inner cities in the 1980s and the harsh federal and state law enforcement responses, many urban youth found themselves part of a burgeoning young black male jailed population. And, out of these years of massive black male incarceration came the prison look of muscular bodies, baggy pants, tattoos, and all wrapped up in a hyper-masculine persona. This prison aesthetic plays a major role in Hip Hop culture.[17]

In contemporary culture, the media have become central to the constitution of social identity. Teenagers get their desires for the latest fashions from movie stars, popular magazines, and television. Many American Southerners—white and black—look to *Southern Living* magazine, or the cooking shows of Paula Deen and Patrick and Gina Neely to put them in touch with a way of life that has been lost to modernization and homogenization of American culture. In many ways our identity is often rooted in what we choose to purchase, what we choose to consume. So it is in Hip Hop culture today. What is being put out for consumption by various media outlets as the ideal Hip Hop masculinity is that of the cool posing male from the inner city. Thus the cool posing toughness of ghetto, or the ghetto aesthetic, is the primary image of black manhood we see today. We can see it in movies set within an African American cultural context or in the Hip Hop industry itself. Byron Hurt points out in *Beats and Rhymes* that the cool posing toughness of current Hip Hop is also encouraged by record and movie companies that are seeking to make millions of dollars around the world, selling a particular type of black manhood. Or as Chuck D, former front man for the rap act Public Enemy, comments in Hurt's documentary on the black on black crime referenced so often in Rap lyrics: "black death has been pimped by corporations."[18] The marketing of the "roughneck ghetto thug" brings us to the final contributory factor that forms the popularity of cool posing toughness in Hip Hop: the commercialization of thug life.

One of the major features of contemporary music is its link to advertising and marketing strategies. In this day and age, television viewers seldom, if ever, hear an originally written jingle for a product. Instead advertisers, hoping to cash in on the popularity of hit songs from the field of Rock or Rap, use hit songs to peddle everything from cars to running shoes. Most Rap songs unabashedly function as walking advertisements for luxury cars, designer clothes, and liquor. In his article on the global presence of Hip Hop culture, James McBride comments:

> Agenda Inc., a "pop culture brand strategy agency" listed Mercedes-Benz as the number one brand mentioned in *Billboard's* top 20 singles. Hip Hop sells so much Hennessy cognac, listed at number six, that the French maker, deader than yesterday's beer a decade ago are now rolling in suds. The company even sponsored a contest to win a visit to its plant in France with a famous rapper.[19]

Hip Hop and the rapacious logic of the marketplace are now joined at the hip. Hip Hop, an art form that began as a celebration of the political and social isolation experienced by the working poor of New York City, is now used by multinational companies to sell coolness, a hip lifestyle and a bit of the transgressive. Hordes of American teenagers have flocked to the nation's shopping malls to buy their way into cool urban toughness. While for many inner city residents, this toughness is linked to survival in violent drug infested neighborhoods, many suburban kids are attracted to the cool illicit factor. So when the late rapper Biggie Smalls started to wear the Tommy Hilfiger line of clothing, the brand became cool and much sought after. Rap artists such as JayZ and Sean "Puffy" Combs, among others, have their own clothing line and brand of liquor. Yet, one should not be surprised at this development. The market is driven by one overarching imperative: making a profit. Whether it was Rock'n Roll, Disco, and now Rap music, companies are always looking for new ways to sell anything. But as Chuck D of Public Enemy points out, it is not product placement or endorsements that are the real threat to music creativity, but the promotion by record companies of a particular type of music. Commenting on one of the most violent and misogynistic forms of Rap—Gangsta Rap—and its relationship to major recording labels, social critic Eithne Quinn writes:

> Gangsta rap is not a monolithic expression of nihilism, nor is it a counter-hegemonic voice of sophisticated racial and class analysis. Its expressions vary, even within the work of a single artist. And despite the brash and exaggerated tales of antiauthoritarianism, some politically subversive (anti-police) gangsta rap has been censored by record executives who simultaneously endorse black-on-black violence in lyrics.[20]

The marketing departments of record companies have had the most lethal effect on the images, values, and the ideas connected to Hip Hop culture over the last twenty years. "Many talented young artists are convinced, compelled, commanded to shun substance over style, to promote promiscuity over principle, to dump decency for delinquency." A look at the development of rap music in the American South and how the music industry shaped the growth of Southern rap is a telling story of the hegemonic forces at work in this nation, and the forces at work shaping gendered, racial, and regional identities.

While Southerners were virtually absent from the national Hip Hop landscape through the 1980s, they started showing up in the early 1990s and, by the end of the decade, they were involved in the creation of 30 to 40 percent of the singles on the Hip Hop charts. Then, around 2002, the market share exploded and the figure went up to 50 to 60 percent. Roni Sarig, an observer of popular American music, who has written extensively on Hip Hop, noted that "during the week of December 13, 2003, the top six slots (and ten of the top twelve) on the Billboard Hot 100—that's the pop chart that includes all genres of music, not just Hip-Hop—were occupied by Southern urban artists, labels, or producers." In December of 2004 *Vibe* magazine—the *Rolling Stone* for the Hip Hop reader enthusiast—reported that 43.6 percent of urban radio airplay featured Southern artists, compared to 24.1 percent East Coast, and just 2.5 percent West Coast. The remaining percentage, about 30, was taken up by rappers based in the American Midwest, particularly St. Louis, where many of the artists have strong Southern connections.[21] After an initial reluctance coming from the Hip Hop community, Southern rap, a.k.a. Dirty South Rap, was acknowledged as an important and innovated development in the Rap game. This was also acknowledged by the larger entertainment community when the 2005 film, *Hustle & Flow*—the story of a Memphis two-bit hustler and pimp who becomes a rap star—won an academy award for best original song, "It's hard out here for a Pimp," by the Memphis-based Rap group 3-6 Mafia. As could be expected this caught some by surprise. And, it caused Jon Stewart that year's Oscar host to quip, "In the tally for Academy Awards, 3-6 Mafia One, Martin Scorcese 0."[22]

As Southern Hip Hop, with its presentation of a diverse black life south of the Mason-Dixon Line, began gaining national attention in the mid-1990s, mainstream Hip Hop music began to present black men more and more as the thug or intimidating neighborhood gangsta. The arrival of West Coast rapper Dr. Dre and his seminal hit album, *The Chronic* (1991), made Gangsta Rap a national phenomenon. Record producers and recording labels began looking for the next great "thug gangsta act." The ideal of the thug really comes into its own by the early 1990, and begins to dominate the Hip Hop coming out of the East Coast and West Coast. Yet, Southern rap was different. Images of manhood in the early days of Dirty South Rap were much more diverse.

The themes found in Dirty South Rap and the reasons for its popularity have been well documented. Writing in *Southern Cultures* Darren Grem pointed out the key features that compose Southern Rap are the musical legacies of the South, namely: gospel, rock'n'roll, the blues, and the high hat sound of Stax Soul, all of which many of the artists attempt to deliver with their southern accents, drawls, and idiomatic expressions.[23] And like their earlier Hip Hop counterparts in New York City or Los Angeles or Oakland, Southern artists rapped about the conditions of their lives using the cultural and musical heritage that surrounded them, thereby melding a regional, racial, and gendered identity. In looking at Southern rap three major thematic categories have developed, all reflecting the uniqueness of the regions from which these themes were born.

In the early days of Southern rap, an urban sound developed out of Southern Sunbelt cities such as, Houston, Memphis, and Atlanta. The contents of this urban-based sound spoke of the deprivations, challenges, and feelings of isolation felt by certain elements of the Southern black urban poor. Many of these artists lived in the shadows of economically thriving cities, surrounded by wealthy and racially segregated suburbs, and a black population that found itself fracturing along class lines. Some important groups in this category would be: Goodie Mobb (Atlanta), 3-6 Mafia (Memphis), Geto Boys (Houston), and early Outkast (Atlanta). From these urban Southern rappers—and others like them—came a skillful exploration of the irony of modern urban life and the challenges faced by young black males, which led many to choose a life of hustling in a culture where crime is the only option of the economically vulnerable. The Atlanta-based Goodie Mobb sang of hustling whites, who they called "Clampetts," after the family name of the hillbilly family in *The Beverly Hillbillies* television show of the 1960s. The Mobb condemned those whites who came to their Southside Atlanta neighborhoods looking for drugs or women. Yet, these very same "Clampetts" were staunch supports of the rising Southern republican juggernaut of the 1980s and their accompanying conservative policies, some of which were the new harsh crack cocaine laws sweeping the country in the late 1980s and early 1990s.

The Houston-based Geto Boys, another early urban Southern Rap group, were one of the few really hardcore early Southern Rap acts. As one writer characterized their lyrics:

> [The Geto Boys] . . . captured in one frame: the absurd, the grotesque, the hardcore, the pathetic, the black comedy. If these guys had little else in common with William Faulkner and Flannery O'Connor, they were at least firmly in territory that Dixie artists had cultivated for generations.[24]

Faulkner and O'Connor would indeed find the Geto Boys interesting. Their very presence and names were enough to conjure up images of the "absurd" and "grotesque." At one time the group was composed of members with the monikers of Willie D, Scarface, and Bushwick Bill, a one-eyed four foot dwarf. The presence of the four-foot Bushwick Bill on stage challenged the tough gangsta images coming from the West Coast rappers of the time. In fact, the story of Bushwick Bill's eye loss is a telling example of some of the pressures facing young black men.

One night in May 1991, while drunk, depressed, and suicidal, Bill went to his girlfriend's house, armed with a handgun, and asked her to shoot him. As one would guess, she refused. He then threatened their baby. After a struggle, the gun went off, piercing Bill's left eye, leaving a bullet lodged in his skull. He survived, but lost his eye. He would later popularize this incident in a song called *Ever So Clear*, named after the alcohol Everclear on which he got drunk that night. But the song is more than just the rendering of an unfortunate incident. Bill's lyrics reveal the challenges of fame, fortune, and his personal struggles of living up to the ideas of coolness and an aggressive manhood that permeates Hip Hop culture.

Southern Rap also contains a "country-fried" element defined by its celebration of the joys and hardships of rural Southern life. Many of these artists extolled the beauty of the Southern countryside, a love for the land and its food, a rejection of the materialism connected with the glamour of city life, the importance of religious faith, and, mirroring the ironic acceptance in mainstream Hip Hop culture of the "n" word, these southern-fried rappers willingly took on the once pejorative moniker, "country" as a symbol of their pride in their rural Southern heritage. Prominent among this group would be the Nappy Roots (Kentucky), David Banner (Mississippi), and an early Timbaland (Virginia), especially his early collaborations with Petey Pablo (North Carolina) and the white Southern rapper Bubba Sparxx (Georgia). In "country-fried" Southern Hip Hop manhood and regional identity are made virtuous and defined by their connections to the land. This is done through a discourse rooted in older and longstanding American traditions of anti-urbanism, anti-intellectualism, and the romantic notion of American rural life as redemptive. So, when the Nappy Roots celebrate the hospitality, generosity, and love of neighbors that marks the idealized lives of rural Southerners—both black and white—as they do in their single "Po Folks," or sing of "country boys on the rise" from their biggest hit, "Awnaw," they are tapping into ideas that are as old as this republic and date from the agrarian republicanism of Thomas Jefferson in the eighteenth century; ideas seen later in the transcendentalism of Ralph Waldo Emerson and Henry David Thoreau in the nineteenth century.

The final thematic category of Southern Rap is "crunk," which of the three elements within Dirty South Hip Hop, most mirrors current mainstream Rap music. "Crunk" as a term has an ambiguous origin. At times it is used as a euphemism for sexual intercourse. But more often than not, most see its origin as a combination of two words, chronic and drunk.[25] Given this lineage, it is to understand that "crunk" Rap is party music. Like the majority of Southern Rap, "crunk" features frenetic bass heavy beats and repetitive lyrics, but unlike other forms of the Dirty South sound, "crunk" is about the party and having a good time. There is more going on with "crunk" than simply "getting high" or "getting off." David Banner a rapper whose style goes back and forth from country-fried to crunk remarked on his music and its connection with the blues:

> The blues is the way people express the pain. That's what Crunk music is to me. . . . [It's that] God please help us! That release of energy. Even though Crunk is party music, you're only partying to get away from the pain. So if I can have a song talking about busting a Motherfucker up, just so you don't have to, I take that responsibility wholeheartly (sic). I know Tupac kept me from doing a lot of things to a lot of people.[26]

Crunk at its best celebrates the manhood developed out of the juke joints, gin houses, and street corners of the Jim Crow South; places in which black men sought release from the grind of second-class manhood and a denied citizenship. In these places drinking, dancing, and good-natured male boasting offered many black men a temporary escape. Here can be found one of the defining features of early Southern Rap, the artists performed not only with voice, but also with body. Crunk artists are especially known for having created a number of dances that have swept through Hip Hop circles. Of course East Coast and West Coast Hip Hop possessed dance, but it was the athletic elaborated break dancing that composed one of the key elements of Hip Hop. And more often than not, these West Coast/East Coast MC's were "too cool" to dance themselves. Crunk artists developed the Hip Hop dances the "Tootsie Roll" and "Bankhead Bounce," as they rapped about Daisy Duke (a character from the TV show Dukes of Hazzard) and her tight cut-off jean shorts. Rather than emphasize the skill of the individual break dancer, Crunk artists celebrate the communal and the party, with the only requirement being the ability to "shake your booty."

But just as masculinity in mainstream Rap has become dominated by the thug and gangsta, so that transition is happening in Southern Rap. The rise of rappers such as Ludacris and T.I. (both from Atlanta), or Rich Boy (Mobile, Alabama) and the later work of Nelly (St. Louis) mark the end of the diverse images of manhood and Southern life seen in the early days of Dirty South Rap. More and more Southern Hip Hop lyrics are dominated by dirty jokes, sexually explicit lines, physical posturing, emasculation of other men and the love of violence. What is happening here? As in the earlier expressions of Hip Hop culture from the East Coast and the West Coast, major record labels are pushing a certain image of manhood, that of the "G," the "gangsta," a man who is hard, intimidating and is comfortable with violence. But this image could not have successfully taken hold if it did not resonate within the minds of Americans. Writing on the image of manhood that now dominates mainstream Hip Hop, Henry Louis Gates states:

> [true manhood in hip-hop culture] stands for untrammeled masculinity precisely as the Marlboro Man did a few decades ago. Here is the postmodern cowboy, untamed, unruly, and unbelted. He is vilified, yes; but this frontier culture has always had an ambivalent attitude toward its villains, possessed by a sense of their dangerous glamour. Wyatt Earp is a hero of the American frontier, but so is the outlaw Jesse James.[27]

The misogynistic and violent manhood rapped about in much of today's Hip Hop music is simply part and parcel of the larger American regulatory discourse that disciplines, not only black male bodies, but all American male bodies into the identity box of the tough guise. Anti-violence educator Jackson Katz comments:

> Masculinity is a pose, a performance. It is not just rap and hip hop music and style that offer this story of sexualized violence and misogyny, but the American culture in general tells boys you become real men through power, control. That respect is linked to physical strength, the threat of violence and the ability to scare people.[28]

The masculine gender imperative in this nation tells young men that being a man means being powerful, being dominant, being in control, and having the respect of your peers. As mentioned above, for some men in this nation, this gender imperative is exercised in symbolic ways: prestige from family background; educational achievement; income; social and political connections; and material acquisitions. But, no matter how this masculinity is exercised, symbolically in the boardroom, or the local hockey rink, or the mean streets of a tough urban ghetto, the DNA of American manhood rests on the foundation of a set of ideas born in the development of this nation.

The idea of manhood that now dominants Hip Hop, and is often expressed in the symbolic way listed above, is built on the historical creation of American white masculine identity. This *ideal* of white masculinity was founded on, and created in the "conquest" of North America by white Europeans and their white American descendants. It is a masculinity based on the subjugation and domination of various American Indian groups and other peoples of color.[29] This masculinity born on the American frontier now occupies our collective fantasies.

And no one man embodies that ideal more than John Wayne. Garry Wills, who wrote a book on Wayne as metaphor comments:

> He [John Wayne] embodies the American Myth. The archetypal American is a displaced person—arrived from a rejected past, breaking into a glorious future, on the move, fearless himself, feared by other, a killer but cleansing the world of things that "need killing," loving but not bound down by love, rootless but carrying the Center in himself, a gyroscopic direction-setter, a traveling norm.[30]

We do well to remember myths express ideology in narrative form, rather that discursive or argumentative structure. Its language is metaphorical and suggestive rather than logical and analytical. Over time, through frequent retellings and deployments as a source of interpretive metaphors, the original mythic story is increasingly conventionalized and abstracted until it is reduced to deeply encoded and resonant symbols, "icons," "keywords," or historical clichés. Thus John Wayne is more than a well-known dead movie star. He is well known to the baby boomers who grew up watching his movies on late night television. Though less well known to generation Hip Hop, Wayne still occupies psychic space within the minds of this younger generation. He embodies the iconic ideal of American manhood. He acts, fights, and kills the way a man is suppose to do those things. He lived (acted) the way God intended an American male to live. Or as the movie character J.B. Brooks puts it in Wayne's last film *The Shootist*, "I won't be wronged. I won't be insulted, and I won't be laid a hand on. I don't do these things to other people, and I require the same from them." This sounds eerily similar to a statement given by El-Hajj Malik Shabazz (Malcolm X), who like the mythic Wayne, was "a displaced person, arriving from a rejected past, breaking into a glorious future and himself fearless," who once told his male followers, "be intelligent . . . be peaceful, be courteous, obey the law, respect everyone; but [if] someone puts his hands on you, send him to the cemetery."[31]

The social critic bell hooks calls the resulting culture coming out of this mythic construction a "culture of domination," a collection of values, beliefs and concepts centered in white supremacy and patriarchy.[32] One should not, and cannot, deny the struggles and brave resistance offered by those conquered and subjugated people against which the models of American whiteness and American manhood were formed. But in the end, Americans of European descent—often aided by people they sought to pacify—made this land in their own ideological image. Or, as Theodore Roosevelt argued for American foreign policy of Imperial expansion over one hundred years ago, " . . . the mighty civilized races which have not lost the fighting instinct [are] by their expansion gradually bringing peace into the world's wastelands, where the barbarian peoples of the world hold sway."[33] Roosevelt imagined a generation of American men—white men—mimicking in the islands of the South Pacific and other "barbaric" places the same conquest that "domesticated" and brought "civilization" to the American West. This "civilizing" process would allow white

American boys to become "real" men and take up their proper roles as latter-day centurions in an American Empire.

A word of caution and clarification is needed here. This accusation of "white male domination" is not new and can be seen as just another charge in the indictment of black America versus white America, or as yet another feminist critique articulating how poorly white men have shaped our society. That would be an unfortunate and simplistic read of my argument. Rather, I want to claim that in varying degrees all of American society—even generation Hip Hop—is complicit and therefore guilty of perpetuating a cultural ideal of manly behavior, which when all is said and done, rests on a foundation of violence, for one cannot dominate or subjugate without the threat of violence.

Since the early 1990s, scholars have commented on the reverse migration of African Americans back to the South, and of black Southerners claiming a place at the table of Southern identity and regional pride. Yet with this newfound sense of regional pride comes a new set of challenges. Challenges not directly associated with race, but with gender identity in general and masculinity in particular. Generation Hip Hop did not invent songs laced with violence, misogyny, and sexual boasting. Rather, they took up the grammar of American manhood.

Notes

1. For census bureau information see: United States Census Bureau Report: The Black Population 2000 (Issued August 2001) & United States Census Bureau Report: The American Community—Blacks: 2004 (Issued February 2007).
2. Jimmie L. Franklin, "Black Southerners Shared Experience and Place: A Reflection," *Journal of Southern History*, Vol. 59 (February 1994), 3-18; James Cobb, "Search for Southernness, Community and Identity in the Contemporary South," Redefining *Southern Culture: Mind and Identity in the Modern South* (Athens: University of Georgia Press, 1999), 125-149.
3. *New Times*, 31 July 1994.
4. Although *Sweet Home Alabama* main protagonist is a white Southern female—actress Reese Witherspoon—the conventions of the "coming home" narrative still hold true.
5. I am lead to pause here and ask: could this "African American coming home" narrative, which is rooted in the American Intellectual tradition of redemptive ruralism, be a sign of a post-civil rights moment of assimilation? Where we see the grafting of black cultural life into the larger American narrative of redemptive ruralism? I think the Southern Agrarians of the 1930s would argue in the affirmative.

6. Derrick Alridge and James Stewart, "Introduction: Hip Hop in History: Past, Present, and Future," *Journal of African American History* (Summer, 2005), 190.

7. D Jay Davey D, *San Francisco Chronicle*, 5 August 2001; Alridge and Stewart, 190-191.

8. In December 2005, the French Parliament called for legal action against French rappers for allegedly "inciting" a series of suburban riots. For an in-depth study of the international roots and influences of Hip Hop culture see, James McBride, "Hip Hop Planet," *National Geographic* (April 2007).

9. Michael Eric Dyson interviewed by Byron Hurt, in *Beyond Beats and Rhymes*.

10. The idea of performativity is taken from the work of Judith Butler, particularly her work in *Gender Trouble: Feminism and the Subversion of Identity* (New York: Routledge, 1990).

11. *A Question of Manhood: A Reader in United States Black Men's History and Masculinity, Vol I* (Bloomington: Indiana University Press, 1999), 1-3.

12. Jackson Katz, interviewed by Byron Hurt, in *Beyond Beats and Rhymes*.

13. The rise of male muscularity as a fetish is not only seen in Hip Hop circles, but in mainstream America as well. One need only look at the growing popularity of Mixed Marital Arts fighting, movie stars with new "sculptured" bodies and the growing industry dedicated to building every American a new body. Some feminists argue that this rise in the popularity of muscularity is traceable to the growing power and influence of American women throughout American society, culture, and politics. Their argument goes that as women rise to fill jobs and political positions through all areas of American life, men look for ways to differentiate themselves from women. One way to do this is through the physical.

14. *Born in a Might Bad Land: The Violent Man in African American Folklore and Fiction* (Bloomington: University of Indiana Press, 2003), 2; Lawrence W. Levine, *Black Culture and Black Consciousness: Afro-American Folk Thought from Slavery to Freedom* (New York: Oxford University Press, 1977), 367-440.

15. "Ghettocentricity and the New Black Cinema," *The Michael Eric Dyson Reader* (New York: Basic Civitas, 2004), 353.

16. "Ghettocentricity," 350. Some of the films that Dyson examines are: *Straight Out of Brooklyn* (1991); *Boyz N the Hood* (1991); *New Jack City* (1991); *Juice* (1992).

17. I have also noticed a rise in muscularity within the ranks of law enforcement officials. It is as if there is a muscle arms race going on between, on one side, city policemen and prison guards, and on the other side, the many young men of color who are in and out of our prisons.

18. Chuck D interviewed by Byron Hurt, in *Beyond Beats and Rhyme*.

19. "Hip Hop Planet: The Roots of the Music That Can't Be Ignored," *National Geographic* (April 2007), 114.

20. Jeffrey O. G. Ogbar, review of *Nuthin' but a "G" Thang: The Culture and Commerce of Gangsta Rap*, by Eithne Quinn, *Journal of American History*, 92, no. 3 (Dec. 2005), 1072-1073.

21. Roni Sarig, *Third Coast: Timbaland & How Hip Hop Became a Southern Thing* (Cambridge, Ma: Da Capo Press, 2007), xiv-xv.

22. At the time, Scorcese was known as the most talented director never to win an Academy Award. This was made all the more controversial as a number of his movies are

considered classics and many of the actors in these movies have received Oscars. He finally received his own Oscar the following year for his direction of *The Departed* (2006).

23. "The South's Got Something to Say: Atlanta's Dirty South and the Southernization of Hip-Hop America" *Southern Cultures* (Winter, 2006), 55-73.

24. Sarig, *Third Coast*, 51.

25. Chronic is the street slang for a potent form of marijuana.

26. Sarig, *Third Coast*, 225-226.

27. *Thirteen Ways of Looking at a Black Man* (Random House, New York 1997).

28. Sut Jhally, Dir. *Tough Guise: Violence, Media and the Crisis in Masculinity.* (Northampton, Mass.: Media Education Foundation Video, 1999), VCR.

29. Some of the best work on this idea is the work of historian Richard Slotkin and his series on violence, mythology, and American identity. Of particular note is the final volume, *Gunfighter Nation: The Myth of the Frontier in 20th Century America* (New York: HaperPerennial, 1993).

30. *John Wayne's America* (New York: Simon & Schuster, 1997), 302.

31. The opening scene of John Wayne's last movie *The Shootist*, 1976. Don Sigel, Dir., *The Shootist*. Dino De Laurentiis Production; "Message to the Grassroots," delivered to the Northern Negro Grass Roots Leadership Conference, Nov. 1963. *Malcolm X Speaks: Selected Speeches and Statements.* Ed. George Breitman. (New York: Pathfinder Press, 1965), 12.

32. *We Real Cool: Black Men and Masculinity* (New York: Routledge, 2004), xii-xiii.

33. Theodore Roosevelt, *The Strenuous Life,* the Digiread Edition (Stilwell, Kan.: Digiread Publishing 2008), 5-13.

Chapter Four
The Rise, Fall, and Rise of the Kingfish— How Southern Politicians Are Successful in the Face of Overwhelming Stereotypes
Kevin Unter, John Sutherlin, and Joshua Stockley

The South in general has been portrayed in an unflattering (and often a disparaging) manner since before the Civil War, Reconstruction and Jim Crow. Alexis de Tocqueville's *Democracy in America* occupies itself with a description of southern life, people and politics as one most would find as biased observations intent on slandering a region instead of providing useful analysis. He states that the Southerner's upbringing "all but ensures that he will be arrogant, quick-tempered, irascible, violent, ardent in his desires, and impatient of obstacles, but easily discouraged if triumph is not immediate." Later, Tocqueville would look forward to the day when all of America would be more like the North than the South.[1] Even popular literature from the likes of Edgar Allan Poe, Arthur Conan Doyle and Mark Twain introduced a plethora of Southern situations and characters that detailed a brutal, racist, and often ignorant people. Further, political cartoonist Thomas Nast, who drew for *Harper's Weekly* until 1886, frequently presented images to the public at-large of a brutal and racist South and then a defeated South shamed into submission by a victorious North. Arguably his most famous and relevant cartoon is the "Compromise with the South" that illustrated how the South costs so many Northern lives and shattered the Union; this was later used by the Republican Party in President Lincoln's reelection campaign.[2]

Another emerging type of media would also have something to add: motion pictures, or movies. *Birth of a Nation* was written and directed by D. W. Griffith and paved the way for countless controversial films dealing with complex political subject matters. Regardless of blatant racist themes and historical inaccuracies, this film, like so many after it, will blend politics and media, particularly the medium of film, in a manner that has lingered.

It is from this background that this chapter begins. Here, the initial focus will be on the expanding nature of the media in the early part of the twentieth century and how it offered commentary on southern politics and southern politicians. But, this is a symbiotic relationship: institutions that control mass information can control mass institutions.[3] Media provides perspectives and shapes images[4] and in many ways defines everything about our world beyond immediate family and friends.[5] Some have suggested that the media has the ability to declare something true or untrue.[6] Still others would contend that the media goes even further by working with government and to a lesser extent social scientists to "socially engineer" policies and solutions to economic and political problems.[7] Regardless of the perspective, few would argue that the media does not impact perceptions and in politics few things are more important than that.

Coupled with the media are perceptions of the South that have been aggravated by stereotypes supported through academic research. The beginning place for most is the Cash account[8] that has been generally echoed in works like *Deep South*,[9] *Southern Politics*,[10] *The Plantation South*,[11] and *The Lazy South*.[12] The summary of these works is essentially that the South is a place where a white caste system is in place and ignorant lazy people are able to flourish. To say that the mass media have not assumed this as fact and reported as such would not be accurate. However, as will be detailed below, the story is much more complex than "ruthless rednecks wreaking ruin" on a helpless black population.

More contemporary accounts present a more multifarious inspection. Gilmore's *Defying Dixie* is arguably the most thorough version of the origins of the civil rights movement that actually began post-World War I with Marxists and other radicals in the south. Her description of white and black socialists and communists (male and female) working together throughout the 1920s is a reminder of how multifaceted race relations were (and are).[13] Other works use a sociological perspective to elucidate about changes in attitudes toward race relations.[14] The point is that many of these more intricate issues are not easy for various forms of media to understand or to convey a message about to a mass audience.

The Roaring Twenties

Politicians have attempted to use the media and its influence since Pericles, perhaps the world's first populist, stood in the middle of Athens and demonstrated his oratory skills. Thucydides chronicled Pericles as did Diodorus Siculus and later on Plutarch. In our modern era, politicians sought out media, primarily newspapers and magazines and then later on radio and television, for support and to manipulate the public's impression of themselves and policies.

When KDKA, the legendary Pittsburgh AM radio station, broadcast the presidential returns for the Harding-Cox election, the courtship between mass media and politics was over and the marriage had begun. Even popular entertainers and movies of that era had a political connection. Al Jolson, for example, wrote and sung the official Republican Campaign Song: "Harding You're the Man for Us." But, certain events and the manner in which they were reported sustained the view by those outside the South that Dixie was backward, ignorant and racist.

The South, though, was not utterly guiltless. In response to increased Ku Klux Klan violence following the Tulsa Race Riots, Oklahoma Governor John C. "Jack" Walton (former Oklahoma City Mayor) declared martial law throughout the state on September 15, 1923, and was impeached by the Legislature.[15] Walton was convicted and removed from office on November 19, 1923. He was charged with the "illegal collection of campaign funds, padding the public payroll, suspension of habeas corpus, excessive use of the pardon power, and general incompetence." In Oklahoma this drama played out as a struggle between the governor and the legislature over his powers to act beyond the state's constitution. This is not to suggest that the Klan was not an important political force in that or other Midwestern and Southern states. In fact, Governor Walton had made it a point to "declare war upon the group" and this certainly placed him in an odd position relative to the legislature and many citizens.[16] On the other hand, the national media, mainly newspapers, lampooned the state for its "support" for the Klan and the impeachment of a Governor that was trying to fight these hooded fanatics. When forty thousand KKK members marched on Washington, D.C. a few months later, it seemed justifiable that the media point out the tribulations that lay ahead of the nation if Southern evils were allowed to encroach upon the rest of the country. Thus, a constant theme of the media is revealed here: the South is made up of dumb racists and we need to do something about it.

Within a few months another national story would hit the south: the Scopes Monkey Trial. Many today consider this to be the "trial of the century." On March 21, 1925, Tennessee Governor Austin Peay signed into law House Bill 185 that stated the following:

> AN ACT prohibiting the teaching of the Evolution Theory in all the Universities, Normals and all other public schools of Tennessee, which are supported in whole or in part by the public school funds of the State, and to provide penalties for the violations thereof.[17]

According to the new law, any teacher found guilty would be fined no more than $500 for each offense. William Jennings Bryan had recently extended his anti-evolutionary campaign to include Tennessee and in many ways this is what prompted Governor Peay. Following the Evolution Act (e.g., Butler Law), Roger Baldwin, the Executive Director of the American Civil Liberties Union (ACLU), placed an advertisement in all major Tennessee newspapers declaring "We are looking for a Tennessee teacher who is willing to accept our services in testing this law in the courts. Our lawyers think a friendly test case can be arranged without costing a teacher his or her job. . . . All we need now is a willing client." By May 5, 1925, John Scopes of Dayton, Tennessee, had agreed to be that willing client.[18] Clarence Darrow would represent Scopes and the ACLU. The *Baltimore Evening Sun* writer H. L. Mencken was sent to cover the trial. This was a media event waiting to happen.

The scene was set as the grand jury indicted Scopes on May 25, 1925. Both Darrow and Bryan deliver impassioned speeches for their respective sides, but Mencken (who clearly favored the defense) reports to the nation how the prejudice and ignorance of these Southern politicians, country preachers, ordinary people, and Judge John Raulston are making a mockery of the American Constitution. He further adds that Governor Peay is "ten times cheaper and trashier" and it is "vain to look for relief in such men."[19]

The foregone conclusion of a guilty verdict was handed out after nine minutes of deliberation, but Darrow and Scopes with the ACLU's support decided to press onward and not pay the $100 fine imposed by Judge Raulston. Bryan died in Dayton a few days after the verdict. Eventually, the Tennessee Supreme Court overturned the Scopes conviction, but not the law. Tennessee's evolution laws were not repealed until 1967. One label used by Mencken to describe the Southerners who supported the Butler Law was "fundamentalist." This is a term that immediately conjures images of a die-hard ignorant bigot. Again, the national media (obviously with local help) cast the entire South, especially its political leaders, in an unsympathetic light.

These events would later inspire Jerome Lawrence and Robert E. Lee to write a play dramatizing this trial and it opened on Broadway in 1955. Stanley Kramer would later direct Spencer Tracey, Fredric March, and Gene Kelly in one of the greatest courtroom movies ever *Inherit the Wind* (1960). Such a play and the film, due in part to their subject matter and greatness, actually further the notion of the South as bigoted and closed-minded. The political fallout remains relevant today when any politician finds himself or herself on the wrong side of this issue.

Toward the end of the decade a prominent figure would emerge from an unlikely place to challenge everybody's assumptions about and then reinforce prejudices regarding Southern politicians. Huey P. Long, the Louisiana "Kingfish" (also called the "Despot of the Delta" and the "Caesar of the Bayou" by his detractors), was elected governor in 1928 and established a political machine that impacted state politics for the next four decades—three of those decades came after his assassination in 1935. While there would be others in Louisiana that were more colorful, such as Hadacol King "Coozan" Dudley Leblanc[20] or the singing Governor Jimmie "You Are My Sunshine" Davis,[21] few ever wielded such influence beyond the Bayou State. Eventually, Long would seek a higher office and none of this could have been done without the media.

In 1928, the Kingfish asked rhetorically:

> Where are the schools that you have waited for your children to have, that have never come? Where are the roads and the highways that you send your money to

build, that are no nearer now than ever before? Where are the institutions to care for the sick and disabled? Your tears in this country have lasted for generations. Give me the chance to dry the eyes of those who still weep here.[22]

So, Louisiana gave Long a chance. Voters loved him, but he was impeached by the State House in 1929. He subsequently beat back the charges in the Senate. According to the Long Legacy Project, this impeachment was driven by Standard Oil and their allies who feared Long's five-cent per barrel of oil tax to build roads would sabotage profits.[23] This was a media festival to say the least. Every major newspaper in the state, but especially the anti-Long *Times-Picayune* (New Orleans), fed readers a daily diet of political intrigue. The Baton Rouge *State-Times* ran extra copies and printed front-page editorials bemoaning the Kingfish's plans on March 18, 1929. This impeachment would be driven by the media from beginning to end.

Unquestionably the low point in the process came when Huey P. Long threatened Charles Manship, who owned both Baton Rouge newspapers, the *State-Times* and the *Morning Advocate*. In an interview with C. P. Liter, a managing editor, Long warned, "Tell Manship that if he don't lay off me, I am going to publish a list of names of the people fighting me who have relatives in the insane asylum."[24] Naturally, this threat was printed in every major newspaper in the state and was carried by some national wire services. Through his own manipulation and threatening gestures (not idle ones), Long was able to halt the process on the Senate side as the decade came to an end. However, the relationship between Long and the media was only beginning.

The Depressing Thirties

When the 1930s began, the United States was in the initial years of the Great Depression. Because of his experience in the South, Long had seen what many there had witnessed, which in the North did not: mass migration of blacks from rural to urban centers.[25] New programs and policies were being proposed by the new President Franklin Delano Roosevelt. But, down in Dixie, an ugly trial was about to begin. And, just like the Scopes Trial, the national media and the ACLU would descend onto a Southern state with a vengeance. Further, just like with Tennessee, the State of Alabama would ensure that Southern stereotypes about race relations and fixed trials and crooked politicians would be afforded.

In the Scottsboro "Boys" case, nine young black men were arrested and convicted of raping two white women on a train. Aware of the problems from the Scopes trial, Judge Alfred E. Hawkins was committed to holding a fair and impartial process, but the local and regional newspapers had already biased people's minds. Most such newspapers often referred to the "Boys" as "savages" and "brutes" that had committed a crime that had been "savored in the jungle by the meanest African corruption" while extolling southern virtues that would justify lynching.[26]

According to the ACLU investigator, Hollace Ransdell, a teacher and journalist, some white Southerners who felt that the "Boys" were innocent still favored execution because of the potential threat this could pose among other blacks.[27] This type of sentiment was a feeding frenzy for the media. Whether in editorials or political cartoons, the Scottsboro case became synonymous with Southern racism. That the International Labor Defense organization and the ACLU were involved did not help the "Boys" either.

For the national media, the verdict was never in doubt because no black man regardless of the evidence could ever get a fair trial in Dixie. Many students as colleges and universities across the south were interviewed about this trial by newspapers from across the United States. The results were shocking to those elsewhere: even educated Southern people, especially men, supported lynching, particularly when it involved white women and black men. And, even when prosecutors spoke of the merits of this case before the jury, it was foreordained that the "Boys" would be found guilty and sentenced to death. Later, the two white women would recant their rape story.

Eventually, there would be a second trial in 1933 for one of the defendants, where Judge James E. Horton would overturn certain convictions and order a retrial. In fact, his role as an impartial jurist ensured that he would be removed from the bench a year later. It would take several years, numerous trials, lots of media attention and reformed segregationist Governor George Wallace to pardon the lone remaining defendant. The stain of Scottsboro and the media's reporting of the tragedy visibly blemished the South. The theme of a black man falsely accused and railroaded by a Southern jury is found in short stories, books, and films. Perhaps Harper Lee's *To Kill a Mockingbird* (1960) is the best example of such a story (and later in 1962 a movie with Gregory Peck). The negative force of this shadows Southern culture to this day.

Still, at least one Southern politician during this time seemed to be making a positive mark on the nation. As the FDR administration waged war on an economic depression that just could not seem to be shaken, Huey P. Long, the Louisiana Kingfish stepped up his efforts to appeal to a national audience. Using the mass media, this time radio, Long cast himself as the populist alternative against the rich and powerful. This did not mean that the national media would always be kind to Long. In the classic work by Allan P. Sindler[28] and the more recent and well-researched T. Harry Williams work,[29] it is obvious that Long was often the target of the media that had thrown their support behind FDR. Although Long had supported FDR in 1932 at the Democratic National Convention, it would not take a lengthy interlude before these two prima donnas would tangle. When Long was sent to Washington D.C. as one of Louisiana's Senators, he gained access to a national stage by which to hammer FDR. Long frequently used his new platform to thrash FDR outright, but he understood that he could not simply beat up on another politician and remain relevant in the press for an extended period.

When Huey Long went to the Senate in January 1932, he was armed with the political skills and media savoir-faire that many could not fathom. Not only was he able to win his own race, Long travelled north to Arkansas to campaign for Hattie Caraway, the first woman elected to the Senate until she was beaten by J. William Fulbright in 1944. The national media, like they were apt to do with Southern politicians, in large part dismissed Long as a "rustic clown, a Southern oddity in the tradition of Dixie demagogues" on a path of "political buffoonery."[30] Many still had in their mind a picture of Long meeting a German diplomat wearing "bright green pajamas" and pleading ignorance of tact and a lapse in judgment for this fashion faux pas. Even FDR had dismissed Long as just another "southern crook."[31]

By that March, he had begun to unveil his "Share the Wealth Program: Where Everyman is a King, but no one wears a crown" (which he had borrowed from William Jennings Bryan). Few in the media were laughing at him then. In fact, many in the media were beginning to contrast him with other world leaders, such as Hitler and Mussolini. Raymond Gram Swing had interviewed all three leaders and stated that Huey P. Long was "the embodiment of the appetite for power" with strong leanings toward National Socialism and Fascism.[32] Perhaps, only Father Charles E. Coughlin, another critic of FDR, was labeled a fascist more often than Long.[33] Strangely enough, both of these used the "new" medium of radio to spread their respective messages.

In fact, in February 1934, Long reached out to millions of Americans through an address on CBS radio to champion his "Share the Wealth Plan."[34] NBC radio would give him thirty minutes to talk to the nation. Some of the major points include:

- Cap personal fortunes at $50 million each (equivalent to about $750 million today)
- Limit annual income to one million dollars each (about $12 million today)
- Limit inheritances to five million dollars each (about $60 million today)
- Guarantee every family an annual income of $2,000 (or one-third the national average)
- Free college education and vocational training
- Old-age pensions for all persons over 60
- Veterans benefits and healthcare
- A 30-hour work week
- A four-week vacation for every worker

While FDR certainly adopted aspects of some of these, clearly many were seen then (and now) as too radical. According to the Long Legacy Project, Huey P. Long received more than 720,000 letters in under a month following his radio address. This far eclipsed anything FDR was getting. Long would later recruit Reverend Gerald L. K. Smith to travel around the country, make radio and newspaper interviews and stir up interest in the Kingfish's plan. It is difficult to speculate on how far Huey P. Long would have made it on the national level. His Share the Wealth Clubs had thousands of chapters and millions of members across the United States. But, on September 8, 1935, Dr. Carl Austin Weiss shot the Senator in Baton Rouge and he died two days later. As in life, the Kingfish's death was a media event covered by newsreels and radio stations.

Still, there was at least another important movement during the 1930s that shaped Southern politics and subsequently how the media interpreted and reported happenings from the South: the Dixiecrats. With the election of FDR and the rise of organized labor with Northern blacks under the regime of the New Deal, white Southern Democrats saw their former position of dominance beginning to erode.[35] FDR was concerned about this and knew he needed continued Southern support, especially in Congress, where committee chairs were often occupied by those from Dixie. According to Walter White, this is why FDR resisted efforts by the NAACP to pass an anti-lynching bill.[36] But, this fracture had formed during the Great Depression when the rural south lost farms and fell even further behind the rest of the nation.[37] FDR and the Democratic Party were on a collision course with white Southern Democrats, but would be delayed because of World War II.

But, before the decade could end, Victor Fleming (based on Margaret Mitchell's novel) would direct one of the most damning and lasting celluloid icons ever: *Gone with the Wind* (1939). This vision of Southern antebellum life and the ruin left in the wake of the Civil War remains a harsh criticism of the South, its culture, and its politics. David Selznick, the producer and the driving force behind the film, was no doubt mindful of the mistakes Griffith had made with *Birth of a Nation* and deliberately soft-peddled some of Mitchell's renderings of black characters and overtly racist themes.[38]

The Fighting Forties

The decade began with one of the best feature films about rural poverty and prejudice ever made: *The Grapes of Wrath* (directed by John Ford). In this adaptation of John Steinbeck's novel, which was set in the Dust Bowl era of the Depression, the Joad family was seen leaving Oklahoma (and presumably their Southern values) for a better life in California. Henry Fonda starred in one of his most memorable roles here. Hollywood, an increasingly important media player by this point, made many such films in this genre. *The Southerner* (1945), which was directed by Jean Renoir, was more stylish attempt but was largely panned by United States audiences. However, the abject poverty of the South is what most remembered about these types of films. Fonda later added another great performance in *The Ox-Bow Incident* (1943) that ricocheted off the Scottsboro trial.

Following World War II, Robert Penn Warren published the Pulitzer Prize-winning novel *All the King's Men*.[39] This work of fiction (although largely based on Louisiana's Huey P. Long) later became a movie directed by Robert Rossen starring Broderick Crawford as the unforgettable character Willie Stark. Perhaps more than any real life image, the conquest of a governor's mansion by a ruthless, rural, populist southern politician is as ineffaceable and indelible of an image ever created by the media.

However, in the "real world" President Harry Truman's pronouncement on civil rights was the trigger on a states' rights gun that had been loaded by FDR. And, Dixiecrats across the South were ready to fire. The blast resulted in a political realignment in the 1940s of the Democratic Party. In 1948, the Democrats included a civil rights plank to the platform as President Truman insisted upon desegregating the armed forces.[40] But, Southerners had been peeved at FDR since the *Agricultural Adjustment Act* of 1933; and again with the Supreme Court decision in *Wickard v. Filburn*, 1942, that upheld an extreme interpretation of the interstate commerce clause that most Southerners felt was unnecessary encroachment of the federal government. That the demand for civil rights was first announced by Minnesota Senator Hubert Humphrey only added to the north-south divide as discussed in the reflective work by Ralph Emerson McGill, the editor for the *Atlanta Constitution* during this era. *The South and the Southerner* (1993) looks back through the McGill's personal experiences with segregationists and activists alike to fill in what the popular media often missed: the human side that was complex and a south that "was more than just one south."[41] Yet, the focus on the media would not be on those economic issues that was driving a wedge between Democrats, but racial prejudice. Once again, the South appeared to be on the wrong side of the race issue and the national media was going to pounce on them.

In July 1948, South Carolina Governor Strom Thurman and Mississippi Governor Fielding Wright would emerge from a Birmingham, Alabama, convention for States' Rights, or Dixiecrats as the Presidential and Vice Presidential nominees, respectively. While issues such as federal involvement into state and local politics were important, it was racial politics that garnered media attention. This was not something that the media manipulated, as the slogan of the Dixiecrats was "Segregation Forever!" That the Dixiecrat Party was "at heart, the most infamously hypocritical and intellectually dishonest political organization every created," according to McGill only made the media's job easier.[42] A literal war of words was fought in newspapers and on radio stations across America. Both sides ramped up their attacks, using images of "adulterous wives" and "bastard children" to describe each other. One Mississippi Congressman may have provided the best visual, albeit gruesome depiction of Truman as having "run a political dagger into our backs and is now drinking our blood."[43]

In the keynote address to the Dixiecrat Convention, Alabama Governor Frank M. Dixon declared that Truman's plan "wants to reduce us to the status of a mongrel, inferior race, mixed in blood, our Anglo-Saxon heritage a mockery."[44] An interesting side about Dixon was that his uncle Thomas Dixon was the author of *The Clansman* (1905), the basis for the film *Birth of a Nation*. The press had an undemanding field day with the Dixiecrats.

While the Dixiecrats' success in the 1948 Presidential Election was minimal, they did carry Alabama, Louisiana, Mississippi, and South Carolina along with one electoral vote from Tennessee. National media outlets, especially Northern newspapers, were quick to point out that these Dixiecrats were backward, out of touch, and the "last gasp of the Old South."[45] This may have been a bit premature because segregationists in the 1950s and 1960s found new life in resisting the Supreme Court decision in *Brown v. Board of Education* (1954), opposing the desegregation of Central High School in Little Rock, Arkansas, and backing new icons like George Wallace (Alabama), Lester Maddox (Georgia), and John Rarick (Louisiana). Richard Nixon's "Southern strategy" legitimated the importance of the South. Further, media itself would take another turn as the medium of television transformed politics.

In 1946, Walt Disney and RKO films released a revolutionary project based on Joel Chandler Harris' Uncle Remus (1881) stories. *The Song of the South* (1946) continues to have vestiges in popular culture and the media today. The movie is part animation and part live action and describes some idyllic post-Civil War American South that never existed. Whether or not the film has any merits as a work of art or as a commentary on Southern culture (real or imagined), it does remain the only thing Disney has ever produced that is banned from distribution in America.

By the time the 1940s came to an end, an amazing book was published and remains a testament for those opposing political and social bigotry, again closely associated with the south. *Cry, the Beloved Country* (1948) by Alan Paton was on the surface a scathing denigration of South Africa's racist policy of apartheid; except when the book was published that system had yet to be imposed. Sidney Poitier would later star in the first film adaptation of the book. The work is abounding with references to Abraham Lincoln and the Old Testament. This book is somewhat hopeful about the future, which is a departure from earlier media themes about race relations. But the reality of segregation and the civil rights movement would cause many to wonder if Paton's notions would remain merely a work of fiction.

The Not-So-Fabulous Fifties

The post-World War II 1950s represented a renaissance for America and the American "Dream." As defined by Guimond, "the Dream has been one of the hardiest perennials in the mass media and American popular culture . . . it has inspired editors, journalists, salespeople, and ordinary citizens who have used the phrase (or the concept behind it) loosely and frequently as a synonym for success, prosperity, equality, economic expansion, and social mobility."[46] While new mediums such as television and cinema were becoming mainstream, the primary mechanism for transmitting images remained the art of photography. The increase in circulation of magazines depicting American life, such as the eponymous *Life, Look, Time,* and even *National Geographic* captured many of the post-war changes that were taking place in America, often in contrast to the manufactured television shows of harmonious family life, such as *The Adventures of Ozzie and Harriet* (1952).

Despite these new media, perhaps the best look into Southern culture was through literature. Writes Roland, "Stimulated by the contrast and paradox of southern change and continuity and perhaps sheltered by a certain 'culture lag' from the outside pressures of literary convention, southern novelists continued to draw upon the southern mystique to sustain a regional literature of national and international acclaim."[47] William Styron's *Lie Down in Darkness* (1951) explores the stark differences between life in New York compared to the South. Often forgotten because of the success of *All the King's Men*, is Robert Penn Warren's collection of poetry entitled *Promises*, for which he won the Pulitzer Prize for poetry, making him the only holder of both that and the Pulitzer Prize for fiction. William Faulkner, winner of the Pulitzer Prize for literature in 1950, was severe in his condemnation of "northern materialism and commercialism, as well as a yearning for the way of life that reflected the nobler southern ideals."[48]

The racial stereotypes of the typical Southerner and Southern politician were confronted most dramatically during the post-World War II era. The integration of the U.S. Armed Forces by President Truman after World War II began to soften the attitudes of whites who fought side by side with blacks although it would not be until 1954 before the U.S. armed forces were completely desegregated.[49] Those newfound perceptions however were still running up against those who still harbored racist perceptions. The film *The Defiant Ones* (1958) in which a black convict (played by Sidney Poitier) and a white convict (played by Tony Curtis) escape from a chain gang while handcuffed to each other. The interaction and sometimes coarse dialog between the two characters is a surrogate for many whites who refused to treat blacks as equals, despite similar circumstances. The limited number of movies or television shows dealing with race is part due to the "newness" by which white Southerners (and the rest of America for that matter) were being confronted by racial issues.

The foundation for changes in race relations is often identified as the May 17, 1954 U.S. Supreme Court decision in *Brown v. Board of Education of Topeka, Kansas*. In actuality though, many Southern states had begun the process of rolling back the idea of "separate but equal" set out in *Plessy v. Ferguson* (1896): the 1950 case of *Sweatt v. Painter* resulted in the state of Texas admitting blacks to the University of Texas law school; as Roland points out, by 1950 alone, more than 200 black students were enrolled in twenty-one graduate and professional schools in eleven of the seventeen states that had once barred them and that by 1953, only five state universities in the Deep South remained completely white.[50]

Spurred by the U.S. Supreme Court decision, the interactions between blacks and whites in the South were becoming increasingly confrontational. Senator Richard B. Russell of Georgia condemned the Court's decision as a "flagrant abuse of judicial power"; Senator Harry F. Byrd of Virginia called it a "serious blow against the rights of the states," and Senator James O. Eastland of Mississippi predicted "southern defiance and victory."[51] In March 1956, a group of nineteen U.S. senators and eighty-one U.S. representatives from the eleven former Confederate states, led by Senator Byrd, issued a manifesto against the U.S. Supreme Court's decision in *Brown*; the manifesto pledged the signers to "use all lawful means to gain a reversal of the decision and prevent its enforcement."[52] These attempts by white politicians at all levels and the boycotts and sit-ins adopted by members of the burgeoning civil rights pioneers were caught by the media and helped fuel the negative stereotypes of Southerners and Southern politicians. Early in 1956, the University of Alabama expelled its first black student "under a shower of eggs and tomatoes."[53] Later that year, William Attwood published an article with accompanying photographs in *Look* that captured the brutal attacks of blacks and policemen by white youths in Clinton, Tennessee, who were resisting efforts at school desegregation. One year later, the stage was reset at Central High School in Little Rock, Arkansas: Democrat Governor Orval Faubus refused the federal order resulting in Republican President Eisenhower sending in U.S. Airborne troops to prevent riots and maintain order. The issue received intense scrutiny as would be expected: in 1958, Relmin Morin of the Associated Press won the Pulitzer Prize for National Reporting "[F]or his dramatic and incisive eyewitness report of mob violence on September 23, 1957, during the integration crisis at the Central High School in Little Rock, Arkansas." As Guimond states, "for the rest of the 1950s and 1960s the mass media presented new and unpleasant stereotypes of ordinary Americans that contradicted the populist cliché that they were a friendly, helpful people."[54]

Politically, the South's solid Democratic roots were showing signs of withering: by the 1950 elections, all twenty-two of the South's senators and 103 of its 105 House members were Democrats. All elected statewide officials, almost all state legislators, and thousands of locally elected officials were Democrats.[55] However, the 1952 presidential election of Republican Dwight Eisenhower showed the beginnings of a division among Southern voters.[56] The disruption of the "Democratic South" continued after the 1948 presidential election as the factions within the South continued with their dissent from the national Democratic party relating to racial issues and the increased role of federal intervention into what these Southern politicians considered to be traditional "state" roles.[57] Republicans forced Democrats into retreat during this decade by taking the high ground on race. The Republicans' 1956 party platform pointed to their record of accomplishment on civil rights, claiming "more progress has been made in this field under the present Republican Administration than in any similar period in the last 80 years."[58] It was under the Eisenhower administration that the country passed the first civil rights legislation since the 1870s—the Civil Rights Acts of 1957 and 1960.[59] As a result of the gains that were being made in the South by blacks, black support for the Eisenhower-Nixon ticket increased from 21 percent in 1952 to 42 percent in 1956.[60]

The Turbulent Sixties

The election of 1960 hinged on civil rights: the Democratic platform called for "every school district to submit a desegregation plan by 1963"; the Republican platform called racial discrimination "immoral and unjust."[61] In the heat of the presidential campaign, Eisenhower was confronted with yet another issue over school desegregation, this time in New Orleans as Louisiana Governor Jimmy Davis (who had been elected on a platform of preserving segregation), sought to prevent the integration of the New Orleans public schools. The black students were eventually allowed into school but not without threat of the deployment of federal troops.[62] Nonetheless, the Democratic candidate, Senator John Kennedy of Massachusetts, with the addition of Texas Senator Lyndon Johnson as the Vice Presidential nominee, beat Vice President Richard Nixon in the 1960 election. Of significance in this race is that Nixon captured more white Southern votes than Kennedy did despite putting Johnson on the ticket.[63]

The growing protests against segregation by what was now called "the civil rights movement" in the early 1960s was being increasingly captured by television with nightly broadcasts of national news events. Actions by Mississippi Governor Paul Johnson to prevent the integration of the all-white University of Mississippi resulted in federal marshals and more troops being sent to the South to enforce court orders. Alabama Governor George Wallace's symbolic blocking of the entrance to the University of Alabama to prevent black students from enrolling was emblematic of the ongoing struggle for civil rights. The televised images of the sometimes violent clashes between ardent segregationists and civil rights pioneers, such as those between T. Eugene "Bull" Conner and black protestors led by Rev. Martin Luther King in Birmingham, Alabama, in 1963— the images of blasting fire hoses and police dogs attacking unarmed protestors— inspired sympathy for blacks throughout the rest of the country. Reverend King's August 1963 speech from the Lincoln Memorial—the "I have a dream" speech— and the deadly confrontation between segregationist whites and black protestors in Selma, Alabama, in March 1965 resulted in landmark federal legislation to put an end to such clashes. Other major events that received significant media attention included the 1963 murder of Medgar Evers (and the resulting trial and non-conviction of his assassin) and the 1964 bombing of a church in Birmingham in which four young girls were killed.

While some desegregation efforts were succeeding, the evidence suggests that such success was symbolic at best. Rather than try to achieve full desegregation, many states in the deep South found it advantageous to allow token desegregation, allowing a few black students to attend otherwise all-white schools rather than shutting down the all-white schools. As late as 1964, 98 percent of the region's black students still attended all-black schools.[64] President Kennedy was indeed active on the civil rights issue, often meeting with civil rights leaders such as Whitney Young, Dr. Martin Luther King, Rabbi Joachim Prinz, A. Philip Randolph, Walter Reuther, and Roy Wilkins. Pictures of their meeting at the White House demonstrated his commitment to equal rights and helped entrench black support for Democrats during the turbulent early 1960s.[65] However, in the South, for many white Democrats, Kennedy's actions were viewed with dismay and anger. Roland writes, "so bitter was this hostility that some groups of school children in the Deep South were reported to have applauded the announcement of Kennedy's assassination."[66]

Efforts to expose larger audiences to the racial issues were not limited to newspapers and magazines, or even nightly television news. The 1962 screen adaption of Harper Lee's *To Kill a Mockingbird* netted Gregory Peck the Best Actor Academy Award. Clearly, more and more people outside the South were becoming increasingly uncomfortable with the intolerance being propagated by a significant segment of American society.

This negativity was felt by national politicians, even in the South. President Lyndon Johnson, in his memoirs, wrote of the national bias against Southerners relative to his election in 1964, that he did not think a Southerner could get elected, or lead the nation in unity because of the inherent bias against Southern manners and more.[67] Wrote Johnson in his book, *The Vantage Point: Perspectives on the Presidency, 1963-1969*, "I was not thinking just of the derisive articles about my style, my clothes, my manner, my accent, and my family . . . I was also thinking of a more deep-seated and far-reaching attitude—a disdain for the South that seems to be woven into the fabric of Northern experience."[68]

In part, Johnson benefitted from the fact that his opponent, Senator Barry Goldwater of Arizona openly opposed the Civil Rights Act of 1964. However, his opposition was based more on anti-federal government intervention into traditional state matters. Goldwater's "southern strategy" was an attempt to reach out to Southern Democrats unhappy with the current Democratic Party and encourage them to join the Republican party or at least vote Republican.[69] Goldwater thought he could build upon the growing Republican support in the South that had supported Eisenhower in 1956 when Eisenhower won five Southern states by appealing to white Southerners' dissatisfaction with Kennedy's and Johnson's civil rights policies. Goldwater believed that the race issue could be exploited at the local and state levels, and even at the federal level. His "states' rights" appeals were aimed directly at the white Southerner.[70] To Democrats, this strategy consisted simply of "recruiting to conservative Republican ranks bigoted Southern red-necks outraged at the wholehearted conversion of the Democratic party to the cause of the civil rights for blacks."[71] Clearly Goldwater misunderstood what he was aiming at as Republicans divested their support for him based on this approach: Goldwater won five Southern states (he won six states total). According to Cosman, "never before had a Republican presidential candidate garnered almost all of his electoral votes in the South while at the same time losing in so reliably a Republican state as Vermont."[72]

The landslide election of Lyndon Johnson in 1964 meant that civil rights for blacks would be pioneered by a Southerner against the vestiges of Southern racism and bigotry. The passage and enforcement of the Civil Rights Act of 1964 and the Voting Rights Act of 1965 ended many of the most blatant practices of state-sponsored racism that separated the South from the rest of America (many Southern states had written segregation into their state constitutions). By 1968 majorities of eligible black adults were registered to vote in every Southern state. African Americans increased to 14 percent of the region's voters in the 1960s. Many conservative Southern whites objected to President Johnson's liberalism on civil rights, economics, social policy, and cultural issues; an estimated 55 percent of Southern whites voted for Goldwater in 1964.[73] From that point on, in every presidential election, the Republican presidential candidate has received more votes from Southern whites than has the Democratic candidate.

The continued national reporting of the civil rights movement yielded another Pulitzer Prize for National Reporting, in 1966 to Haynes Johnson of the *Washington Evening Star* "[F]or his distinguished coverage of the civil rights conflict centered about Selma, Ala., and particularly his reporting of its aftermath." The continued and increasing attention by the media on the division between Southerners and the rest of America placed intense pressure on Southern politicians to moderate or even abandon their segregationist views. That many refused to do so despite the escalating calls to do so only added to the negative stereotypes held by non-Southerners.

In 1967, actor Sidney Poitier once again played a critical role in another movie that highlighted the racial tensions between whites and blacks, and Northerners versus Southerners when he played a Philadelphia police detective investigating a homicide in Mississippi in *In the Heat of the Night* opposite Rod Steiger. The movie would go on to win the Academy Award for Best Picture and Steiger would win the Academy Award for Best Actor (five years prior, Poitier would become the first black male actor to win an Academy Award—a Best Actor for his performance in 1963's *Lilies of the Field*). Films such as this would lay the groundwork for films in later decades that would further explore the racial dichotomy and disharmony.

Several other prominent events in the 1960s demonstrated the fight for civil rights and justice was far from resolution. President Johnson pushed through the Civil Rights Bill of 1968 (which primarily dealt with housing discrimination) just days after Martin Luther King was assassinated in Memphis, Tennessee, over the objections of many Republicans. This had the significance of further alienating the white South.[74] Johnson would not run again in 1968, setting the table for another Democrat to try to hold together the fractious Democratic coalition.

Civil rights and segregation remained at the forefront during the 1968 election. Former Alabama Governor George Wallace, who once stood in the doorway at the University of Alabama in an effort to block black students from entering, announced a third-party candidacy based solely on returning power back to the states to regulate civil rights issues. Interestingly, the Republican candidate, former Vice President Richard Nixon (and 1960 Republican candidate for president), ran on a similar platform, echoing the Southern Strategy of Goldwater. Nixon's 1968 campaign was run in stark difference to his 1960 campaign when he ran on a racially progressive platform and made a personal effort to win black votes; in 1968, Nixon focused directly on appealing to Southern whites, much like Goldwater in 1964.[75] As a result, Nixon won with only a small proportion of the black vote but with a number of Southern states in his column. Said Dent, "we elected a man [Nixon] destined to handle the sensitive desegregation of the South with the velvet-glove approach required to avert bayonets, bullets, and bloodshed."[76]

The election of 1968 revealed some other intriguing results that further muddied the differences in perceptions of Republican and Democrat politicians vis-à-vis southern racial politics. Nixon carried six states in the "peripheral" South plus South Carolina while Wallace won Georgia, Alabama, Mississippi, Louisiana, and Arkansas, and Humphrey carried only Texas, in part due to Johnson's efforts.[77] The deep South's support for an ardent segregationist (Wallace) compared to the remaining southern states support for the Republican (Nixon) led some to equate Republicans with the racist policies of the Dixiecrats and the segregationists. This is an entrenchment of the stereotype that Southern politicians of either major party would have to work hard to overcome.

The Settling Seventies

The growth of the Southern economy in the 1970s—due in part to the lure of lower expenses and thus increased profits—drastically altered Southern living as "sleepy" Southern cities grew in size and importance. For example, greater Atlanta, Georgia, grew in population from 438,000 in 1940 to almost 1.2 million in 1970. Similarly, greater Houston, Texas, the southern center of oil, agriculture, and industry neared a population of almost 1.7 million by 1970.[78] With the influx of people came increased representation in U.S. Congress along with increased clout for those Representatives and Senators. In addition, Southern governors and the mayors of these large cities also enjoyed increased visibility and influence. With the added influence came added media attention, some favorable and some not so favorable. The lingering racial problems kept the images of Southerners fresh in people's minds. Films like *Deliverance* (1972) certainly did not help— while the film was not about politicians, the stereotypes of Southerners as "hicks" and "inbred" meant an immediate association for those claiming the South as their home.

During the 1970s, the Democratic biracial coalition ran up against the practiced "Southern strategy" of President Nixon. George Wallace, having narrowly won the gubernatorial election in Alabama, announced he would run again as a national candidate in 1972. Many of Wallace's supporters had returned to their Democratic roots and their support propelled Wallace to the front of the pack for the Democratic nomination. Nixon's strategy, aimed at bringing middle-class, suburban whites into the Republican party was not as successful as he would have liked. Combined with that was the fact that Nixon's less than enthusiastic efforts to promote the civil rights agenda did little if anything to bring blacks into the Republican tent. Between March and May 1972, Wallace won the Democratic primaries in Florida, Tennessee, North Carolina, Michigan, and Maryland, while finishing strong in Wisconsin, Pennsylvania, and Indiana.[79] Suffice to say, Southern Democrats were in a strong position to nominate an ardent segregationist and "state's rights" politician as their standard bearer. With Northeastern liberal elites having nowhere else to go, Wallace represented a legitimate threat to capture the election of 1972. Unfortunately, Wallace was shot and paralyzed in an assassination attempt on May 15, 1972, and forced to abandon his campaign. With Wallace no longer in contention, the Northern and Midwest Democrats' position on civil rights, especially forced integration of public schools by busing whites into predominantly minority neighborhoods (and vice versa), pushed many of the conservative Southern Democrats back into the Republican camp. The result was a landslide for Richard Nixon, with over 70 percent of Southerners casting their votes for Richard Nixon.[80]

After the election of 1972, national Democrats and especially those in the South realized they had to contain the Republican growth in the region, Republicans having won six of twelve U.S. Senate elections (including electing North Carolina Senator Jesse Helms), and increasing their numbers in the U.S. House of Representatives by seven. Recognizing the need to regain their electoral advantage, Southern Democrats began to soften their campaign rhetoric regarding segregation. These new Democrats avoided the word "liberal," moved away from traditional "integrationist" policies, and used subtly different appeals to embrace diversity.[81] Alexander Lamis described the new changes thusly, "the racial tension that had alienated traditionally Democratic white voters lessened, and at the same time large numbers of blacks carrying strong Democratic Party leanings entered the electorate. The potential flowing from this new situation was not lost on a host of Democratic office seekers who put together potent black-white coalitions in the early 1970s."[82]

This moderation, combined with the end of the Vietnam War and the Watergate scandal which forced President Richard Nixon from office, led to the election of Democrat Georgia Governor Jimmy Carter as president in 1976. Carter was one of several moderate Democratic governors throughout the South during this period, including Louisiana Governor Edwin Edwards (1972), North Carolina Governor James B. Hunt Jr. (1976), and Arkansas Governor Bill Clinton (1978). Said Lamis, "attractive, skillful moderate Democratic leaders capitalized on strong white-voter allegiance to the Democratic Party coupled with black support, которая became solidly Democratic . . . to reduce statewide Republican challenges from 1972 through 1978 to no more than nominal contests."[83]

Carter's election resulted in a swelling of pride and triumph for millions of Southerners as they now had a president from the heart of their region. Liberal journalist Tom Wicker wrote, "Whatever else he may do, Jimmy Carter has removed the last great cause for Southern isolation; and even in the remote little farm towns that dot the Southern countryside, it is already possible to sense that Southerners are coming to believe that they finally belong to something larger than the South."[84] Unfortunately, President Carter failed to measure up to the hopes of Southerners as he would later lose the 1980 election to former California Governor Ronald Reagan, a conservative Republican.

The Realigning Eighties

During the 1980s, Democrats primarily controlled Congress, and Republicans controlled the White House, but many significant leaders and strategists in both parties were Southerners. Jim Wright, Democrat from Texas, was the House Majority Party Leader (1976-1987) and Speaker of the House (1987-1989).[85] Jim Wright expanded the Speaker's role in an attempt to change the institutional balance between Congress and the White House. Notably, he pushed the envelope on the constitutional separation of powers by attempting to gain control over Reagan on foreign policy. Speaker Wright also forced out longtime Democratic committee chairman in order to push his own agenda, and he ran roughshod over historic House procedures to quell Republican-led revolts. Patronage, not meritocracy, was Jim Wright's leadership style; a sharp deviation from former Speaker Carl Albert, Democrat from Oklahoma. Resentment over his tactics, mismanagement of Congressional pay raises, and pending ethic charges regarding a book deal led to a relentless anti-Wright campaign from Democrats and Republicans and, ultimately, his resignation in 1989. Speaker Wright was not a popular individual and was not spared from public criticism. Regardless, Jim Wright left an indelible impact upon the role of the Speaker of the House that would be mimicked by future Speakers in subsequent decades.

During Rep. Wright's tenure, presiding over the Senate as the Senate Majority Party Leader was Robert Byrd, Democrat from West Virginia. Although West Virginia is not regarded by some as a formal Southern state because it was not a member of the original Confederacy, southern West Virginia, where Robert Byrd grew up, is nicknamed "Little Dixie." Senator Byrd served as Senate Majority Party Leader from 1977 to 1980 and 1987 to 1988; he was relegated to Senate Minority Leader from 1981 to 1986 when Republicans briefly became the majority. Senator Byrd managed this feat in spite of having admitted to being a former member of the Ku Klux Klan in the 1940s. It is interesting this past association was rarely mentioned and was not an impediment to his ascension. The nation, and Democrats, seemed to largely forgive Senator Byrd for this association because many Southern officeholders before the 1960s held segregationist and racist views, and he had issued numerous apologies for this earlier association. Senator Byrd was known as a proceduralist and often used arcane or little-known Senate rules to push his agenda. On at least four occasions during his forty-six-year Senate career he was instrumental in amending Senate rules with simple-majority votes, not the usual sixty normally required. Unlike Speaker Wright, Senator Byrd was generally well perceived by the media, even receiving credit for quickly killing any thoughts of impeachment as the Iran-Contra scandal broke.

Serving opposite Senator Byrd as Senate Minority Leader (1977-1981) and Senate Majority Leader (1981-1985) was Senator Howard Baker from Tennessee. The left-leaning *New York Times,* on January 12, 1983, called Senator Baker, "the most moderate, skillful, amiable, eloquent, and effective parliamentarian in Congress."[86] He developed a reputation as a moderate by supporting the Panama Canal Treaty opposed by many Republicans and fighting against Reagan's attempt to cut federal social programs. Senator Baker openly flirted with challenging as a public way to express dissatisfaction Reagan's policies, earning the nickname "The Great Conciliator." Unlike Speaker Wright, he was very popular, and like Robert Byrd, he was known to warm up audiences with his Southern charm. Howard Baker was considered a serious challenger for the presidency to Ronald Reagan in 1980 and asked by many to consider running for president again in 1988.

While Congress was controlled primarily by Democrats and the Democratic Party consisted of many Southern politicians, Southerners were slowly building a home in the Republican Party. Focusing on congressional developments in the 1980s obfuscates the fact that historical political transformations and political legacies were happening at the presidential level. Political movements were being shaped by Southern strategists like Bill Brock and Lee Atwater, pioneering strategies to propel their candidates and party to national ascendancy.

Bill Brock, also a former Senator from Tennessee, is considered by many as the savior of the Republican National Committee (RNC) post-Watergate because he established a highly effective fundraising apparatus to pull the RNC out of debt. Under Brock the RNC diverted resources to assist in the election of Ronald Reagan to the presidency and, more importantly, to target Southern states like Alabama, Georgia, and Florida, which resulted in the defeat of notable Democratic incumbents like Herman Talmadge of Georgia and a brief period of Republican majorities in the Senate. Many of Brock's detractors felt it was foolish to divert valuable resources to the South while the Republican Party was trying to repair its image. With Brock's assistance, the Republican Party won a majority of the Senate for first time since 1954. By the time of Brock's departure, the RNC had developed a formidable fundraising apparatus that allowed Republicans to contest elections at the national, state, and local level across the

United States.[87] Continuing the Brock tradition was a fellow southerner, Lee Atwater.

Lee Atwater was the architect of "slash and burn," whereby "Your opponent can't talk when he has your fist in his mouth."[88] He burst on the scene by running Ronald Reagan's 1980 South Carolina campaign and authoring Reagan's famous campaign lexicon, "welfare queen." Lee Atwater is also credited with saying:

> You start out in 1954 by saying, "Nigger, nigger, nigger." By 1968 you can't say "nigger"—that hurts you. Backfires. So you say stuff like forced busing, states' rights and all that stuff. You're getting so abstract now [that] you're talking about cutting taxes, and all these things you're talking about are totally economic things and a byproduct of them is [that] blacks get hurt worse than whites.[89]

It was Atwater who convinced the Bush campaign to attack Michael Dukakis on the furlough program that allowed Willie Horton, a black man convicted of murder and rape, to brutally slay a white family during a botched robbery. He brazenly declared Horton "may end up to be Dukakis' running mate."[90] To date the Willie Horton campaign advertisement ranks as one of the most effective campaign ads in presidential history. This ruthlessness contributed to Republican victories at the local level in Southern states that Democrats had dominated since Reconstruction. For his success, he was rewarded with the chairmanship of the Republican National Committee from 1989 until his death in 1991. Lee Atwater gave an organizational foundation for Newt Gingrich, Dick Armey, and Tom DeLay to take over the House of Representatives in 1994. Many believe his untimely death in 1991 may have led to George H. W. Bush's defeat to Arkansas Governor Bill Clinton in 1992. The inflammatory life Atwater even became the subject of a documentary, *Boogie Man: The Lee Atwater Story*. Atwater was not a popular individual, the original Karl Rove, and was openly reviled by Democrats and the national media.

Southern influence in the 1980s extended beyond politicians and spawned powerful grassroots movements as well. Perhaps none gained as much notoriety as the emergence of the Christian Right from Virginia in the 1980s. The Christian Right became a potent national political force. The rise of the Christian Right is a testament to the organizational prowess and religious intensity of Southerners. The movement's two central organizers—Jerry Falwell and Pat Robertson—were both native Southerners from Virginia.[91] In the 1960s, Falwell ran a program entitled *The Old-Time Gospel Hour* and regularly featured Southern segregationists like Lester Maddox and George Wallace. He used this successful ministry to launch the Moral Majority in 1979, which played a huge role in mobilizing a majority of evangelical Protestants to vote for the Republican presidential nominee, Ronald Reagan.

The Moral Majority helped secure Republican advancements in the South and in the nation, but was largely criticized outside the South. Many perceived the movement as a classical example of Southern zealousness, feverish religiosity, and bigotry. Falwell's positions on illegal aliens, AIDS, homeless, pornography, homosexuality, women's equality, and, most notably, apartheid were regular fodder for newspapers. The televangelist scandals at the end of the 1980s effectively ended the Moral Majority's reign over the Christian Right movement and, with great fanfare, Falwell shut down the Moral Majority in 1989. This would not be the end of the Christian Right movement.

The Promising Nineties

Ushering in the 1990s was the second part of the Christian Right movement in the form of Pat Robertson, the son of former Democratic U.S. Senator Absalom Willis Robertson of Virginia. Though originally a televangelist and founder of the Christian Broadcast Network, Pat Robertson ran for president in 1988 after three million supporters signed petitions urging him to run. His presidential campaign ultimately failed, but the momentum from the campaign was used to create the Christian Coalition, which played a decided role in both Republican and Democratic contests throughout the nation. Robertson and Ralph Reed used the Christian Coalition to gain control of several state and local party machines, to develop state-of-the-art voter databases, and to establish an intricate fundraising apparatus. In the late 1980s and early 1990s, the Christian Coalition voting guide became one of the most powerful voting guides in the nation. Politicians carefully monitored their votes on known Christian Coalition issues to avoid being listed in their guides as anti-Christian. Their voting guide became a deadly get-out-the-vote instrument and could reliably turn out large blocks of votes for Religious Right candidates. The Christian Coalition played a critical role in helping Newt Gingrich create Republican congressional majorities in the 1990s and launching an opposition to the presidency of Bill Clinton. Alas, the Christian Coalition succumbed to the same forces as the Moral Majority for all the same reasons.

Wildly lambasted by many Americans with scathing publicity from the national media, the Moral Majority and Christian Coalition made the Christian Right a powerful political force in national, state, and local politics and they owe their existence to Southerners. In spite of persistent criticism and parody for their platforms and views, Jerry Falwell and Pat Robertson unleashed a spirit of religious fervor and harnessed this fervor into an authoritative political movement that served as the blueprint for modern Christian Right organizations like Focus on the Family.

It could be argued no politician typified the Southern political archetype more in modern times than Bill Clinton—born in poverty, Southern drawl, Southern charm, gifted storyteller, Southern Baptist, and womanizer. Dismissed as a small-town country bumpkin, Bill Clinton went from governor of the smallest Southern state to President of the United States in an unparalleled fashion by utilizing the exact same "slash and burn" strategy devised by Lee Atwater. In fact, he did with arguably greater success and less media negativity. While Atwater was reviled, Clinton was revered, almost forgiven for his transgressions because he was, after all, just a typical Southern country boy. Refusing to fall victim on the issue of race like Dukakis, Clinton, then still Arkansas governor, presided over the execution of Ricky Ray Rector, a legally retarded African American convicted of murder. At an event sponsored by Jesse Jackson's Rainbow Coalition, Clinton publicly criticized the comments of rapper Sister Souljah who had said she never met a white person she liked. Clinton said, "If you took the words 'white' and 'black,' and you reversed them, you might think David Duke was giving that speech."[92] His comments were positively received.

Considered a long shot, Bill Clinton used his Southern charm and magnetism to make people feel like they were the most important person in the world and whose ideas were the only ones that mattered. He also used it to bail himself out of trouble and defeat political rivals. Prior to the New Hampshire primary double disaster struck that would have ended any normal campaign, in fact it did end the candidacy of Gary Hart just the year before. First, Gennifer Flowers produced tapes showing she had had an affair with the governor. Second, *The Wall Street Journal* published letters and documents chronicling his attempt to avoid being drafted. In response Bill and Hillary Clinton did a post-Super Bowl interview on national television on *60 Minutes* about the state of their marriage, thrusting his charm and magnetism before a national audience. For his efforts he was dubbed the "Comeback Kid" and went on to win the nomination and the election. Clinton was considered to be a dazzling campaigner and a dazzling communicator. He deflected Whitewater, a budget shutdown, the Monika Lewinsky affair, and impeachment on his way to an approval rating at 66 percent—the highest end of office rating of any president since World War II.[93]

The popular acceptance of Bill Clinton's image and stereotypes of Southerners left little to the imagination with the film *Primary Colors* (1998), a not so veiled caricature of Bill Clinton's 1992 campaign. John Travolta as Governor Jack Stanton played a convincing philanderer and storyteller, yet deft and magnetic politician. Travolta's performance was reminiscent of Charles Laughton's Southern archetype personified in *Advise and Consent* (1962) and Willie Stark in *All The King's Men* (1949). *Primary Colors* became a best seller and was nominated for several awards, including two categories by the Academy Awards.

The mastermind behind the scenes, also captured eloquently by the film *Primary Colors*, was James Carville of Carville, Louisiana. Carvilles shared Lee Atwater's sentiments, "When your opponent is drowning, throw the son of a bitch an anvil."[94] Carville famously observed that Pennsylvania, for all practical purposes, was Alabama sandwiched in between Philadelphia and Pittsburgh. That is, if Democrats want to win perennial swing states, then they had to put forth a candidate and argument that would resonate in the South, whether they care about the region or not, because the concerns of the South were the concerns of the nation. This was the exact same argument put forth by Lee Atwater in the 1980s and it paid the exact same dividends for Clinton as it did for George H. W. Bush. Giving Clinton the theme, "It's the economy, stupid," Carville put together a campaigning and governing formula allowing Clinton to win the 1992 presidential election and to govern for next eight years. Clinton's presidency arrived at a time when Republicans had held the White House for twenty-six of the last thirty years; the only other four years when fellow southerner Jimmy Carter sat in the Oval Office. For all of the stereotypes of Southerners, Democratic presidential success only occurred via Southerners.[95]

The biggest threats to the Clinton presidency—the post-Monica Lewinsky affair, impeachment proceedings, and budget shutdown—were engineered by the charismatic and energetic Newt Gingrich, Republican Representative from Georgia. His ascension was memorable for a number of reasons: first, he was, for several years, the only Republican representative from Georgia; and, second, one of only a handful of Republican representatives in the entire South. He managed to rise from fringe Southern Republican to mastermind of the most remarkable partisan transformation in the history of the House of Representatives. Gingrich was elected by contrasting the pristine work ethic of Cobb County, a wealthy and predominately white suburb of Atlanta, with the "welfare state" of predominately black Atlanta. In May 1988, Gingrich made a name for himself among Republicans when his confrontational and aggressive efforts led to ethics charges being brought against Democratic Speaker Jim Wright, who had allegedly circumvented campaign-finance laws and House ethics rules with a book deal. He was rewarded by being elected House Minority Whip. Wright's resignation began a two decade absence of Southerners from leadership positions within congressional Democratic ranks.[96]

In 1994, with the help of fellow Southerner Dick Armey, Newt Gingrich unveiled the *Contract with America*, a list of ten reform promises should Republicans obtain a congressional majority. More than half of the text was taken from Ronald Reagan's 1985 State of the Union Address. Signed by all but two Republicans, this platform helped Republicans win fifty-four seats and take control of the House of Representatives for the first time since 1954. Newt Gingrich was subsequently elected Speaker of the House, fellow Southerners Dick Armey and Tom DeLay became House Majority Leader and House Majority Whip respectively. For the first time since Reconstruction, the House of Representatives was controlled by the Republican Party and its leadership was entirely Southern.[97] This Southern tandem would run the Republican Party until 2005.

Eventually, Newt Gingrich suffered from the same reputation as Lee Atwater and Speaker Jim Wright—harsh, argumentative, and relentlessly confrontational—and met the same fate as Speaker Wright. The very qualities that led to his rise, also led to his dismissal. For example, his disastrous budget showdown frightened many Republican moderates, drew a ton of media criticisms, and generated tremendous public backlash. He was not afraid to reward loyal followers with prestigious committee assignments at the expense of senior members. He used the rules to effectively shut out the Democratic opposition. Gingrich became the Republican everyone loved to hate. Despite the fact that he guided the Republican Party to three consecutive majorities in Congress for the first time in seventy years, Republicans feared his mounting ethics charges and a recent $300,000 ethics fine would cost Republicans a majority. His high disapproval ratings, public confrontations, and reactive policy decisions were enough to encourage Bob Livingston, a Republican Representative from Louisiana, to lead a challenge for his Speaker's position. Gingrich resigned in 1998, closing one of the more colorful Speaker chapters in House of Representatives history.

The Southern takeover of Congress and the Republican Party was cemented. In Gingrich's place, Dick Armey and Tom DeLay became de facto and legislative leaders of the Republican Party and House of Representatives. From 1995 to 2003, Dick Armey served as House Majority Leader and Tom DeLay served as House Majority Whip. Tom DeLay, affectionately known as "The Hammer" for his enforcement of party discipline and reputation for wreaking political vengeance on opponents, later assumed the position of House Majority Leader from 2003 to 2005. He too resigned in the wake of ethics charges in his home state of Texas and incredibly high disapproval ratings. Also a "love-to-hate" Republican, Tom DeLay was a very powerful and effective congressional leader.[98]

Over in the Senate, Southerners asserted themselves and took control. The principal Southern architect in the Senate was Trent Lott, Republican from Mississippi. He was first elected to the House of Representatives in 1972 and became House Minority Whip in 1981; the first Southern Republican to hold such a high leadership position in the House. He held this position until 1988 when he left the House to run for the U.S. Senate. In 1995, Lott became Senate Majority Whip and the first individual to hold the position of whip in both houses of Congress. Shortly thereafter, Lott became the Senate Majority Leader when Bob Dole resigned to run for President in 1996.[99] To become Senate Majority Leader he defeated Thad Cochran, his fellow and senior Senator from Mississippi. In the Senate Lott carried out the Contract and oversaw Clinton's impeachment amidst criticisms that Republicans were short of the two-thirds majority required to convict. After mounting public criticisms he later agreed to suspend impeachment proceedings against Clinton.

Trent Lott's coup de grace came four years after Newt Gingrich, when at Strom Thurmond's 100th birthday party he said, "I want to say this about my state: When Strom Thurmond ran for president we voted for him. We're proud of it. And if the rest of the country had followed our lead, we wouldn't have all these problems over all these years, either."[100] *The Washington Post* declared, "Lott played right into the hands of opponents who are eager to paint the Republican Party's Southern ascendance as nothing more than old-fashioned bigotry." In the same article, David Frum stated, "Lott's unwise words have reduced the ability of all Republicans to speak frankly about race and racial problems."[101] Denounced as a typical southern racist in a party striving to move beyond the image of David Duke, Trent Lott resigned his Senate Majority Leader's position December 20, 2002. He was replaced by Bill Frist, Senator from Tennessee, who would hold the position from 2003 until his retirement in 2007. Interestingly, Lott did not resign from office and, in a masterful stroke of career revival, regained a leadership position on November 15, 2006, when he was named Minority Whip over Lamar Alexander of Tennessee. Lott won his job back with the same steady, quiet leadership and admiration from his colleagues that led to his initial success. Furthermore, his organizational abilities and his avoidance of extreme policy positions stood in stark contrast to what the Republican Party became under the leadership of Bill Frist, who was ultimately undone by his role in the Terry Schiavo case.[102] While Southerners were making the news in the Republican Party, Wendell Ford, Democrat from Kentucky, quietly served as Senate Minority Whip from 1991 to 1999.

The history of congressional leadership from the 1980s to the present is a history of Southern congressional leadership. Southerners were either occupying the White House or fashioning a campaign strategy to occupy the White House. With his election in 2000, George W. Bush joined the likes of Lyndon Johnson, Jimmy Carter, and Bill Clinton. The strategy fashioned by his political architect, Karl Rove, was identical to Lee Atwater and James Carville. Rove utilized race and slash and burn; Bush utilized southern charm and good ole' boy simplicity. If anything is unusual about national politics in 2009, then it is the decided absence of Southerners. Not since Reconstruction has there been such a void of Southern leadership in the House, Senate, or White House—even the President's Cabinet and Congress' Committees are strangely missing a Southern feel.

The 1990s saw no shortage of films about the South or in the South, indicating the enduring perceptions and stereotypes about the South continue to exist. Whether watching *A Time to Kill* (1996) about a black man who killed two white men, who raped and tortured his ten-year-old daughter; *The Chamber* (1996) about a young lawyer attempting to save his estranged grandfather, an unrepentant member of the Klan, from the Mississippi gas chamber for a 1967 bombing that inadvertently killed two children; *The Firm* (1993) about a man who finds himself working for a Memphis law firm with connections to the underworld that no one leaves alive; or *Runaway Jury* (2003) about an expert for a big gun manufacturer who attempts to rig a jury in New Orleans; the South is hot, humid, racist, violent, crooked, and ignorant. Southern films advertently or inadvertently fuel these stereotypes, yet are so easily believed because of the presence of these stereotypes. Consider the list of Southern films: *My Cousin Vinny, Driving Miss Daisy, Fried Green Tomatoes, Cookies Fortune, O' Brother Where Art Thou, Ghosts of Mississippi, Mississippi Burning, A Lesson before Dying, Nashville, Coal Miner's Daughter, Midnight in the Garden of Good Evil, Sweet Home Alabama, Eve's Bayou, Steel Magnolias, Sounder, Divine Secrets of the Ya Ya Sisterhood, Hope Floats, The Apostle, Forrest Gump,* and *Cape Fear.* All of them dwell upon these stereotypes; the caricatures of one are easily blended into others. Even contemporary political movies—*All the Kings Men* (remake) and *O' Brother Where Art Thou*—choose the Southern past as their setting because present audiences continue to believe and accept the myth of the South as a Bananna Republic. Even recent television hits, *My Name Is Earl*, portray Southerners as ignorant, undereducated hicks living in mobile homes.

In a literary manner harkening to W. J. Cash's *The Mind of the South*, Peter Applebome argues in *Dixie Rising: How the South Is Shaping American Values, Politics, and Culture* that we are witnessing the "Southernization of America." For Applebome, this is not a good thing. The South is a region of feverish religiosity, intense conservatism, antigovernment sentiments, white supremacy, stagnation, RC Cola, Moon Pies, Confederate flags, NASCAR, poverty, and populists. He writes, "It's already pretty clear that the easy answers and repackaged nostrums out of the South's past are as hollow as plastic pipe, and the racial scapegoating and public disinvestment that crippled the South for so long will do the same for the nation."[104] Despite his clear disdain for cultural elements of the South, he concedes that the South is the indisputable epicenter of politics and he traces ground zero to Cobb County, Georgia.

The Vacant 2000s

If anything has been unusual about national politics in 2009, then it is the decided absence of the South from the White House and congressional leadership. Not since Reconstruction has there been such a void in the House, Senate, or White House—even the President's Cabinet and Congress's Committees are strangely missing a Southern feel.

One of the emerging figures has been Eric Cantor, the House Minority Whip from Virginia. Rep. Cantor has already drawn comparisons to Newt Gingrich and is considered by some as the next rising star. Adam Nagourney of *The New York Times* called him "in the Gingrich mold" and Rick Klein at *ABC News* called him "the Newt Gingrich of his generation." Yet, in many ways, Rep. Cantor is a different Republican. First, he is Jewish. Second, he is soft-spoken and exhibits no trace of a Southern accent. However, it is party discipline and knack for ideas that has many people remembering the Gingrich years. In the most recent vote on the Obama stimulus package, not a single Republican voted with the Democrats. Either way, the comparisons to Newt Gingrich are a testament to the South's legacy in Congress. In addition to Cantor, some of the early possible candidates for 2012 are Southerners—Mike Huckabee of Arkansas, Jeb Bush of Florida, and Bobby Jindal of Louisiana are among the frequent presidential possibilities. The South is scarcely present in the Democratic Party, but Democrat Jim Webb of Virginia is emerging as significant political figure. He presently lacks the seniority to hold a chairmanship or leadership position, but many feel this is about to change.

Today even the educated are not immune to playing upon Southern themes of racism, poverty, and education. A survey of recent titles in the subfield of Southern politics underscores this point: *The End of Southern Exceptionalism*, *The Hand of the Past in Contemporary Southern Politics*, *The New Politics of the Old South*, and *Foxes in the Henhouse* are all great examples. *The New Politics of the Old South* opens with V.O. Key's quote, "in its grand outlines the politics of the South revolves around the position of the Negro."[103] *The End of Southern Exceptionalism* reminds its readers that "Southern politics was, is, and will principally be about race."[105] Refreshingly, *The Hand of the Past in Contemporary Southern Politics* concedes race played a role and that past traditions are still evoked in contemporary campaigns, but wants its reader to remember "a forgotten point that change overlays a strong southern tradition."[106] The South is different today, but many contemporary non-political scientists have had trouble recognizing this.

Like W. J. Cash and Peter Applebome, Joe Bageant, in his book *Deer Hunting with Jesus*, describes the South as "the great beery, NASCAR-loving, church-going, gun-owning America that never set foot in Starbucks."[107] Bageant, who hails from Winchester, Virginia, goes so far as to describe his own town as "unacknowledged working class poor: conservative, politically misinformed or oblivious, and patriotic to their own detriment."[108] In fairness, his disdain is not aimed so much at Southerners in general, rather what he perceives to be as Southerners being duped by the false promises of populists like George W. Bush. Either way, he implies the South is ignorant and prone to political deception.

Political scientist and liberal blogger, Thomas F. Schaller, argues in *Whistling Past Dixie* that Democrats should simply ignore the South. In his opinion, the region's legacy of prejudice and racism fall outside issues traditionally espoused by Democrats. Instead, Democrats should focus on the West and Southwest portions of this country. His book has resonated with many non-Southern liberals throughout the nation, sparking debates among liberals on sites like Daily Kos and Talking Points Memo, who tend to agree the nation would be well-served without the support of the backward, irrational, racist South.[109] In contrast, Steve Jarding and Dave Saunders argue in *Foxes in the Henhouse: How the Republicans Stole the South and the Heartland and What the Democrats Must Do to Run 'em Out* that, "Democrats need to figure out how to break through the culture of America."[110] Here a distinction is noteworthy. It is not how to break through the culture of the South, but the culture of America. They partially agree with Bageant and Applebome that Southern culture is demarcated by Southern Baptists, NASCAR, hunting, high school and college football, country and bluegrass music, populism, and a legacy of race. However, if any party aspires to build a real governing majority, it will have to at least compete seriously in the South. Jarding and Saunders insist that the Democrats' problem is not Southern voters, but the way non-Southern Democrats relate, or do not relate, to the South. They see former President Bill Clinton and former Virginia Governor Mark Warner as perfect examples of how Democrats can resonate in the South.

Conclusion

Today the South continues to receive significant attention from bloggers, authors, movie producers, journalists, and political scientists. This treatment is peculiar because no other region in the United States continues to be viewed in such a monolithic fashion despite indisputable evidence that the South has become an incredibly diverse region noted for economic prosperity, policy innovation, university growth, and successful politicians. The specter of racism, rural poverty, lack of education, and romantic views of the past haunts politicians from the South. Regardless of Southern political successes and achievements, bloggers, authors, movie producers, journalists, and political scientists are quick to remind every Southerner of David Duke, George Wallace, and Huey Long, of segregation and integration, of *Deliverance* and banjos, and a host of other negatives that the South has and will continue to endure.

Notes

1. Alexis De Tocqueville, *Democracy in America* (New York: Addleton, 1899).
2. Thomas Nast, "Compromise with the South," *Harper's Weekly*, September 3, 1864, accessed October 15, 2009, http://www.sonofthesouth.net/Thomas_Nast.htm.
3. Doris Graber, *Mass Media and American Politics* (Washington D.C.: Congressional Quarterly Press, 1980).
4. Jennings Bryant and Dolf Zillmann, *Perspectives of Media Effects* (Hillsdale, N. J. : Lawrence Erlbaum Associates, 1986).
5. Walter Lippman, *Public Opinion* (New York: Macmillan Press, 1922).
6. Michael Shudson, "The Politics of Narrative Form: The Emergence of American Political Issues," *Daedalus* 111(1982): 97-112.
7. Ronald Rice and Charles Atkin, *Public Communication Campaigns*, 2nd ed. (Newbury Park, Calif.: Sage Publications, 1989).
8. Wilbur Cash, *The Mind of the South* (New York: Alfred A. Knopf, 1941).
9. Allison Davis, *Deep South: A Social Anthropological Study of Caste and Class* (Chicago: University of Chicago Press, 1941).
10. V. O. Key, *Southern Politics* (New York: Vintage Books, 1949).
11. Katharine Jones, *The Plantation South* (Indianapolis, Ind.: The Bobbs-Merrill Company, 1957).
12. David Bertelson, *The Lazy South* (New York: Oxford University Press, 1967).
13. Glenda Gilmore, *Defying Dixie: The Radical Roots of Civil Rights, 1919-1950* (Chapel Hill: University of North Carolina Press, 2008).
14. Edgar Thompson, *Plantation Societies, Race Relations and the South* (Durham, N.C.: Duke University Press, 1975); Edward Ayers, *The Promise of the New South* (New York: Oxford University Press, 1992); John Beck, Wendy Jean Frandsen, and Aaron

Randall, *Southern Culture: An Introduction* (Durham, N. C.: Carolina Academic Press, 2007).

15. Oklahoma Department of Libraries, "100 Years of Oklahoma Governors," accessed October 15, 2009, http://www.odl.state.ok.us/oar/governors/walton.htm.

16. Oklahoma Historical Society, "Governor Walton Declares Statewide Martial Law, 1923," September 16, 2007, accessed October 15, 2009, http://www.okhistory.org/okjourneys/martiallaw.html.

17. UMKC School of Law. (1925). Tennessee Anti-Evolution Statutes, Public Acts of the State of Tennessee Passed by the Sixty-Fourth General Assembly, accessed October 30, 2011, http://law2.umkc.edu/faculty/projects/ftrials/scopes/tennstat.htm.

18. PBS, "The Monkey Trial," *American Experience* (Boston: WGBH Productions, 2002).

19. State of Tennessee, "Tennessee Evolution Statutes," accessed October 15, 2009, http://www.law.umkc.edu/faculty/projects/ftrials/scopes/tennstat.html.

20. Martin Clay, *Coozan Dudley Leblanc: From Huey Long to Hadacol* (Gretna, La.: Pelican Publishing Company, 1973).

21. Gus Weill, *You Are My Sunshine: The Jimmie Davis Story* (Waco, Tex.: Word Books, 1977).

22. *Long Legacy Project*, accessed October 15, 2009, http://www.hueylong.com/index.php.

23. *Long Legacy Project.*

24. G. Croft Williams, *A Social Interpretation of South Carolina* (Columbia: University of South Carolina Press, 1946).

25. Gilmore, *Defying Dixie.*

26. Dan T. Carter, *Scottsboro: A Tragedy of the American South* (Baton Rouge, LA: LSU Press, 1979).

27. Hollace Ransdell, "Report on the Scottsboro, Alabama Case," accessed October 15, 2009, http://www.law.umkc.edu/faculty/projects/ftrials/scottsboro/SB_HRrep.html#REPORT%20ON %20THE%20SCOTTSBORO,%20ALA.

28. Allan Sindler, *Huey Long's Louisiana: State Politics, 1920-52* (Baltimore: Johns Hopkins Press, 1956).

29. T. Harry Williams, *Huey Long* (New York: Vintage Books, 1981).

30. Sindler, *Huey Long's Louisiana: State Politics, 1920-52*, 26, 28.

31. William Hair, *The Kingfish and His Realm* (Baton Rouge, La.: Louisiana State University Press, 1991), 108.

32. Raymond Swing, *Forerunners of American Fascism* (New York: J. Messner, Inc., 1935), 99-100.

33. James Shenton, "Fascism and Father Coughlin," *The Wisconsin Magazine of History* 44(1960): 6-11.

34. *Long Legacy Project.*

35. Kari Frederickson, *The Dixiecrat Revolt and the End of the Solid South: 1932-68* (Chapel Hill: University of North Carolina Press, 2001).

36. Walter White, *A Man Called White: An Autobiography of Walter White* (New York: Arno Press, 1967).

37. Dewey Grantham, *The South in Modern America: A Region at Odds* (New York: Harper Collins, 1994).

38. Leonard Leff, "David Selznick's *Gone with the Wind*: The Negro Problem," *The Georgia Review* 38(1984):146-149.

39. Robert Penn Warren, *All the King's Men* (New York: Harcourt, Brace & Company, 1946).

40. Augustus Cochran, *Democracy Heading South: National Politics in the Shadow of Dixie* (Lawrence: University of Kansas Press, 2001).
41. Ralph McGill, *The South and the Southerner* (Athens: University of Georgia Press, 1992), 7.
42. McGill, *The South and the Southerner*, 15.
43. Jane Dailey, Glenda Gilmore and Brent Simon, *Jumpin' Jim Crow: Southern Politics from Civil War to Civil Rights* (Princeton, N. J.: Princeton University Press, 2000), 86.
44. Lois Gordon and Alan Gordon, *American Chronicles: Six Decades in American Life, 1920-1980* (New York: Atheneum, 1987), 121.
45. Key, *Southern Politics*, 156.
46. James Guimond, *American Photography and the American Dream* (Chapel Hill: University of North Carolina Press, 1991), 10.
47. Charles P. Roland, *The Improbable Era: The South Since World War II* (Lexington: University Press of Kentucky, 1975), 139.
48. Roland, *The Improbable Era: The South Since World War II*, 7.
49. David Nichols, *A Matter of Justice: Eisenhower and the Beginning of the Civil Rights Revolution* (New York: Simon & Shuster, 2007).
50. Roland, *The Improbable Era: The South Since World War II*, 34.
51. Dan Wakefield, "Respectable Racism: Dixie's Citizens' Councils," *Nation*, October 22, 1955, 339.
52. Roland, *The Improbable Era: The South Since World War II*, 37.
53. I. F. Stone, *The Haunted Fifties* (New York: Vintage Books, 1963), 108.
54. Guimond, *American Photography and the American Dream*, 198.
55. Earl Black and Merle Black, *Divided America: The Ferocious Power Struggle in American Politics* (New York: Simon & Shuster, 2007), 74.
56. Black and Black, *Divided America: The Ferocious Power Struggle in American Politics*, 35.
57. Dewey Grantham, *The Life and Death of the Solid South: A Political History* (Lexington: University Press of Kentucky, 1988).
58. Donald B. Johnson and Kirk H. Porter, *National Party Platforms, 1840-1972* (Champaign: University of Illinois Press, 1973), 554.
59. Edward G. Carmines and James A. Stimson, *Issue Evolution: Race and the Transformation of American Politics* (Princeton, N. J.: Princeton University Press, 1989), 37.
60. David A. Nichols, *A Matter of Justice: Eisenhower and the Beginning of the Civil Rights Revolution* (New York: Simon & Shuster).
61. Nichols, *A Matter of Justice*, 257.
62. Nichols, *A Matter of Justice*, 261.
63. Grantham, *The Life and Death of the Solid South*.
64. Earl Black and Merle Black, *Politics and Society in the South* (Cambridge, Mass.: Harvard University Press, 1987).
65. Getty Images, "Civil Rights Leaders Meet with John F. Kennedy," accessed October 15, 2009, http://www.gettyimages.com/detail/3333637/hulton-archive.
66. Roland, *The Improbable Era: The South Since World War II*, 75.
67. Harry S. Dent, *The Prodigal South Returns to Power* (New York: John Wiley & Sons, 1978), 3.
68. Lyndon B. Johnson, *Vantage Point: Perspectives on the Presidency, 1963-1969* (New York: Holt, Rinehart and Winston, 1971), 95.
69. Nichols, *A Matter of Justice*.

70. Bernard Cosman, *Five States for Goldwater: Continuity and Change in Southern Presidential Voting Patterns* (Tuscaloosa: University of Alabama Press, 1966).
71. William A. Rusher, *The Rise of the Right* (New York: William Morrow and Company, 1984), 156.
72. Cosman, *Five States for Goldwater: Continuity and Change in Southern Presidential Voting Patterns*, 39.
73. Black and Black, *Politics and Society in the South*, 80.
74. Carmines and Stimson, *Issue Evolution: Race and the Transformation of American Politics*, 116.
75. Carmines and Stimson, *Issue Evolution: Race and the Transformation of American Politics*, 118.
76. Dent, *The Prodigal South Returns to Power*, 4.
77. Grantham, *The Life and Death of the Solid South*.
78. Roland, *The Improbable Era*, 147.
79. Grantham, *The Life and Death of the Solid South*.
80. Richard Scammon, *America Votes* (Washington, D.C.: Congressional Quarterly, 1973).
81. Grantham, *The Life and Death of the Solid South*.
82. Alexander Lamis, *The Two-Party South* (New York: Oxford University Press, 1984), 5.
83. Lamis, *The Two-Party South*, 120.
84. William Leuchtenburg, *The White House Looks South* (Baton Rouge: Louisiana State University Press, 2005), 388.
85. All years of service for U.S. Representatives and U.S. Senators courtesy of the *Biographical Directory of the United States Congress, 1774-Present*, accessed October 15, 2009, http://bioguide.congress.gov/biosearch/biosearch.asp.
86. James Restin, "Baker's Whispering is Significant Sign," *New York Times*, January 12, 1983. http://news.google.com/newspapers?nid=2194&dat=19830112&id= JqQyAAAAIBAJ&sjid=Fu8FAAAAIBAJ&pg=4534,483187 (accessed October 31, 2011).
87. William Bennett, *America: The Last Best Hope, Volume II* (New York: Thomas Nelson, 2007), 181.
88. Lloyd Green, "Clinton as Atwater," March 23, 2007, accessed October 15, 2009, http://politicalmavens.com/index.php/2007/3/23/clinton-as-atwater.
89. Green, "Clinton as Atwater."
90. Thomas Edsall, *Building Red America* (New York: Basic Books, 2006), 223.
91. Mark Rozell and Clyde Wilcox, *The Christian Right in American Politics* (Washington D.C.: Georgetown University Press, 2003).
92. Dick Morris, "In Contrast to Obama, Hilary Plays the Race Card," January 16, 2008, accessed October 15, 2009, http://thehill.com/.
93. Bill Clinton, *My Life* (New York: Alfred A. Knopf, 2004).
94. Matt Bai, "The Way We Live Now: South Poll," *New York Times*, January 20, 2008, accessed October 15, 2009, http://www.nytimes.com/2008/01/20/magazine/ 20wwwln-lede.t.html?_r=1.
95. Bai, "The Way We Live Now: South Poll."
96. Earle Black and Merle Black, *The Rise of Southern Republicans* (Cambridge, Mass.: Belknap Press, 2002).
97. Black and Black, *The Rise of Southern Republicans*, 162.
98. Edsall, *Building Red America*, 124.
99. Black and Black, *The Rise of Southern Republicans*, 168.

100. Edsall, *Building Red America*, 126.

101. Thomas Edsall and Brian Faler, "Lott Remarks on Thurmond Echoed 1980 Words," *Washington Post*, December 11, 2002, accessed October 15, 2009, http://washingtonpost.com/ac2/wp-dyn/A37288-2002Dec10?language=printer.

102. Charles Bullock and Mark Rozell, *The New Politics of the Old South*, 3rd ed. (New York: Rowman and Littlefield, 2007), 94.

103. Peter Applebome, *Dixie Rising* (New York: Harvest Books, 1997), 22.

104. Key, *Southern Politics*, 1.

105. Shafer and Johnston, *The End of Southern Exceptionalism*, 4.

106. James Glazer, *The Hand of the Past in Southern Politics* (New Haven, Conn.: Yale University, 2005), 8.

107. Joe Bageant, *Deer Hunting with Jesus* (New York: Crown Publishers, 2007), 6.

108. Bageant, *Deer Hunting with Jesus*, 6.

109. Thomas Schaller, *Whistling Past Dixie* (New York: Simon & Shuster).

110. Steve Jarding and Dave "Mudcat" Sanders, *Foxes in the Henhouse* (New York: Simon & Shuster, 2006), 14.

Chapter Five
Magnolias and Manufacturing: Southern Imagery in Mississippi's Promotional Publications, 1945-1955
Burt Buchanan

> *An interesting and philosophical explanation of low incomes in Mississippi and the South is the socio-economic one which is advanced and cherished by Northerners. Most Northerners will tell you, without being asked, what is wrong with the South. Their answers are simple: Southerners are by nature indolent; they are addicted to gambling, fornication, fishing, hunting and loafing; they have been debilitated by the heat; they are entranced with the "moonlight and magnolia" tradition of the ante-bellum south; and their cardinal fault is that they are not 100 percent dedicated to the making of money.*
> —*Martin Colby Schnitzer, 1960.*[1]

The Mississippi Agricultural and Industrial Board's (A&I) publication, "Mississippi Magic: The BAWI Bulletin" 1945-1955, manufactured an image of a waiting state full of possibility and promise for potential industrial/manufacturing firm interested in relocating. The publication was the key advertising tool for the A&I Board. The magazine was the central marketing tool for the entire Balance Agriculture with Industry (BAWI) program. It had the task of promoting industry as well as continuing to showcase the many advantages of possible relocation to the state.

The Great Depression devastated Mississippi's mostly agrarian economy.[2] Cotton prices plummeted during this period. Cotton was the state's chief crop. What few jobs and little industry Mississippi possessed quickly disappeared as the nation's economy plummeted into collapse.[3] The state was left with massive unemployment and a damaged agricultural-based economy possessing little prospects. Mississippi was one of the poorest states in the union.[4]

In 1937, Mississippi Governor Hugh L. White introduced to the state legislature a new act designed to change the economic landscape of the state. His "Balance Agriculture with Industry" program sought to supplement the existing agrarian economic base with a more industrialized and hence diversified economy.[5] White, in the early 1930s, saw from personal experience his own hometown lose its last surviving industry. He knew too well the economic devastation that could occur when a community relied too heavily upon a single source of income.[6]

For most of the state of Mississippi that single source was agriculture. White's new plan included a new incentive plan of bringing new industrial and manufacturing plants to the state.[7] Municipal bonding was undertaken to fund incentives to prospective manufacturing locations. In addition, the BAWI program established several new state agencies. Among them was the Mississippi Advertising Commission.[8]

The Mississippi Advertising Commission was the advertising and marketing arm of BAWI. Governor White saw the need for Mississippi to be marketed to prospective industrial organizations. He knew Mississippi in the eyes of the nation was a backward region without much promise. Part of the promotion of the state was an all-out public relations campaign primarily in the print media. The Mississippi Advertising Commission, which became the Agricultural and Industrial (A&I) Board, began to publish "Mississippi Magic: The BAWI Bulletin" in 1945. Its sole purpose was to promote the state. Marketing the state's possibilities for manufacturing sites and travel and tourism was a new and bold concept. A national marketing plan followed, which began by placing advertisements in numerous regional and national publications.

"Mississippi Magic's" mission remained constant; the marketing of the state of Mississippi. These efforts to market a state in the wake of modernization efforts, poor economic conditions, and social upheaval proved difficult. "Mississippi Magic" showcased Mississippi using much of the imagery that other regions of the nation possessed about the South. Notions of what the South was had been retained by much of the nation. The publication and its advertising initiatives capitalized on these ideas and the imagery surrounding the South.

The Mississippi Advertising Commission which published "Mississippi Magic: The BAWI Bulletin" played a key role in depicting the state as a haven for potential industry and tourism through the projection of Southern imagery, in a time when Mississippi had in reality, few tangible benefits to offer. An unemployed, unskilled workforce, a damaged agrarian state economy, limited infrastructure, and a segregated society were all Mississippi could offer. However, "Mississippi Magic" was there from its first issue, touting the state as an untapped resource for industry, a haven for the out-of-state tourist, and a playground for year-round recreation. The magazine used much of what other regions of the nation thought of as "Southern" to market the state. Southern charm, young, and beautiful women, bucolic land, and an almost religious reverence to the past that can be seen as key selling points for Mississippi in the publication.

Of particular importance is the "BAWI Bulletin: Mississippi Magic's" efforts from 1945 to 1955, to advertise and market the state using Southern imagery in such a time of economic and sociopolitical difficulties. This particular time period best expressed the fervor and prevalence of the state's advertising efforts. By 1953, Mississippi had set new records with many advances in agricultural and industrial growth.[9] The state during this period markedly increased its economic viability with "Mississippi Magic" as its primary marketing tool. The publication's mythic devotion to Southern imagery was also at its most flagrant.

Southern stereotypes in particular have become popular research topics for scholars. However there has been relatively little research that looks specifically at how such stereotypes might be utilized in successful marketing campaigns.[10] During the same period, "Arizona Highways" was published in Arizona (1939). It utilized the local Native American population and surrounding mystique in much the same way "Mississippi Magic" utilized images of the Southern way of life.[11] It attempted to bring in tourism to the region by overtly marketing an image and state of mind concerning the desert Southwest. Native Americans were considered as part of the allure of the region much in the way African Americans seemed to be a part of the "Southern experience" in Mississippi.[12]

The beginnings of stereotypical imagery many associate with the South date back to fictional exaggerations of prewar accounts of grandiose Southern lifestyles.[13] The origins of this amalgam of the Southern stereotype were actually conceived and perpetuated by the North.[14] Some of the most prominent symbols of the South were produced in the North. New England's Harriet Beecher Stowe gave literature Uncle Tom. Literature aside, prints from Nathaniel Currier and James Merritt Ives depicted blatant celebrations of pastoral plantation life. Lyricists such as Stephen Foster with his "My Old Kentucky Home" and "Old Folks at Home" also aided in developing a specific mythology surrounding the South.[15] These and other works did much to originate and perpetuate a Southern mythology in the minds of not only Northerners but Southerners as well.

Francis Pendleton Gaines was perhaps the first historian to explain the North and South were actually partners in the "creation of a pseudopast—what the poet Stephen Vincent Benet called the 'sick magnolias of the false romance.'"[16] Both regions agreed that specific picturesque portions of the antebellum South were in need of preservation to forever cement the concept in the American consciousness. Perpetuating this mythology would fulfill tastes for American aristocracy, caste and feudalism.[17] This co-creation of a Southern mythology, a Southern mystique is clearly perpetuated in the pages of "Mississippi Magic" for purposes of economic expansion.

The personally directed promulgation of the BAWI program by Governor White occurred just as several major motion pictures were appearing in theaters all over the nation. Stories of the South involving plantation life and the aristocratic, agrarian way of life began in 1930 with the release of "Dixiana," continuing with "Mississippi" in 1935 and culminating with the 1939 release of *Gone with the Wind*.[18] In particular, portrayal of Southern women immortalized by Bette Davis in *Jezebel*, in 1937 did much to perpetuate the myth of the Southern woman as a beautiful temptress who lived by the whim of her "untamed heart."[19]

The image of the South that Hollywood perpetuated so well was one had not been susceptible to the modern economic tough times. The idea the image was outdated, inaccurate historically, or the South had not suffered in the Depression could be for a moment forgotten by the moviegoer. Moviegoers were caught up in the grandeur and majesty of *Gone with the Wind*.[20] The perception of the South many people possessed, came from these and other films. The nation needed to forget its own modern economic troubles and was ripe for acceptance of these traditional notions that fashioned so well these ideas surrounding the South. The BAWI plan would incorporate this mythology into its overall strategy of marketing Mississippi for new and expanding manufacturing and industry.

Martin Colby Schnitzer pointed out certain traditions make the South overall receptive to industry.[21] Southerners, he added, have been used to living under an oligarchy.[22] First it was the landowners from the ante-bellum period, now it is the plant.[23] In addition, Schnitzer added that many Northerners had somewhat of a "tobacco road" stigma toward the South.[24] Even still, the A&I Board still stressed many of the more traditional ideas of the region in its advertising and in "Mississippi Magic."

The image of Mississippi as portrayed in the pages of "Mississippi Magic" was that of an idyllic, agrarian society of white citizens waiting for industrial development and the economic boom it would bring. As part of the statewide public relations campaign one pamphlet, "Mississippi: A Land of Industrial Opportunity," in 1937 published a photograph depicting one hundred or so young, white women appeared with the caption, "friendly, happy employees."[25] The same publication in its labor section, mentioned that the Mississippi labor force was 99.6 percent native born. Industries would encounter, it continued, a "type of employee that fair employers need and want."[26]

African Americans were all but invisible in the BAWI advertising and marketing campaign. Mississippi as most of the Deep South was steeped in the "separate but equal" Jim Crow social structure. Most facilities denied admission to blacks. From sports centers to restaurants, from schools to libraries, black citizens were barred from any such white establishments.[27] In addition, whites controlled the governments of every town and city with the exception of Natchez. It is estimated that whites held over 95 percent of all county offices statewide.[28] Whites would also control all BAWI industrial development in Mississippi.

Any desirable, non-agricultural jobs were reserved for what state industry promoters called, "native Anglo-Saxons." BAWI industry employed practically no blacks. Their jobs continued to be limited to mainly domestic and manual labor.[29] Any BAWI jobs created would go only to native born, white men and women.

Education for African Americans was separate but at no time was it ever equal to that of whites.[30] Black education system was systematically maintained at a substandard level. This would ensure that blacks would be unable to compete with whites economically and politically. It also perpetuated a needed supply of low-wage labor.[31] Any industrial and manufacturing jobs created by BAWI initiatives would be certain to go to white workers.

The image portrayed in the marketing strategy of the state-run Mississippi A&I Board showed an eager, traditional state waiting for industry to transform it. It successfully ignored African Americans in the advertising campaign, except for the rare, depiction of local black residents. One particular reference was included in the 1941 "Mississippi Tourist Guide," published by the Mississippi State Board of Development, an arm of the A&I Board. It portrayed pages and pages of whites enjoying a variety of outdoor, recreational activities. Among these was a depiction of two black children drinking from a well. The caption merely read, "Delta Pickaninnies."[32] African Americans were only mentioned as additions to the local atmosphere and mystique of the state. Blacks were all but excluded from the benefits of the BAWI plan in Mississippi. References to blacks in the marketing strategy were included only as components of the Southern milieu, an occasionally visible part of life in Mississippi.

The genesis of "Mississippi Magic" was a systematic public relations and advertising campaign devised to perpetuate the aims of the BAWI program. Governor White directed a carefully planned media campaign directed toward prospective industrial/manufacturing organizations. In addition, the advertising targeted potential tourists as well. This provision for external advertising was built in to the BAWI effort and was an integral part of its success. In 1937, White delivered to every member of the Mississippi Legislature a public relations campaign press kit containing numerous pamphlets and reprints of advertisements that were to appear in national publications.[33]

White, in a letter introducing the press kit, emphasized the importance of advertising. Moreover, he stressed to legislators that they were, more than any other residents of Mississippi, "in a position to interpret the fundamental facts contained in these pages for the welfare and betterment of our people."[34] The kit contained copies of numerous major advertisements that were soon to be printed in national newspapers and magazines. Moreover, several pamphlets were included in the kit. One was targeted to prospective tourists. The "Mississippi Tourist Guide" opens by greeting the reader with a call to the warmer climate of the state.

It continues by inviting the reader to "desert for a time at least the crowds and congestion of nervous metropoli [sic] to seek the relaxation of a gentle Southern sun and the pleasant welcome of a people hospitable by habit. Mississippi invites you to find in the heart of the Old Deep South and ease of living that is happy and contagious."[35] The pamphlet is replete with images of the antebellum south. Photographs included those of young women in hoop skirts posing in front of large plantation homes, images of people at play at the Gulf beaches, and illustrations of the completed, paved highways crisscrossing the state. Two double pages entitled "The Present" and "The Past" seemed to blur the chronological timeline between the ante-bellum past and present era. The present showed plantation homes and stately oaks coated with Spanish moss, ladies in hoop skirts, and people arriving to a home in a horse-drawn carriage. The past depicted yet still more ladies in antebellum fashions, a photograph of Windsor Ruins, a popular plantation site in western Mississippi, and several Confederate war memorials."[36]

Another pamphlet in Governor White's kit was entitled "Mississippi: A Land of Industrial Opportunity."[37] More formal in design, it too opened with a letter of greetings from White. It assured the reader of a commitment to industry and a spirit of cooperation between the state and any industrial organization interested in relocating its facilities south. The pamphlet served as an enticement to prospective industrialists, boasting of the state's pro-business legislative climate, abundant natural resources, inexpensive energy, transportation infrastructure and even success stories of industry already operating in Mississippi.[38] Above all, the primary enticement for manufacturing was that of cheap and abundant labor. The kit's pamphlets once again touted a friendly, virtually all native-born workforce, eager to accept jobs in relocated factories.[39]

Governor White's innovative kit was the initial push in the advertising of the state as a haven for manufacturing. The Mississippi Advertising Commission was the first marketing entity for BAWI followed by its later incarnation as the A&I Board. Aggressive use of advertising provided a place for the plan to "hang its hat on" promoting the state and its possibilities to those potentially investing.[40] In June of 1945, the inaugural issue of the "BAWI Bulletin" was published pledging its determined efforts to Mississippians of relocating industry and manufacturing to the state. Little more than a mimeographed newsletter, these early issues of the publication began the strategy that continued for many years.[41] The first issue reported on "industrial prospects," organizations that requested information on relocating. Next was information on local initiatives and bond issues that began bringing manufacturers to various municipalities statewide.[42] In August 1945, the A&I Board embarked upon an industrial advertising campaign that lasted for fourteen months with ads appearing in numerous national newspapers and magazines.[43]

The issue included reprints of the state's previous national advertisements, a practice that continued for many years.[44] Finally, the issue reminded readers that

Mississippi's men and women returning from the armed services as well as others deserved gainful employment.[45] The agricultural base would not be sufficient to keep everyone working. There was no time to be lost. With the war winding down, industry would be searching for site locations as never before. A concerted effort was needed by all to secure industry for the benefit of Mississippi and all Mississippians.[46]

The August 1945 issue devoted even more space to the BAWI program's national advertising efforts.[47] It delineated the advertising campaign launched that month. There was to be an eight-month long campaign of ads to run in five national publications. The ads were directed to manufacturers looking for Southern locales. In addition, the issue contained a reprint of the press release that accompanied the ads. The issue also marked the official change of the Mississippi Advertising Commission to the Mississippi Agricultural and Industrial Board.[48]

The September 1945 issue reminded readers that since gas rationing was history and the recent unpleasantness of shortages and austerity was behind the nation, tourism was expected to be on the rise nationwide.[49] The A&I Board announced press releases of "Travel and Trade" opportunities. The issue encouraged local community residents to do everything in their power to make their communities attractive to the tourist trade.[50] In addition to attracting manufacturing and industry, the board encouraged the proliferation of the tourism within the state.

The January 1947 issue updated readers on the status of the publication of a new sixteen-page two-color process travel folder. It served to answer questions prospective tourists might have concerning Mississippi's numerous attractions.[51] "Mississippi, Heart of the Southland" featured two dozen photographs of items of general tourist interest. Among the photos were images of key state paved highways, locales for hunting and fishing, as well as accommodations. The folders were targeted to out-of-state residents contacting local Mississippi chambers of commerce.[52] The pamphlets depicted the state as an unspoiled playground for the tourist complete with images of people engaged in a variety of leisure time activities. The brochure hinted that the reader could take part in a simpler, uncomplicated lifestyle, away from the hectic pace of urban metroplexes and the northern pace of life.[53]

The February 1947 issue of the "BAWI Bulletin" included an article on out-of-state reports regarding Mississippi public health. It reported on a rather lengthy article previously published by the *St. Louis Post-Dispatch* in its January 23, 1947, issue. The article pointed out that the Mississippi State Board of Health was rated as "one of the most efficient organizations of its kind in the United States."[54] The article went on to say that Mississippians have made outstanding health strides, another selling point for prospective businesses. The issue also stated that reprints of the *Post-Dispatch* article were available for sending to sources outside the state.[55] This third-party rating of the state's public health system served as a reminder to potential investors that their prospective rural, poor labor source would have access to adequate healthcare.

As 1947 drew to a closed, the "BAWI Bulletin" marked the new year with the beginning of a more sophisticated version of its publication. The July 1948 issue would also mark the publication's transition to its name, "Mississippi Magic." From then on, the publication would simply be known as "Mississippi Magic."[56] The magazine was no longer a typed, mimeographed newsletter, but a small magazine with an average of ten to fifteen pages per issue. It would continue its efforts to lure industry to the state as well as tout the program's statewide success stories. In addition, it would continue to use the charm and mystique of the South, old and new to accomplish its mission.[57]

The July 1948 issue of "Mississippi Magic" offered readers a rationale behind the name change. It began stating the change was not by chance. Careful thought and preparation went into the changes, "as most suitable to the history of Mississippi—past, present, and future."[58] The article traced the discovery of the great river, whose name the state bears, by Hernando DeSoto in May 1541. The "magic" of Mississippi, both the state and river, is discussed via all the natural and historical points of interest that abound. A discussion of the physical beauty of the state of Mississippi followed. The article culminated in a rather poetic description of the economic prosperity that has descended upon the state.[59] "Mississippians today turn a proud ear to the hum of farm machinery being echoed by the busy noise of nearby factories, taking Mississippi's crops and abundant natural resources and putting them through manufacturing processes to make them useful to the people of the world."[60]

The heralding of the magazine's new name reminded readers the southern, natural, unspoiled beauty of the state made it a natural destination for vacationers. The scenic highways, historic charm of the early settlements along the Gulf Coast, the old plantation homes in Natchez and the National Military Park in Vicksburg, all beckoned tourists to come and sample the many attributes of the South, both old and new.[61]

The article closed by further touting the "Southern lifestyle" adding that it "is a pleasing blend of the leisurely Southern way-of-life that is traditional, with an aggressive ambition which is constantly developing the state in many magic ways."[62] Other Southern iconic images included two tow-headed boys proudly posing with their catch of white perch on Lake Washington in Mississippi's Delta region. The caption described the area as a destination for vacationers during the hot summer days. "Fishing's good," it continued with mention of the boys' catch.[63] The "magic" of Mississippi was that it had started to become a paradoxical mixture of the traditional Southern way and of modern agricultural and manufacturing methods, bringing in progress and change.

In August 1948 a follow-up article appeared in response to its first printed issue. One comment read; "Congratulations on the faceliftin' job done [sic] on the 'BAWI Bulletin.' It now has the 'eye appeal' of a Biloxi bathing beauty."[64]

Many comments from readers from all over the state and the nation praised the new look of the issue. This particular comment however from a Clay county businessman, incorporated Southern language and iconic imagery of the beautiful Southern woman.

In the October issue of that same year, several reprints were included of advertisements that appeared in national publications during that month.[65] "Mississippi Has—Roads, Romance, Recreation for a Year 'Round Vacation" reads one ad.[66] Images of one of the state's many newly paved highway system roads, a man and three ladies seated at a fountain, dressed in antebellum garb in front of a plantation home and a young, attractive woman water skiing completed another of the ads.[67] Again the line between past and present is slightly blurred in the ad, promoting ever more the imagery of the "Old South."

Again in 1949, for its February issue, "Mississippi Magic" had on the cover a photograph of a Natchez antebellum plantation home with two couples dressed in 1860s clothing. Azaleas in full bloom flanked both sides of the couples as they stood, frozen in a dance step on the front steps beneath four massive Corinthian columns.[68] As a companion to the cover, an article appeared telling of a *National Geographic* article entitled, "History Repeats in Old Natchez," featuring the Natchez pilgrimage.[69] Once again, Mississippi banked on the media drive Southern stereotypes to draw attention to the state.

In 1949, the state A&I Board opted to cash in on yet another commonly held concept people have about the South. The idea of "southern hospitality" had come to be well-established and generally accepted among most people. The A&I Board effected plans for a concerted, statewide program in Mississippi called "Hospitality Month."[70] Designed to increase the tourism industry in the state, the program began as a series of meetings to organize committees and devise promotional activities.

Governor Fielding Wright in his efforts at modernization and urbanization of Mississippi set forth in his 1949 proclamation that May would forever be known as "Hospitality Month." The purpose was manifold; to create a consciousness of the state's chances for bringing in tourism dollars, to develop an awareness among communities the economic potential of tourism, to coordinate and strengthen these efforts, to establish a regular state vacation season, to gain favorable national publicity, and to indirectly promote the state by building civic pride and favorably impressing business and industrial leaders who may choose the state as a vacation destination.[71]

From that point forward, "Hospitality Month" was a regular feature of the A&I Board's advertising and marketing efforts. A cornerstone of the May observation would be forever more the "Miss Hospitality" contest. The June 1949 issue of the magazine featured the first ever "Miss Hospitality," with a biography, an explanation of how she was chosen from thirty-seven contestants, and a generalized itinerary of events she would attend. She appeared on the issue cover in June, in a photograph depicting her crowning by the governor.[72] The obvious exploitation of the hospitality mystique the South has long possessed was a logical and effective method of spreading awareness of the potential for state tourism. The September 1949 issue featured an oil portrait of the 1949 "Miss Hospitality," who had placed second in the "Miss America" pageant that same year.[73] Later in the December issue, a reprint of an advertisement appeared on the back cover. Clothed in a striped top, shorts, and sandals, "Miss Hospitality" is inviting the reader to spend a winter vacation in Mississippi. The copy by her photo reads, "With a smile as warm as a Mississippi day in January . . . lovely Miss Katherine Wright—Mississippi's official travel hostess—says, welcome to the Hospitality State."[74] This mixture of Southern hospitality and the most beautiful young women that the state had to offer were keen examples of the exploitation of prominent ideas of what people from other regions and for that matter, most Southerners thought of as uniquely "Southern."

The A&I Board continued its efforts at advertising and marketing Mississippi through the 1950s. The same successful strategy of incessantly touting new and expanding industry in the pages of "Mississippi Magic" continued as well. The February 1950 issue featured a photograph of Governor Fielding L. Wright at a Sweet Potato Day observance. He is pictured crowning Miss Jackie Rogers of Collins, the 1950 reigning Sweet Potato Queen.[75] Articles surrounding the photograph discussed recent industrial "prospects," where people and organizations from various locations have asked for information regarding industrial possibilities within Mississippi's borders. Another article laid out an overview of how a local chamber of commerce had initiated its own industrial development plan.[76] However, by far the largest focal point of the page was the crowning of the Sweet Potato Queen. This juxtaposition of industrial discussion and the beauty of local women was common in the issues of "Mississippi Magic" during this period.

The July issue of 1950 continued the exploitation of Southern imagery, specifically the concept of the natural beauty of Southern women, to sell the state. On the cover was the 1950 winner of the "Miss Hospitality" contest, on the arm of Governor Fielding Wright. He appeared dressed in a white Tuxedo and she in a formal gown with a tiara and "Miss Hospitality" sash.[77] In addition to the news and information on new and expanding industrial development in the state, there was something new. For the first time, there appeared a double-page spread of the contestants for that year's "Miss Hospitality" contest. Small oval portraits dotted an outline of the state of Mississippi, with the names and hometowns of each contestant.[78] The A&I Board began a bold new step to deliberately catalyze overt sexuality and the beauty of these contest winners with Southern imagery to attract potential industry and tourism to the state.

In November of the same year, the issue featured a photograph of a trio of three "Miss Hospitality" contestants who "are helping to sell Mississippi to tourists." The young women are shown taking a break from the activities during the 1950 "Miss Hospitality" contest. They are reclining on a grassy knoll at "Ole

Miss," wearing identical sports shirts and shorts, given to them, the caption notes, by a distant admirer. The admirer was a judge at one of the recent "Miss Hospitality" contests.[79]

That same November issue went a step further in using the Southern mystique to publicize Mississippi's possibilities as a potential site for industry. The magazine reported on a large publicity campaign sponsored by a group of Mississippi manufacturers. The campaign launched to promote industrial growth in the South specifically attempted to call attention to the region as a desirable place to live and as a potential site for new industry. In order to accomplish the goal, the group of manufacturers ordered the printing of several million dollars in facsimile Confederate money. The faux currency was to be handed out to "stimulate the interest and pride of Southerners in the South," once again borrowing on the media-derived imagery and notions of the Old South. Contests were sponsored and prizes were offered as well.[80] Such deliberate usage of Confederate imagery to promote the South was a homegrown attempt to call attention to the area.

In March 1952, the issue covers pictured trees in full bloom against a spring sky full of white, fluffy clouds. The "Our Cover" section of the magazine exclaimed the arrival of the spring season after a mild winter. It went on to say that thousands of visitors heading for Mississippi for Mardi Gras and area pilgrimage festivities would be treated to the blooming of various trees and shrubs that "brought exclamations from winter weary Northern tourists."[81] The exaltation of things Southern continued as the issue told of how Northerners could come to Mississippi and enjoy not only the beauty of the state in full bloom, but the warm temperatures as well. The agreeable climate has long been a drawing point for the South in luring tourism by people of colder regions of the nation.

The same March 1952 issue reported on the A&I Board's presence at the annual Chicago Outdoor and Travel Show. The two photographs depicted the exhibit appearing at the show. At the top of the 30-foot exhibit was the lettering, "MISSISSIPPI . . . YEAR-ROUND PLAYGROUND and THE HOSPITALITY STATE." The left side of the exhibit featured nearly life-sized images of young women in hoops skirts, posed all around the columned entrance of another mansion home. In the center, was a viewscreen where visitors were treated to a film produced by the A&I Board. It touted the vacation and tourist opportunities that the state had to offer. Next to the viewscreen was a diorama of a coastal scene complete with palm trees and lighthouse. On the right side of the exhibit were large photographs of various mansion homes as part of the state's annual pilgrimage tours.[82]

The second photo appearing in the issue was a close up of that year's "Miss Hospitality" who was offering an A&I Board tourism brochure to a smiling couple. Dressed in a dark colored antebellum type gown, her job was to stand in front of the exhibit and pass out an array of brochures to passersby.[83] Again the image of the Old South, even updated and almost stylized, is a powerful tool in conjuring up the mystique for the average Chicagoan attending the travel show.

The September issue of 1952 showed a photograph of the Windsor ruins, near Port Gibson, Mississippi. The "Our Cover" section discussed the "once magnificent" five-story structure. It explained to the reader that the twenty-two Corinthian columns were all that remained of the palatial antebellum home. After a brief history of the home, the article stated that the observatory had once been an observation point during the War between the States. The "Federals" had used the home as a hospital. In addition, Mark Twain had used the house as a navigation point during his days piloting a Mississippi Steamboat along the nearby river.[84] Once again, the publication used the history of the Old South as a method to attract attention to the state as a potential site for industry and as a locale for tourism. The idea was the visitor could be a part of a rich and colorful history by relocating or visiting the state.

The December 1952 issue of "Mississippi Magic" contained two notable examples of this continued usage of Southern beauty and stereotypical imagery. First, a photograph of "Miss Hospitality" 1952 Suzanne Paul showed her seated at a desk writing "a letter of invitation to middlewestern television viewers to visit the Hospitality State." The copy went on to explain how that year's winner was to appear in television spots to be aired "over northern stations."[85] For many Midwesterners and Northerners in 1952, "Miss Hospitality" appearing in television commercials would personify the South. The A&I Board's promotion of the South by the use of beautiful women proved to be an important tool in the successful marketing of Mississippi.

Next, the back page of the issue contained a reprint of the A&I Board's most recent advertisement in its campaign. The ad had a caption at the top that read "Time for a ... Southern Exposure." The photograph was yet again a depiction of five beautiful, young women dressed in antebellum gowns standing at the gate of a plantation home. It was a winter travel ad to boost tourism to the state. The print ads that were to appear in the February 1952 issues of *National Geographic*, *Holiday Magazine*, and *Cosmopolitan*, were part of an overall campaign that included television advertisements to air in Northern and Midwestern states.[86] Although the advertisement obviously was calling attention to annual pilgrimage activities, the intent was a reinforcement of the traditional images of the Old South in the minds of readers.

The December 1955 issue of "Mississippi Magic" featured a cover picturing the century-old "Little Chapel of the Cross," a chapel in Madison county. The "Our Cover" section once again spun a tale of the Old South. The slave labor-produced structure was ordered built by a visiting widow, whose daughter was to be married there. The young woman fell in love and became engaged to Henry Vick, the founder of Vicksburg. Vick, the article went on to say, was killed in a duel in New Orleans just four days before the wedding was to take place. He fired his own shot into the air to keep a promise he made to his betrothed to never kill a man. The heartbroken young woman, it was said, later married a minister, but never gave her heart to this husband. Instead, she "remained the bride of a ghost."[87] Here again the publication makes use of tales of the Old South to propagate the mystique.

On the back cover of the December 1955 issue, once again the A&I Board showed readers its exhibit used in travel and tourism shows. This year, the Mississippi exhibit was on display at the Louisville Sports and Travel Show in Kentucky. This time the exhibit featured more pictures of what Mississippi had to offer potential visitors.[88] On the left of the exhibit was a rendering of a young woman swinging on a tree swing dressed in a frilly dress reminiscent of antebellum garb. The oak tree is draped with Spanish moss, and behind the woman is a distant view of farmland.

The next portion featured a group of beachgoers and a depiction of a group of sailboats on the Mississippi Sound. Next was a painting of two women in antebellum dresses standing out in front of a Greek revival plantation house. The final portion of the exhibit featured three photographs. The first featured an image of a bather at the beach flanked by a lighthouse. The second photo showed modern machinery harvesting a cotton crop. The final photo depicted various activities going on at one of the state's many state parks. Two young women in bathing suits supervised the booth during the eight-day show, handing out brochures on the many attractions that Mississippi had to offer potential tourists.[89] Although a modern appeal, the idea of the embodiment of beauty and charm by attractive young Southern women in bathing suits is a strong image synonymous with the South.

The Mississippi A&I Board with its "Mississippi Magic" used a variety of media-driven examples of what many people had come to think of as Southern. Comprising the monolithic concept associated with "the South" were uncomplicated, smiling people, beautiful women often dressed in hoop skirts in front of plantation homes, Civil War iconic imagery, famous hospitality, and most of all, a slower-paced, an uncomplicated way of life. In addition to a strong inclusion of local success stories in attracting and maintaining industry, the magazine capitalized on what came to mind for most people when they thought of "the South." Overt sexuality in the form of "Miss Hospitality" exploited the idea of Southern beauty and charm among the region's women. Promotion of the state was often left to these simple notions and concepts.

The early work of the Mississippi Advertising Commission and the A&I Board paid off when in 1965 a major announcement came. The state after three decades of work, Mississippi had more industrial workers than agricultural workers.[90] The program did leave a legacy of industrial growth in the state over several decades. The marketing machine started by Governor Hugh White in the 1930s did its job and that was to advertise and market the state of Mississippi to prospective industry and tourism. The Mississippi A&I Board's job of promoting Mississippi as a destination for industry and tourism alike can be seen through the pages of "Mississippi Magic." The Board used an idea that many people had of the south, specifically Mississippi, and used it as a cornerstone of a determined marketing campaign that spanned many years.

The publication continued to evolve and incorporated technological improvements as time went on. However, the publication in its first decade projected the most overt and pointed exploitation of things Southern to market Mississippi to industry and tourism. At a time when Mississippi had very little to offer, the A&I Board sold an idea that resulted in an influx of tourism dollars as well as an industrial expansion that surpassed all of the other Southern states during this period under study.

"Mississippi Magic" in its pages from 1945 to 1955 portrayed the state as a destination for both industry and tourism. The myth and mystique of the South were used as tools in this all-out advertising campaign to target Mississippi to others. The magazine portrayed the state in a manner that was comfortable to Southerner and Northerner alike. Mississippi as a state capitalized upon such notions of the South, and included them into the BAWI initiative, even though its benefits were not equally distributed among its citizens. Southern myth as developed by media was perpetuated to lure visitors and industrial expansion to Mississippi at a time when Southern reality was not nearly as pleasant as the Southern fantasy.

Notes

1. Martin Colby Schnitzer. "The Use of Inducements by States and Communities in the Promotion of Industrial Development, with Special Reference to Mississippi." Ph.D. diss., University of Florida, 1960, 121. Schnitzer, a Southerner, recounted his personal experiences with Northerner colleagues and business associates.
2. Eric Charles Clark. "Industrial Development and State Government Policy In Mississippi, 1890-1980." Ph.D. diss., Mississippi State University, 1989, 359.
3. Clark, "Industrial Development."
4. Clark, "Industrial Development."
5. Hugh L. White. "Mississippi Bids for Industry." *Review of Reviews* 93, no.6 (Winter 1936): 30.
6. White, "Mississippi Bids," 29.
7. White, "Mississippi Bids," 30.
8. White, "Mississippi Bids," 31.
9. Phil Stroupe. "Mississippi Closes 1953 with Biggest Industrial Growth in History," *Jackson Daily News*, January 3, 1953, Section 1, 12.
10. Most of the literature concerning Southern stereotypes has been social and regional in nature. It discusses such disenfranchisements of peoples from Southern, Indian, and Appalachian regions. Dwight B. Billings, Gurney Norman, and Katherine Ledford,

eds. "Confronting Appalachian Stereotypes: Back Talk from an American Region." Lexington: University Press of Kentucky, 1999.
11. John M. Coward. "Selling the Southwestern Indian: Ideology and Image in Arizona Highways, 1925-1940." *American Journalism*, 20 (Spring 2003): 13-31.
12. Coward, "Selling the Southwestern Indian."
13. Edward D. C. Campbell Jr. *The Celluloid South: Hollywood and the Southern Myth* (Knoxville, Tenn.: University of Knoxville Press, 1981), 5.
14. Patrick Gerster and Nicholas Cords. "The Northern Origins of Southern Mythology," *Journal of Southern History*, 43, no. 4 (1977): 568.
15. Gerster and Cords, "The Northern Origins," 568.
16. Gerster and Cords, "The Northern Origins," 572.
17. Gerster and Cords, "The Northern Origins," 572.
18. Campbell, *The Celluloid South,* 75.
19. Ida Jeter. "Jezebel and the Emergence of the Hollywood Tradition of a Decadent South." *The South and Film,* ed. Warren French (Jackson: University of Mississippi Press), 1981, 37.
20. Campbell, *The Celluloid South,* 75.
21. Schnitzer, "The Use of Inducements," 40.
22. Schnitzer, "The Use of Inducements," 41.
23. Schnitzer, "The Use of Inducements," 41.
24. Schnitzer, "The Use of Inducements," 53.
25. "Mississippi: A Land of Industrial Opportunity," pamphlet included in the BAWI advertising kit, 1937, Mississippi State Department of Archives and History, Jackson, Mississippi.
26. "Mississippi: A Land of Industrial Opportunity."
27. Neil R. McMillen. *Dark Journey: Black Mississippians in the Age of Jim Crow* (Urbana: University of Illinois Press, 1990), 11.
28. McMillen, *Dark Journey,* 37.
29. McMillen, *Dark Journey,* 156.
30. McMillen, *Dark Journey,* 72.
31. McMillen, *Dark Journey,* 73.
32. "Mississippi Tourist Guide," Mississippi State Board of Development, Advertising and Industrial Division, 1941, 60. Mississippi State Department of Archives and History, Jackson, Mississippi.
33. Legislative Packet from the Mississippi Advertising Commission to members of the 1937 state legislature, Mississippi State Department of Archives and History, Jackson, Mississippi.
34. Governor White's Introduction letter from the BAWI advertising kit sent to each member of the 1937 Mississippi legislature, Mississippi State Department of Archives and History, Jackson, Mississippi.
35. BAWI advertising kit, Mississippi Tourist Guide, 1937, Mississippi State Department of Archives and History, Jackson, Mississippi.
36. BAWI advertising kit, "Mississippi: A Land of Industrial Opportunity."
37. BAWI advertising kit, "Mississippi: A Land of Industrial Opportunity."
38. BAWI advertising kit, "Mississippi: A Land of Industrial Opportunity."
39. BAWI advertising kit, "Mississippi: A Land of Industrial Opportunity."

40. Eric Charles Clark. "Industrial Development and State Government Policy in Mississippi, 1890-1980," Ph.D., Mississippi State University, 1989, p. 361.
41. Clark, "Industrial Development and State Government Policy," 281.
42. "BAWI Bulletin, Balance Agriculture with Industry," premiere issue, June 1945, 2. Mississippi State Department of Archives and History, Jackson, Mississippi.
43. Clark, "Industrial Development and State Government Policy," 281.
44. Clark, "Industrial Development and State Government Policy," 281.
45. "BAWI Bulletin," June 1945, 3.
46. "BAWI Bulletin," June 1945, 3.
47. "BAWI Bulletin, Balance Agriculture with Industry," premiere issue, August 1945, 1. Mississippi State Department of Archives and History, Jackson, Mississippi.
48. "BAWI Bulletin," August 1945, 1.
49. "BAWI Bulletin, Balance Agriculture With Industry," premiere issue, September 1945, 1. Mississippi State Department of Archives and History, Jackson, Mississippi.
50. "BAWI Bulletin," September 1945, 1.
51. "BAWI Bulletin, Balance Agriculture with Industry," premiere issue, January 1947, 3. Mississippi State Department of Archives and History, Jackson, Mississippi.
52. "BAWI Bulletin," January 1947, 3.
53. BAWI pamphlet, "Mississippi, Heart of the Southland," January 1947, Mississippi State Department of Archives and History, Jackson, Mississippi.
54. "BAWI Bulletin, Balance Agriculture with Industry," premiere issue, February 1947, 3. Mississippi State Department of Archives and History, Jackson, Mississippi.
55. "BAWI Bulletin," February 1947, 3.
56. Mississippi Magic, July 1948, 1.
57. Mississippi Magic, July 1948, 1.
58. Mississippi Magic, July 1948, 1.
59. Mississippi Magic, July 1948, 1.
60. Mississippi Magic, July 1948, 1.
61. Mississippi Magic, July 1948, 1.
62. Mississippi Magic, July 1948, 1.
63. Mississippi Magic, July 1948, 1.
64. Mississippi Magic, August 1948, 1.
65. Mississippi Magic, October 1948, 10.
66. Mississippi Magic, October 1948, 10.
67. Mississippi Magic, October 1948, 10.
68. Mississippi Magic, February 1949, 1.
69. Mississippi Magic, February 1949, 10.
70. Mississippi Magic, March 1949, 1.
71. Mississippi Magic, March 1949, 1.
72. Mississippi Magic, June 1949, 1.
73. Mississippi Magic, September 1949, 1.
74. Mississippi Magic, September 1949, back cover.
75. Mississippi Magic, February 1950, 5.
76. Mississippi Magic, February 1950, 5.
77. Mississippi Magic, July 1950, 1.
78. Mississippi Magic, July 1950, special insert.
79. Mississippi Magic, November 1950, 8.

80. Mississippi Magic, November 1950, 8.
81. Mississippi Magic, March 1952, 1.
82. Mississippi Magic, March 1952, 9.
83. Mississippi Magic, March 1952, 9.
84. Mississippi Magic, September 1952, 1.
85. Mississippi Magic, December 1952, 10.
86. Mississippi Magic, December 1952, back cover.
87. Mississippi Magic, December 1955, 1.
88. Mississippi Magic, December 1955, 1.
89. Mississippi Magic, December 1955, 1.
90. John Perkins. "State Finally Reaches Economic Landmark," *Jackson Daily News*, May 4, 1965, Section 1, 2.

Chapter Six
Recognizing the Past, Celebrating Change: The "Mississippi Believe It!" Campaign Redefines the South
Wendy Atkins-Sayre

The new South is enamored of her new work. Her soul is stirred with the breath of a new life. The light of a grander day is falling fair on her face.

—Henry Grady, 1886[1]

When Henry Grady, editor of the *Atlanta Constitution* and advocate of the South, first uttered those words before a New York audience in 1886, there is little doubt that he hoped his campaign to change the image of his beloved Southern states would take hold immediately. Despite Grady's attempts and years of additional campaigns to change the public's perceptions of the South, however, the image of the racially segregated, technologically backwards, and intellectually stunted region persists. As Larry Griffin points out, "Each region of the United States has a particular identity hewn from history and culture. Yet none is as distinctive as the American South, and none has been imbued with such historical weight in the nation's making or afforded such metaphorical significance in its collective memory and mythological self-understandings."[2] The state of Mississippi struggles with a particularly negative image. A *Washington Post* columnist describes the state's "pop culture image" as "barefoot, tobacco-chewing, cousin-affectionate rednecks who park their pickups right out front of the double-wide."[3] *New York Times* columnist Brenda Goodman notes, "For decades, a search at the bottom of the nation's barrel of rankings has always seemed to come up with the same state. When anyone wants to know the nation's poorest state, or its fattest, or least educated, or sickest, or most corrupt, the answer has most often been Mississippi."[4] Stereotypes aside, the state does struggle with a challenging public image.

Debuting in 2006, the Mississippi, Believe It! (MBI) campaign was designed to change this negative image. The Cirlot Agency, the Jackson-based public relations firm that created the advertisements, describes the collection of posters and print ads as, "a public service campaign designed to inform and educate the citizens of Mississippi, as well as the rest of the country, about the wonderful people, aspects, and facts associated with the state of Mississippi."[5] The inspiration for the campaign, as Rick Looser, chief operating officer of the Cirlot Agency, explains it, was an encounter with a twelve-year-old boy on an airplane. After Looser explained that he was from Mississippi, the boy queried, "Do you see KKK people on your street every day?" And "Do you hate all black people?"[6] This encounter, one to which many Southerners can relate, gave the agency good reason to begin creating a publicity campaign targeted at boosting Mississippi's sour image. That image, of course, is one that has plagued the state for a number of years. Although Henry Grady's rhetoric was crafted at a time when the South faced a more complicated "image issue"—post-Reconstruction—there are many parallels between the discourses. Southerners felt the need to woo the North—to restore its image. Grady faced a tough sell, however, as Mississippi does today.

When New York Representative Charles Rangel, for example, recently quipped, "Who the hell wants to live in Mississippi?" he did so knowing that it was a safe question because Mississippi continues to bear the brunt of Southern-focused humor.[7] Despite its rich cultural heritage and strides in creating racial reconciliation, Mississippi faces its share of image problems. Stereotypes aside, "When income, poverty, infant mortality or literacy are measured, Mississippi ranks at or near the bottom of all 50 states" and "trails only Louisiana as the least livable place."[8] Mississippi may be the ultimate example of Southern stereotypes, but the South in general often falls victim to negative images. As Cobb notes:

> As the civil rights movement unfolded, "Dixie" soon evoked a vision, not of happy darkies on the plantation but of decidedly unhappy rednecks waving the Confederate flag and spewing contempt or national authority. In fact, an accumulated panorama of appalling and indelible imagery, from a beaten and bloated Emmett Till to the raw brutality of Selma, presented the South as . . . a place that hardly seemed part of America at all.[9]

This image of the South, and Mississippi in particular, has profound effects on the people of the South, affecting everything from identity to commerce. Consequently, messages like those found in the MBI campaign, help to reshape the image that Mississippians and other Southerners attempt to overcome.

This essay accounts for the MBI campaign by rhetorically analyzing the advertisements.[10] A close reading of the visual and discursive elements of the advertisements indicates that the campaign, like Henry Grady's "New South" rhetoric, attempts to reshape the image of the Southern region. In doing so, the message is targeted at Northerners and is based on an acknowledgment of past mistakes, a desire to show a changed region, and attempts to build identification between Southerners and outsiders. The essay will develop by first discussing the historical and contemporary context for the campaign, then turning to rhetorical analysis of the advertisements, before drawing conclusions about the campaign as a whole.

The Southern Problem: Overcoming the Past

The Mississippi, Believe It! campaign, seen through paid advertisements, distributed posters, and a web site, debuted in 2005 and has reached over 120 million people.[11] Featuring a number of famous Mississippians and sporting a sarcastic tone at times, the advertisements often take a humorous shot at stereotypes about the state and the South, more broadly. "What's unique about the ads," the chief operating officer of the Cirlot Agency says, "is that they're in your face, in a gentle Southern way. We're not afraid to confront the criticism head on."[12] The agency describes the campaign as being primarily targeted at Mississippi children and, consequently, distributed a set of the campaign posters to every public and private elementary and secondary school, as well as all state colleges and universities.[13] The campaign was featured on NBC's *Today Show* and in several national newspapers and magazines such as the *New York Times*, *Washington Post*, *USA Today*, and the *Economist*.[14] As a result of these efforts, the campaign has received a fair amount of attention. Designed to "leave viewers with a lasting, positive impression to combat the negative baggage that [Mississippi] has carried for far too long," the message is a tough one to sell, given the history of the state.[15]

Mississippi's negative image is not without warrant. As John Dittmer describes it, the state is often imagined to be "America's dungeon."[16] With the end of the Civil War and the start of Reconstruction, African Americans in the state began to see significant changes in their lives, with many serving in government positions. By the late 1870s, however, White conservatives were successful at chipping away any gains that blacks had won under Reconstruction.[17] Racial segregation, for example, was one of the early signs of regression. By the 1940s, Dittmer argues, "many of the gains made by blacks in the post-Civil War years had been swept away."[18] Black-owned businesses were going under, farmland ownership was dropping, and violence against African Americans was on the rise. Adding to the turmoil was the rise of Jim Crow laws which mandated segregation, starting with an 1888 law that segregated railroad passengers.[19] Violence was also an issue, with six hundred lynchings taking place between 1880 and 1940 in Mississippi.[20] As Harold and DeLuca explain, "Under Jim Crow, lynched black bodies were offered as evidence of white supremacy.

They were the 'strange fruit' swinging in the Southern wind of racial hatred; their 'bulging eyes and twisted mouths' mutely testifying to the horrible extremes of white power."[21]

Despite these conditions, the Civil Rights movement was slow to come to Mississippi. Most of the early civil rights actions were primarily led by Mississippians, without support from national organizations or the federal government.[22] In the late 1940s and 1950s, many African Americans in Mississippi were working in "slave-like" positions—working in agriculture, as opposed to factory jobs. Consequently, despite poor living conditions, many black Mississippians were not in a position to begin work for civil rights. Additionally, the state was not a priority for the National Association for the Advancement of Colored People (NAACP), which believed that change needed to begin in more progressive states before it could happen in such strongly segregated states such as Mississippi.[23] In fact, the NAACP and the Southern Christian Leadership Conference had never been very successful in recruiting members in the state because African Americans were afraid of getting involved or were uninterested in the movement.[24]

The 1955 case of Emmett Till changed the civil rights scene in Mississippi, however. Till, an African American teenage boy from Chicago was in Money, Mississippi, visiting his grandmother. After interacting with a white woman in a grocery store (the stories vary from Till talking to the woman, squeezing her hand, or wolf whistling at her), Till was taken in the night by the woman's husband, beaten, tied to a cotton gin fan, and thrown in a river.[25] Till's distorted body, pulled from the river after several days, became a visual symbol of the civil rights cause[26] and a vivid reminder of the troubled and violent environment in Mississippi. More importantly, the case drew reporters from major news outlets to the state, creating fear among Mississippi whites that "their state was being maligned by outsiders determined to destroy the southern way of life."[27] The attention of the nation on the state began the modern Civil Rights movement in Mississippi.[28]

In the summer of 1961, the Freedom Riders became a concern to Southern states. Civil rights activists boarded buses and traveled south to test the segregation laws and the Kennedy administration. As Murphy argues, "The Freedom Riders exploited the conflict between federal and local law and, through direct action, created dangerous fissures within the American system of government."[29] Finding resistance in Mississippi, the state became a primary location for Freedom Rider activity and, consequently, a hotbed for civil rights actions. Civil rights activists quickly encountered a violent reaction when challenging voting rights and segregation laws. The summer of 1963 saw the assassination of Mississippi civil rights leader Medgar Evers. His death brought national attention to the state, with President John F. Kennedy meeting with the family shortly after his Arlington National Cemetery burial.[30] In the summer of 1964, hundreds of volunteers for Freedom Summer began to enter the state. Primarily white, middle- and upper-class, elite college students, the volunteers spread out across the state to help with voter registration and to teach in Freedom

Schools. Despite training and warnings of possible violence, the disappearance of volunteers Andrew Goodman, James Chaney, and Michael Schwerner in Neshoba County, Mississippi (and the subsequent finding of their bodies) made the seriousness of the civil rights work apparent.[31] Mississippi was back in the headlines with this case, displaying a painful reminder of the resistance to change. Clearly the history of racial discord and the popular image of the state that emerges from that history are part of the past that Mississippi finds so difficult to escape.

Mississippi has, of course, made great strides in racial reconciliation in the last four decades. For example, the state has the greatest number of elected black officials, educates around 4,000 African American students in the major state universities and colleges each year, has seen an improving economy, indicating future potential for lowering poverty rates, and continues to nurture a rich cultural heritage, with many notable African American authors and musicians.[32] The problems that the state faces, however, continue to be overwhelming. Mississippi has the highest poverty rate, the lowest median household income, and is the third worst-educated state, with only 16.9 percent of the population having completed a college degree.[33] The state battles a low high school graduation rate (about 74 percent), with only about 69 percent of African American students graduating.[34] Primary and secondary schools are largely racially segregated.[35] There is an embarrassing income disparity between black and white Mississippians.[36] And Mississippians have yet to elect a black politician to a statewide position, despite an almost 36 percent black population and a plethora of black state legislators.[37] There is no doubt that the state has made improvements and has received little positive publicity in return; however the problems that the state continues to struggle with are not easily ignored. Changing the image of Mississippi is not a step that will happen quickly. Despite these challenges, however, the state continues to attempt to focus on its strengths and overcome its negative image.

Henry Grady faced a similar problem in attempting to gain favor with the North after the Civil War. As Bryan writes, "Bewildered by the destruction and decay of their traditional way of life, Southern people sought out spokesmen to explain the events of their past and to guide them toward a more prosperous future."[38] In trying to sell the South's industrial possibilities, the editor of the Atlanta *Constitution* spoke to Northern audiences about the new peace that was emerging in the South—"a region so thoroughly transformed and cleanly disconnected from its past that it would in reality be not so much a 'New South' . . . as a 'No' South,' fully assimilated and essentially indistinguishable from the rest of American society."[39] Speaking before the New England Society of New York City in 1886, Grady presented what came to be known as his New South speech. He opened the speech with a quotation from Benjamin Hill, a Georgia politician: "There was a South of slavery and secession—that South is dead. There is a South of union and freedom—that South, thank God, is living, breathing, growing every hour."[40] Grady focused on describing the changed South, allowing a renewed faith in the region. Not only was the South reconciled, Grady argued that it was prospering: "The new South presents a perfect democracy. . . . Her soul is stirred with the breath of a new life. The light of a grander day is falling fair on her face. She is thrilling with the consciousness of growing power and prosperity."[41] Grady's appeals, although targeted at Northern investors, also spoke to the powerful Southerners. Although the "New South" spoke of wiping out "the place where Mason and Dixon's line used to be," it also embraced the "Lost Cause."[42] As Cobb argues, "the New South creed painted an almost seamless and undeniably seductive mural in which a glorious past, a reassuring present, and a glittering future were fully integrated and virtually indistinguishable."[43]

The immediate response to the speech was positive. Bryan points out "most major New York newspapers devoted much space to praising the 'New South' speech with the grandest hyperbole. Reporters specifically applauded the speech as important in helping to unify North and South with a common appeal to industrial growth."[44] In fact, Grady received numerous speaking requests after this initial speech and presented a similar message on several occasions.[45] The New South message of the "God ordained birth of a new being on traditional Southern soil," may not have permanently changed the image of the South, but did have some effect on Northern and Southern audiences.[46]

Like Grady's appeal to a "New South" ideal, the MBI campaign attempts to explain the controversial past of the state, while embracing the positive parts of the history and celebrating the cultural richness of the area. Although the campaign focuses on the state of Mississippi, the advertisements could easily be read as a campaign in support of the Deep South as a whole. Given this understanding of the controversial past that Mississippi faces and the attempts that Grady made to overcome a controversial Southern past, this essay now turns to a close reading of the advertisements.

The New "New South"

The collected MBI advertisements provide insight into the self-perception of the state and the message that is constructed in response to that image. Targeted at Northerners, the advertisements recognize the past, while emphasizing a changed region and attempting to build identification with the rest of America.

Speaking to the North

One of the first noticeable characteristics of the advertisements is the audience. The creators of the campaign identify two primary audiences: Mississippi citizens and those outside of Mississippi. In targeting the children of Mississippi with the advertisements, the public relations firm argues that

> it is important for the children of Mississippi to be aware of the facts about the state—including the people, accomplishments, capabilities and positive history—so that they will be proud of their home state and its heritage. By informing children of the many good things about the state, they will become "homegrown" ambassadors for the state.[47]

The language in this description of the purpose of the campaign indicates a belief that the state has been misunderstood not only by outsiders, but also its own citizens.

Despite this stated purpose, however, an analysis of the advertisements indicates a focus on those living outside of the state. That audience could be composed of Northerners, given the history of the state, although it is never explicitly stated. The language indicates a conversation with an audience unconvinced of the strengths of the state. Several of the advertisements, for example, address stereotypes about the South. One poster proclaims in bold lettering across the top of the page: "Yes, we can read. A few of us can even write."[48] Below the words are images of some of the state's most famous authors—Richard Wright, Eudora Welty, William Faulkner, and John Grisham, for example. The advertisement concludes by comparing the state to the rest of the nation: "No other state in the country can claim as many honored, awarded, and revered writers as Mississippi. Yes, Mississippi. Where words transcend." As in the headline, the wording seems to be targeted at an outsider—someone who is questioning the worth of the state. Using a strategy of *prolepsis*, that is, responding to an objection yet to be made, the message is constructed as if answering frequently launched attacks against the state. The final statement— "Where words transcend"—can be read in multiple ways. Perhaps this is meant to indicate the word, the art of writing, can bridge differences between the state and outsiders. Recognizing the talent is found in the state and the universality of the work emphasizes the shared substance of those from the Deep South and those outside of the South. Alternatively, the message can be read as being targeted at Mississippians ("Yes, Mississippi"), emphasizing the ability of literature to transcend racial divisions. In this case, the words acknowledge the troubled past of the state, but indicate a reconciliation.

A stronger example of the campaign addressing an audience of outsiders is found in an advertisement celebrating the musical heritage of the state: "Y'all may think we talk funny, but the world takes our music seriously."[49] In this case, the targeted audience is clearly not an insider ("Y'all may think . . . "), but is instead part of an external group. The choice of a Southern colloquialism to begin the sentence emphasizes the perceived differences between the South and the rest of the nation. It also subtly changes the tone of the advertisement, inviting the reader to imagine an individual with a "Slow. Southern. Drawl." making this statement (as emphasized later in the ad). Featuring the images of Mississippi musicians such as Bo Diddley, Muddy Waters, Elvis Presley, and Faith Hill, the message emphasizes the importance of the state's contribution to the music world. "For decades," the ad claims, "Mississippians have been scoring the soundtracks of peoples lives." As in the previous example, the ad argues that art brings people together. Overlooking perceived differences between individuals, a respect for music created by Southerners indicates the need to move beyond past stereotypes. This desire to gloss over differences, however, indicates that the purpose of the message is not only to change Mississippians' perceptions of the state, but to appeal to outsiders and their focus on division.

This appeal to an outside audience continues throughout most of the advertisements (including those analyzed in the following section). Like Grady's appeal to the Northerners for a change of heart about the South, the MBI campaign attempts to sell the state to outsiders by dispelling stereotypes and highlighting accomplishments, all the while directing the comments to outside naysayers.

The focus on those outside of the state, contrary to the claims that the public relations firm makes about the purpose of the campaign, indicates a need to confront negative images of the state held by others. In fact, the advertisements seem to define the South in relation to the North. The South has continually battled this issue in trying to place itself within the image of mainstream "America." As Cobb argues, "mythical non-South had become virtually synonymous with the idea of America itself."[50] The "standard" parts of America have excluded the South in an attempt to create a more consistent image of the country. The South became the "Other," the inexplicable. Cobb continues,

> As the leaders of the young republic struggled to gain the acceptance and respect of other nations, northern architects of national identity soon realized that their vision of America would not only be much simpler to construct but also much easier to look at and far more emphatic and unequivocal in meaning if they simply focused on what they saw, or sometimes chose to see, in the states above the recently drawn Mason-Dixon line.[51]

Thus, the South was defined outside of the image of "America" and seen as an anomaly. Consequently, not only is the region forced to address the North in attempting to gain favor (as in the case of Grady), but it must also attempt to define itself in relation to the Northern states.

A Troubled Past

Aside from the issue of audience, however, the advertisements also form a message similar to Grady's appeal. There is an acknowledgment and rejection of past mistakes, an indication of change, and an attempt to build identification with "outsiders." The messages act as an example of atonement rhetoric. Koesten and Rowland argue that repentance (acknowledgment of wrongdoing and reconciliation), prayer (self-reflection and indication of change), and charity (reparation) are "at the core of atonement."[52] Acting as a "form of symbolic action to serve as curative function," this atonement message allows the state to repair the negative image that it continues to face.[53]

Acknowledgment of past wrongdoings is indicated in several of the advertisement headlines. For example, the history of racial division and violence in the state is not possible to ignore, however the ads skillfully acknowledge the past, while encouraging the audience to embrace a changed image of the state. One advertisement proclaims in bold letters across the top of the page: "No Black. No White. Just the Blues." Pictured below this claim are images of some of Mississippi's most famous blues musicians—Howlin' Wolf, B. B. King, and Muddy Waters, for example. As in the previously discussed ads, the words indicate that the division that was once present has been overcome through art. "Some see the world in black and white. Others see varying shades of gray. But Mississippi taught the world to see . . . and hear . . . the Blues."[54] The words in the headline—"No Black. No White"—call forth images of segregation signs of the past. Acknowledging the past atrocities, the advertisements move on to the future—"Just the Blues"—encouraging audience members to move with the state in transcending racial lines.

Similarly, another advertisement invites viewers to "Meet a Few of Our New 'Good Ole Boys'" while showing the photos of African American men and women, white women, and a Choctaw Indian man who have all held political offices in the state.[55] The assumption that this ad confronts—that the state is stuck in the past with racist and sexist policies—appears to be incorrect. In this case, the visual element is an important aspect of the message, allowing the ad to make the claims of the advertisement even more obvious. "The 'good ole boy' network alive and well in Mississippi? Not hardly," the ad reads. The evidence of the diverse group of politicians seems to support the idea of a changed state. "Good ole boys?' Try 'great young visionaries.' That's more like today's Mississippi." Rather than maintaining images of a segregated South, the discursive and visual elements of the ad invite the viewers to envision the New South. Although the images of leaders appear in separate frames, they bring such a diversity of people together in two rows of photographs that the images indicate, using a strategy of enumeration, that diversity abounds in the state leadership structure. The words in this text acknowledge the troubled past, but the images invite viewers to focus on the changed present.

Change of Heart

Likewise, the MBI ads indicate that Mississippi has reflected on its past actions and is now a changed state. The "No Black. No White" and "Meet a Few of Our New Good Ole' Boys" ads indicate that racial and gender barriers are eroding in the state. Even more explicitly, however, one advertisement suggests social transformation. The headline proclaims, "MISSISSIPPI. The First to Have a Change of Heart . . . and Lungs . . . and Kidneys."[56] The focus of the advertisement is on a black-and-white photograph of an older white male with black horned-rimmed glasses. Wearing a surgical cap on his head and mask draped around his neck, the man is clearly a medical doctor. In fact, after reading the text of the advertisement, the reader discovers that this is an image of Dr. James Hardy, the Mississippi doctor responsible for the nation's first heart, lung, and kidney transplants. Setting aside the text of the advertisement for a moment, however, and focusing solely on the headline and photograph, there is a double-meaning at work. The medical meaning—indicating organ transplants—is clear from the wording and imagery. What is also implied, however, with the "change of heart" phrase is that the state has evolved in its way of thinking. The black-and-white photograph of the white-haired, white man could have been taken in 2006 or in 1956, when this same man labeled as "having a change of heart" in Mississippi might have taken on a very different meaning. Certainly, Mississippi was not the first Southern state to begin rethinking racial issues, however, the imagery and the context of the other advertisements making a nod to past racial discord indicates that this message can be read into the ad. The text then invites readers to think along these lines: "Yes, Mississippi. We were the first in the world to have a change of heart. Now isn't it time the rest of the world had a change of heart about Mississippi?" Thus, the readers are asked to mimic the behavior of the man in the photograph and have a change of heart—to question pre-held beliefs.

Another advertisement indicates a more material change in the state. The ad features a photograph of Oseola McCarty, an African American woman who "lived modestly, never even owning a car" but who donated $150,000 to the University of Southern Mississippi for scholarship money.[57] The headline reads "State of Grace" and explains that, "We always hear about Mississippi being last. Last in this, last in that. Well, at last, Mississippi is first . . . in generosity."[58] The text continues to explain this claim, asserting that Mississippi ranks highest in charitable donations in relation to income. Highlighting this fact in light of other state hardships, the viewer is asked to focus on the state's strengths. Although the focus is on the act of one woman, the headline ("State of Grace") directs the reader's attention to the fact Oseola McCarty's act is only one of many in the state. Moreover, the fact McCarty was an African American woman who chose to give back to the state that might not have been very gracious to her for most of her life indicates a theme of change and forgiveness.

The ads make an important move to recognize past mistakes and then focus on the positive. Similarly, Grady did not ignore the history that lead to the South's demise. Instead, he valorized the skill with which the South was able to overcome, in his mind, those past divisions. "The relations of the southern people with the negro," he said, "are close and cordial."[59] In both messages—Grady and MBI—there is a felt need to acknowledge past mistakes, but also to indicate change. That confessional allows audience members to reconcile discomfort over the past while celebrating the present.

Crafting Identification

A significant purpose of the MBI campaigns is focused on erasing stereotypical images of the state in hopes of emphasizing the similarities between Southerners and "outsiders." For example, in addition to the previously discussed advertisements which seem to be targeted at outsiders, other advertisements poke fun at perceived differences. In the style of *prolepsis*, a series of advertisements counters stereotypes: "Yes, we have running water . . . right next to the world's finest kitchen appliances";[60] "Yes, we wear shoes. A few of us even wear cleats";[61] "Yes, our roads are paved . . . AND we have the best student drivers under the sun."[62] The text of these ads provides support for the claims by highlighting the accomplishments of state entrepreneurs, athletes, and students. Responding to these stereotypes, as ridiculous as they may sound, provides a humorous way to invite viewers to question the remaining stereotypes that they may have about the state. If the campaign is able to effectively undermine some misunderstandings, they are also able to build up feelings of identification. Instead of feeling that the South—and Mississippi in particular—is a foreign land, they can celebrate the unique qualities of the state (literary figures, musical artists, athletes, etc.), while also concluding that the South has changed and is more similar to the rest of the nation.

Implications of the New "New South"

Although Grady's rhetoric and the MBI advertisements were created over 120 years apart, the comparisons between the two messages are telling. In both cases, the primary audience of the message is the Northern states. Forced to turn their eyes to the North, the South continues to not only ask for acceptance and, to some degree, forgiveness, but to gain enough confidence in the Southern region that investments will be made. Despite reluctance on the part of Southerners to need Northern approval, their messages continue to be driven by this desire.

At the same time, both Grady's rhetoric and MBI ads also speak to a secondary audience in the South. Cobb explains how the New South message also appealed to Southerners:

> Defeated and embittered, southern whites drew determination and hope from the New South's promises of an affluent golden age just ahead. They also found pride and reassurance in its celebration of a carefully constructed golden age behind, the glorious and heroic heritage of the Old South and the Lost Cause.[63]

It would be impossible for Grady to ignore Southerners with his message, needing their support of the reformed South image that he crafted. The nod to the strengths of the South allowed Southern audience members to maintain a sense of pride and identity, while also becoming open to Grady's idea of a future South. Although the primary audience with the New South rhetoric was Northerners, Southerners could find a message of their own. The MBI advertisements have a similar split in audiences. Despite the stated claims of the Cirlot Agency that the messages are targeted at the children of Mississippi, analysis shows that the message is largely centered on changing the minds of outsiders. Confronting stereotypes, touting accomplishments, and celebrating the unique characteristics of the state allows the campaign to attempt to change the image of the state that outsiders tend to have. Importantly, however, it also allows Mississippians the opportunity to recover the state's history (in noting the state's cultural heritage and accomplishments), while also reshaping the way they think about their image of the state. For that reason, the advertisements have potential for bringing the various audiences together—those within the state and those outside Mississippi—and strengthening the overall image of the state.

Additionally, both discourses (Grady and MBI) focus much effort on arguing that the South is able to conform to the Northern norm. In Grady's case, he argued that the South had learned its lesson and that it was now living in racial harmony and moving toward a grand future. The MBI advertisements continually come back to the theme of normalcy. With the end of the Civil War and, again, with the end of the 1950s and 1960s Civil Rights movement, the South was seen as the "other," "America's opposite, its negative image, its evil twin."[64] While the South attempts to deemphasize the differences between the regions, however, there is a larger need to maintain that distinction. As Griffin argues, the juxtaposition of North and South allows the country to define itself more specifically.[65] "When one understands the South," Griffin states, "as the negation of America . . . one is likely to understand more deeply what America is, and what it is (or ought to be), in particular, is the opposite of the South."[66] It is this definition by negation that allows the country to reflect on how it should imagine itself. Of course, it is unfortunate that a particular region should stand in for the negative. Mississippi, in particular, has acted metonymically, symbolizing the racial violence and hatred that is, in fact, found in all parts of the country.[67]

Although this negation may be unfair to the region, it does provide a particularly poignant reminder of the extremes to which society will go in order to guard its power. Consequently, although the state, and the region more broadly, should continue work to move beyond the racist image of the South, it is understandable that the area continues to be seen as a symbol of racism.

Finally, the issue of race in both discourses is particularly telling. Grady's attempt to paint the relationship between black and white as "close and cordial" was certainly more difficult that the MBI campaign's attempt to describe Mississippi as "No Black. No White" or "having a change of heart."[68] There is no doubt that racial relations have improved in Mississippi and the South more broadly. It is impossible, however, to ignore past racial discord. Griffin argues that the "South's past" continues to hold "profound moral significance, for the region, the nation, and beyond. In a very special and important way, then, that past can't die. Can't become fossilized, can't be relegated to history books or museums; it can't become simply 'past'."[69] The MBI advertisements seem to recognize that importance and acknowledge the troubled past. At the same time, the ads encourage viewers to celebrate the changes that have occurred in the state. Just as the New South rhetoric silenced discussions of continued racial discord in the South, however, the MBI advertisements also tend to overlook state-level issues that continue to be unresolved.[70] As indicated earlier in the essay, Mississippi continues to face problems that center on race. A pessimistic reading of the ads would argue they are merely serving as smokescreens. A more optimistic take on the ads would suggest that the state do what it can to make improvements (in the economy, educational system, politics, etc.) and, at the same time, continue to make improvements in racial relations. Given the recency of the campaign, the success of these goals is impossible to assess.

The South, and Mississippi in particular, continues to battle a public relations nightmare. Griffin explains the "the South's past, especially its racial past is, to quote Faulkner again, 'not even past.' Indeed, that past—a past of racial injustice and brutality, of freedom rides and anti-desegregation riots by white university students—is recycled, and then recycled again."[71] Despite changes in the South, it is the brutal and embarrassing images of the racially segregated South of the Civil Rights movement that continue to linger in many minds. Public relations campaigns may begin to chip away at that image, but the reality of the situation is that Mississippi still faces some troubling issues. The point of this analysis is not to condemn the Mississippi, Believe It! campaign. In many ways, the state has no other option but to continue fighting to alter perceptions of the region. At the same time, the ads should be placed in perspective and should more fully recognize the many areas where improvements need to continue to be made. As with Grady's New South rhetoric, there is the potential for this message to hinder or even silence those who continue to question the strength of the region. Consequently, while it is important to celebrate the state and encourage future change through outside investment and travel, it is also important to continue asking questions about why the negative images of the state, and the South more broadly, continue to exist.

Notes

1. Henry W. Grady, *The New South: Writings and Speeches of Henry Grady* (Savannah, Ga.: Beehive Press, 1971), 11.
2. Larry J. Griffin, "The American South and the Self," *Southern Cultures*, 12 (2006): 7.
3. Neely Tucker, "Now in Mississippi: Four S's, Four I's, and a Dollop of P.R.," *Washington Post*, December 3, 2006, para. 8, accessed October 29, 2008, Lexis-Nexis.
4. Brenda Goodman, "Heard the One About Mississippi? It's Fighting Back," *New York Times*, November 8, 2006, para. 1, accessed February 12, 2009, Lexis-Nexis.
5. "Frequently Asked Questions," Cirlot Agency, para. 1, accessed February 12, 2009, http://mississippibelieveit.com/faq.
6. Robert. S. McCain, "Legends of Mississippi; Nation's Poorest State Spreads Richness of Character," *Washington Times*, December 5, 2006, para. 4, accessed October 29, 2008, Lexis-Nexis.
7. Julianne Malveaux, "Mississippi: Much to Admire, Warts and All," *USA Today*, December 15, 2006, para. 2, accessed October 29, 2008, Lexis-Nexis.
8. Malveaux, "Mississippi," para. 4.
9. James C. Cobb, *Away Down South: A History of Southern Identity* (New York: Oxford University Press, 2005), 1.
10. The agency has produced a total of seventeen advertisements. For this research project, I limited the reading to eleven advertisements, eliminating those that seemed primarily focused not on responding to particular state stereotypes, but on highlighting state accomplishments. The advertisements can be viewed at: http://www.mississippibelieveit.com/.
11. "Fact Sheet," Cirlot Agency, accessed February 12, 2009, http://www.mississippibelieveit.com/faq/MBI08FactSheetNatl.pdf.
12. "Mississippi Campaign Shoots Down Negative Stereotypes," Cirlot Agency, para. 4, accessed February 12, 2009, http://www.mississippibelieveit.com/faq/MBI08release.pdf.
13. "Frequently Asked Questions."
14. "Frequently Asked Questions"; Goodman, "Heard the One"; Malveaux, "Mississippi"; "Mississippi Turning; State Promotion," *The Economist*, January 6, 2007, accessed October 29, 2008, Lexis-Nexis; Tucker, "Now in Mississippi"; Kitty B. Yancey, "Ads Throw Cold Water on Mississippi Stereotypes," *USA Today*, December 1, 2006, accessed October 29, 2009, Lexis-Nexis.
15. "Mississippi campaign," para. 10.
16. John Dittmer, *Local People: The Struggle for Civil Rights in Mississippi* (Champaign: University of Illinois Press, 1995), 9.
17. Dittmer, *Local People*.
18. Dittmer, *Local People*, 13.
19. Dittmer, *Local People*.
20. Dittmer, *Local People*, 13.
21. Christine Harold and Kevin M. DeLuca, "Behold the Corpse: Violent Images and the Case of Emmett Till," *Rhetoric & Public Affairs*, 8 (2005), 268.
22. Dittmer, *Local People*.
23. Dittmer, *Local People*, 29.

24. Dittmer, *Local People*.
25. Dittmer, *Local People*.
26. Harold & DeLuca, "Behold the Corpse."
27. Dittmer, *Local People*, 56.
28. Dittmer, *Local People*.
29. John M. Murphy, "Domesticating Dissent: The Kennedys and the Freedom Rides," *Communication Monographs*, 59 (1992), 66.
30. Juan Williams, *Eyes on the Prize: America's Civil Rights Years, 1954-1965* (New York: Penguin Books).
31. Doug McAdam, *Freedom Summer* (New York: Oxford University Press, 1988).
32. "2008 Economic Forecast," *Mississippi Business Journal*, 30 (January 14, 2008), B62, accessed March 20, 2009, EBSCOHost database; Mississippi Institutions of Higher Learning, *Institutional Research: Degrees, Five Year Trend Data, by Ethnicity and Gender* (2008), accessed April 15, 2009, from http://www.ihl.state.ms.us/research/stats.html; Tucker, "Now in Mississippi."
33. "Mississippi Turning."
34. Mississippi Department of Education, "Mississippi Department of Education Announces Graduation, Dropout Rates for Class of 2007," June 11, 2008, accessed April 15, 2009, http://www.mde.k12.ms.us/Extrel/news/2008/08GradDropoutRates.html.
35. Charles C. Bolton, *The Hardest Deal of All: The Battle Over School Integration in Mississippi, 1870-1980* (Jackson: University Press of Mississippi, 2005).
36. "2008 Economic Forecast."
37. Tucker, "Now in Mississippi."
38. Ferald J. Bryan, *Henry Grady or Tom Watson? The Rhetorical Struggle for the New South, 1880-1890* (Macon, Ga.: Mercer University Press, 1994), 17.
39. Cobb, *Away Down South*, 68.
40. Bryan, *Henry Grady or Tom Watson?*, 44-45.
41. Grady, *New South*, 11.
42. Cobb, *Away Down South*, 77.
43. Cobb, *Away Down* South, 98.
44. Bryan, *Henry Grady or Tom Watson?*, 47.
45. Bryan, *Henry Grady or Tom Watson?*
46. Bryan, *Henry Grady or Tom Watson?*, 60.
47. "Frequently Asked Questions," para. 10.
48. "Yes, We Can Read. A Few of Us Can Even Write," Cirlot Agency, accessed February 12, 2009, http://www.mississippibelieveit.com/ads/print_read.html.
49. "Y'all May Think We Talk Funny, But the World Takes Our Music Seriously," Cirlot Agency, accessed February 12, 2009, http://www.mississippibelieveit.com/ads/print_music.html.
50. Cobb, *Away Down South*, 2.
51. Cobb, *Away Down South*, 3.
52. Joy Koesten and Robert. C. Rowland, "The Rhetoric of Atonement," *Communication Studies*, 55 (2004), 73.
53. Koesten and Rowland, "Rhetoric of Atonement," 71.
54. Elipses in original; "No Black. No White. Just the Blues," Cirlot Agency, accessed February 12, 2009, http://www.mississippibelieveit.com/ads/print_blues.html.
55. "Meet a Few of Our New 'Good Ole Boys,'" Cirlot Agency, accessed February 12, 2009, http://www.mississippibelieveit.com/ads/print_boys.html.

56. "Mississippi. The First to Have a Change of Heart . . . and Lungs . . . and Kidneys," Cirlot Agency, accessed February 12, 2009, http://www.mississippibelieveit.com/ads/print_hearts.html.
57. "A State of Grace," Cirlot Agency, accessed February 12, 2009, from http://www.mississippibelieveit.com/ads/print_oseola.html.
58. "State of Grace," para. 1.
59. Grady, *New South*, 9.
60. "Yes, We Have Running Water . . . Right Next to the World's Finest Appliances," Cirlot Agency, accessed February 12, 2009, http://www. mississippibelieveit.com/ads/print_viking.html.
61. "Yes, We Wear Shoes. A Few of Us Even Wear Cleats," Cirlot Agency, accessed February 12, 2009, http://www.mississippibelieveit.com/ads/print_shoes.html.
62. "Yes, Our Roads Are Paved . . . AND We Have the Best Student Drivers Under the Sun," Cirlot Agency, accessed February 12, 2009, http://www.mississippibelieveit.com/ ads/print_solarcar.html.
63. Cobb, *Away Down South*, 68.
64. Griffin, "American South," 7.
65. Larry J. Griffin, "Southern Distinctiveness, Yet Again, or, Why America Still Needs the South," *Southern Cultures*, 6 (2006), accessed February 23, 2009, Gale Cencage Literature Resource Center.
66. Griffin, "Southern Distinctiveness," para. 18.
67. Cobb, *Away Down South*; Griffin, "Southern Distinctiveness."
68. Grady, *New South*, 9.
69. Griffin, "Southern Distinctiveness," para. 9.
70. Cobb, *Away Down South*, 334.
71. Griffin, "Southern Distinctiveness," para. 7.

Chapter Seven
Poor as Job's Turkey: Back to the Land as a Rhetoric of Authenticity in Foxfire's Appalachia
Jason Waite

This chapter asserts the Foxfire project of Southern Appalachia constructed, rhetorically, an alternative Appalachia and then deployed that alternative as the "authentic" Appalachia. Alternative to what? Appalachia has a long history of being marginalized. Many people, when asked to name the first thing that comes to mind at mention of the word "Appalachia," will say something like "hillbilly," "poverty," or "ignorance" or they'll start humming "Dueling Banjos." Foxfire worked to change such perceptions of the people of Appalachia. And, coupled with such change, Foxfire's "authentic" Appalachia is linked to nostalgia for "simpler times" that is evident in the counter-culture of the 1960s.

Foxfire was initially a "progressive" high school English project conceived in 1966 by Elliot Wigginton, whose goal was to teach basic writing skills to students in a rural school located in Rabun County, Georgia. The project was grounded in Southern Appalachian culture and endeavored to promote "a sense of place and appreciation for local people, community, and culture."[1] Wigginton asked his students to go out into the surrounding communities and interview people (e.g., relatives and neighbors). The interviews cover a wide range of topics including maintaining households, crafting musical instruments, and caring for animals. The students transcribed the interviews, adding necessary background information, and published them as articles in *The Foxfire Magazine*. Eventually, articles from several editions of the magazine were collected and published in book form. The types of articles the project published, as evidenced by the success of the magazine and books, seemed to strike a chord in a large number of people who found themselves disillusioned by the mainstream culture of their time.

A Brief Picture of Appalachia

About 115 miles northeast of Atlanta, nestled among 4,000 foot peaks in the Blue Ridge Mountains, sits Rabun County, Georgia. The county, composed of some 371 square miles, was populated in 1960 by 7,456 people and in 1970 by 8,327 people.[2] Rabun County was (and still is) very rural and in many ways isolated, mirroring much of Appalachia in the 1960s (and to some extent, today). Along with isolation come issues of apparently aberrant distinctness and what seems to be less opportunity, less validation, less of nearly everything. For instance, Appalachian studies scholar Branscome, writing in 1969, noted that fully 65 percent of Appalachia's students, at that time, would not graduate from high school, and less than 30 percent of Appalachia's farm students and only 40 percent of non-farm students would complete ten grades of school.[3]

To preface these figures, Branscome notes "more than three-quarters of a million young people sit in the hollows and hills [of Appalachia] unmotivated, uneducated, and unemployed."[4] Branscome and many others of his time have painted a vivid picture of Appalachia, one that perhaps unwittingly reifies stereotypes often associated with the region (e.g., the ignorant and lazy "hillbilly") and represents the characteristic lack portrayed so vividly in adjectives beginning with the prefix "un" so often used to describe it.[5] When Branscome says that people are "unmotivated, uneducated, and unemployed," the conjured image is, on the one hand, of people who have not been given the same opportunities to succeed or live fulfilling lives as others. On the other hand, the image is of a people who don't have much to offer, of people who, in their unmotivated, uneducated stupor cannot even see the value of remaining in school beyond the tenth grade.

Branscome's account is not without precedent; we can see it extending from a long line of othering that emerges not only from scholarly work but also from government sponsored popular media. For instance, the New Deal's Farm Securities Administration (FSA) was involved in the creation of thousands of photographs from the mid-1930s through World War II, which were made available to popular magazines and other media outlets.[6] The government sponsored these photographs, as Finnegan has pointed out, in order to "chronicle American life in a time of great social upheaval [the Great Depression]."[7] Finnegan's work has been, in part, to explore how the FSA photographs were used by magazines to, among other things, "frame discussions of poverty."[8] Many of the photographs, like those in Agee and Evans, feature tumble-down shacks that functioned as homes for the rural poor.[9] These poor people are often depicted as dirty, barefoot, and forlorn, as though they are broken and in desperate need of fixing. These images are troubling in that viewing Appalachia (as well as the rural poor of other regions) in terms of an unseemly condition that needs to be fixed quite possibly maintains that condition.

This is not to say there are not problems in Appalachia; rather it is to say that viewing something in terms of what it is not creates the risk of forever defining the thing in terms of being partial or unfinished, or in the extreme, substandard. This is not the only view of Appalachia, though. Indeed, there is a long history of Appalachian self-reliance and ingenuity that tells a story that is much different from one that is permanently prefixed with "un." That is, an alternative to looking at Appalachia in terms of what it is not and thereby defining it as lacking certain things that must be given from the outside, involves focusing on how Appalachians have lived fulfilling lives marked with ingenuity and resilience. Not the least prominent voice of such an alternative view has been the Rabun Gap-Nacoochee School (RGNS).

RGNS is a private, co-ed school supported by the Presbyterian Church. It was established, initially as the Rabun Gap Industrial School, at its present location—Rabun Gap, Georgia, in 1905 by Andrew Jackson Ritchie. Ritchie, it is contended, was Rabun Gap's very first college graduate, having achieved the hitherto unheard of feat of attending, and graduating from, Harvard.[10] After graduating from Harvard, Ritchie went on to teach at Baylor for some time and then decided to return to his home in Rabun County where he founded the school. The name of the school changed from the Rabun Gap Industrial School to the Rabun Gap-Nacoochee School in 1926 when nearly simultaneous fires destroyed the main buildings of the Rabun Gap school and another similar school called the Nacoochee Institute, and the two schools merged.[11]

The school has an interesting history of raising interest in and participation in formal educational processes. In 1917, Ritchie instituted the "Farm Family Program" which created a means by which the children of poor area farmers, who often plied their trade in remote mountain locations, could attend school. RGNS would allow whole families to come to the school's grounds and live in houses that it owned. The parents in these families would operate the school's farm while their children attended classes, and the children would do farm work when not in class. The "Farm Family Program" thus made attending school possible for children who might otherwise have been forced, whether by ignorance or economic necessity, into full-time farm work with no time left over for formal education.

RGNS's agenda of raising interest in formal education (represented by the "Farm Family Program") seemed to have lived on. Sixty-one years after its founding, another such approach, this time in actual curriculum, was instituted at the school, namely Foxfire.

The Birth of Foxfire

In 1966, freshly minted from Cornell's Master of Teaching program, Eliot Wigginton arrived at RGNS to teach English. Wigginton says that the only reason he went to Rabun Gap was because he wanted to live there.[12] His experience with the Rabun County area began when he was a child and his father took a job as a professor of landscape architecture at the University of Georgia in Athens. Wigginton's father, says education theorist John Puckett, "was a close friend of Mary Hamdidge, founder and spiritual leader of the Jay Hambidge Art Foundation," where Wigginton lived for a short time upon returning to Georgia.[13] The Foundation was instituted in 1934 by Mary Hambidge, who named it after her late husband.[14] The mission of the center is to "support the arts by providing the setting, the solitude and the time necessary for creativity," and it "pledges to offer a nurturing, secluded retreat for artists."[15] Wigginton credits the center as being the place where Foxfire was, in part, born.[16]

That the idea for Foxfire emerged, in part, while Wigginton was living on the grounds of an artist retreat whose founder believed "creativity was nurtured by working in close harmony with nature" and which has as an objective of contributing to the understanding of the Southeastern United States as a force in the arts[17] is significant in the sense that Foxfire, as we shall see in more detail later, functions in large part to construct a picture of the Appalachian people of the Rabun County area as creative and close to nature.

Wigginton was the only teacher RGNS had ever hired without an interview, a fact that seemed to give him extraordinary confidence: "I had an A.B. in English and an M.A. in teaching, and I thought I was a big deal—a force to be reckoned with."[18,19] This confidence, as Wigginton elucidates in the introduction to *The Foxfire Book*, soon began to bleed humility:

> About six weeks later, I surveyed the wreckage. My lectern (that's a protective device a teacher cowers behind while giving a lecture nobody's listening to) was scorched from the time Tommy Green tried to set it on fire with his lighter—during class. Charles Henslee had already broken off the blade of his Barlow knife in the floorboards. Every desk was decorated with graffiti. My box of yellow chalk was gone and so were the thumbtacks that had held up the chart of the Globe Theatre. The nine water pistols that I had confiscated that very afternoon had been reconfiscated from under my nose. And it was with a deep sigh that, as I launched one of several paper airplanes within easy reach, I began to ponder greener pastures. Either that or start over.[20]

Foxfire, Wigginton tells us, was developed in an attempt to start over and was centered in the rural, Appalachian culture of Northern Georgia. Wigginton, in hopes that his students would learn basic writing skills, asked them to go out into their communities and interview people and find out "how they dealt."[21] In the introduction to *Foxfire 2*, Wigginton gives an example of what a preface to an assignment might sound like:

> Perhaps you're the kind who once knew a grandfather who was extraordinary, maybe for no other reason than that he didn't give a flying damn that he was poor as Job's turkey as long as everyone he cared about was dry and warm, and that there was hot food on the table, and a couple of good neighbors, and time to hike up into that cove above the cabin to see if there were any four-prongers this year in the 'sang patch. Or maybe for the fact that he was one of those rascally scoundrels who ran a liquor still in a basement right in the middle of town and vented his smoke out the same chimney the court house used. Like that.[22]

After conducting interviews, the students would write an article. Many of the articles were edited and then published in Foxfire magazine and many of the magazine articles were collected and published in the popular Foxfire book volumes. As of now, there are twelve Foxfire book volumes and numerous special volumes, including the *Foxfire 40th Anniversary Book*. There have also been several descendants of the Foxfire program, located throughout the United States and abroad, perhaps most notably Salt, founded by Pamela Wood in Kennebunk, Maine.

Wigginton's elucidation of his dilemma as a young teacher and the assignment preface cited above set the stage, in mythical terms, of the problem (namely, an unwillingness of his students to participate in a traditional English curriculum that seemed to them irrelevant) and a potential solution to the problem (developing a curriculum that did seem relevant). The assignment preface characterizes Appalachians as apart from, and perhaps superior to, the culture that sponsors education as a progressive force that leads people into lives that are supposed to be more fulfilling, productive, and useful. For instance, saying that someone is poor and does not care about it as long as certain needs are met, represents an opposition to common associations of financial success with success writ large. Adding to what it says, the way it is phrased (e.g., "four-prongers this year in the 'sang patch") mirrors the Appalachian dialect. Through its mirroring of this vernacular dialect in a description of a school assignment, we see Foxfire embracing the apartness of the region and, in a sense, using it to teach rather than to exclude. Indeed, the Appalachian dialect is featured in many of the Foxfire pieces because presenting the stories of the informants in their own words figures prominently.

A good example of both of these aspects of the assignment preface can be found in an article published in *The Foxfire Book* called, "This is the way I was Raised Up" by Mrs. Marvin Watts, a Foxfire informant. Following an editorial preface that acknowledges that the piece is "presented exactly as it was given to us":

My dadie raised the stuff we lived one he groed the corn to make our bread he groed the cane to make our syrup allso groed they Beans and Peas to make the soup beans out of and dired leather Britches beans and dried fruit enough to last all winter He Killed enough meat to last all winter . . . he diden have mutch money for anything . . . One Xmas Santa Clause gave us three or four sticks of candy and a ornge . . . and we was as pleased as if he had give us a box full of candy.[23]

In addition to the thick, yet accessible, representation of the Appalachian dialect, the passage indicates that being poor is no obstacle to happiness; indeed, the passage reinforces the virtue of self-reliance because it communicates an ability to be fully satisfied with less—three or four sticks of candy is just as good as a whole box.

Moving forward, Wigginton's description of how Foxfire was born works rather elegantly as a metaphorical representation that might be seen as sort of creation myth. Whether or not his students were actually trying to burn down their English classroom, evoking a sort of cleansing fire in his telling of the initial situation is revealing in the sense that any productive work in that classroom was going to have to be centered in something other than the sort of "Great Books" curriculum that is indicative of the traditional English class. In presenting Mrs. Marvin Watts' account of her childhood, Foxfire gives us a glimpse at this new, "authentic" Appalachian center.

Further, asking students to go out and interview members of their communities about "how they dealt" operates to relocate the center of learning, in some respects, from the traditional classroom to wherever one finds a person willing to be interviewed. Interestingly, where the Farm Family Program brought people from the farm to the school, Foxfire does the reverse, sending the students back to the farm, so to speak. As such, by coupling "authentic Appalachian-ness," through dialect and attitudes toward wealth, with a movement from the traditional center of education—the school—to the very places that represented the need for the type of reform that school often provided, Foxfire, it would seem, was attempting to re-value education on a grand scale.

This movement is significantly steeped in John Dewey's notions of experiential education. Dewey describes experience as integral to education saying, "I assume that amid all uncertainties there is one permanent frame of reference: namely, the organic connection between education and personal experience."[24] Dewey says that believing that "all genuine education comes about through experience does not mean that all experiences are genuinely or equally educative."[25] Key to Dewey's argument is that in addition to not all experiences being equally educative, some experiences can also have the reverse effect, impairing education. Wigginton's representation of his dilemma at the beginning of his teaching career can be explained by such impairment, making the advent of

Foxfire and in particular the experience culled from the process of doing the interviews, the central point of departure in Wigginton's attempt to solve the problems of impairment he told us his students were experiencing. Wigginton claims to have come to Dewey after he started the Foxfire project, but when he finally did read Dewey, he was taken aback:

> One paragraph into Experience and Education . . . and things began to crystallize. By the time I had finished it, I was shaking my head in amazement. On every one of its less than a hundred pages, insights had leaped out into the air and I had found myself pounding the arm of my chair and saying, "that's right, damnit, that's exactly right. That's just the way it is." All those discoveries I thought I had made about education, Dewey had elucidated into complete clarity fifty years and more before.[26]

As such, Dewey seems to have provided, for Wigginton, a theoretical endorsement for the activities he asked his students to engage in, adding credibility to the project. Though Wigginton saw his approach to experiential education as incomplete and in need of further work in order to perfect, he saw in his institution of the Foxfire project, and particularly in its journalistic work, a means by which a teacher could facilitate the "right kind of experience."[27]

Integral to this "right kind of experience" is Foxfire's approach to journalism, which describes the form of the Foxfire stories. Foxfire's type of journalism is integral because, through it, the Foxfire students were at least partly responsible for putting Appalachia into the seething cauldron of social and political upheaval that pitted conservative forces against the radical progressivism of the counter-culture of the 1960s and early 1970s. Before discussing Foxfire and the 1960s in depth, it is necessary to discuss more thoroughly the social conditions that serve to define Appalachia in the ways mentioned above and begin to suggest how Foxfire provided an alternative.

Appalachia, A Region Apart

As mentioned earlier, the Appalachia that existed when the Foxfire project began was in peril. Children were living in such abject poverty that there seemed to be no escape, and this seemingly hopeless situation created cause for doubt. Why should the Appalachian people trust a regime, represented by schools, that has perpetually cast them in the role of so much chattel that can be used for whatever purposes their masters devise? Through this marginalization, Appalachian culture was forcibly—through economic and physical violence and training—repressed, which created even more fuel for doubt of both self and other.

Further, this casting as chattel comes through in so-called factual accounts of conditions of poverty in the sense that such facts have a tendency to dehumanize the things they describe. This dehumanization, though in many cases surely not intended to do so, reifies the subaltern subject position of Appalachians and ultimately, it would seem, undermines the purposes for which the factual description was undertaken. This perpetuates an environment of doubt when people attempt to help the poor to "overcome" their poverty.

In *The Other America*, Michael Harrington provides a compelling portrait of conditions of poverty. Though Harrington deals mostly with the urban poor, his basic portrait has extended to all regions—writing in 1962:

> Tens of millions of Americans are, at this very moment, maimed in body and spirit, existing at levels beneath those necessary for human decency. If these people are not starving, they are hungry, and sometimes fat with hunger, for that is what cheap foods do. They are without adequate housing and education and medical care . . . this poverty twists and deforms the spirit. The American poor are pessimistic and defeated, and they are victimized by mental suffering to a degree unknown in Suburbia.[28]

Focusing more closely on the Appalachian region in the 1960s, the President's Appalachian Regional Commission [PARC], indicated particularities:

> Appalachia has natural advantages which might normally have been the base for a thriving industrial and commercial complex. . . . Yet this natural endowment has benefited too few of the 15.3 million people of Appalachia. The average Appalachian, whether he lives in a metropolis, in town, on the farm, or in a mountain cabin, has not matched his counterpart in the rest of the United States as a participant in the Nation's economic growth.[29]

Although these passages (and the greater works they represent) describe poverty in the 1960s and fall in line with other portraits of poverty, they tend to objectify the poor in the sense that they deal with facts and figures and allow these to do the work of describing "people."

On the other hand, in a decidedly different way, James Agee and Walker Evans document (some two and a half decades before Herrington and PARC), the lives of three Alabama tenant-farmer families over the course of four weeks in the summer of 1936 in a decidedly different way.[30] Their project was initially supposed to result in an article for *Fortune* magazine but was never published as such. Interestingly, Agee seemed too to be at odds with his own qualifications to undertake such a project—speaking of himself and Evans in the third person,

> And it seems curious . . . that, with all their suspicion of and contempt for every person and thing to do with the situation, save only for the tenants and themselves, and their own intentions, and with all their realization of the

seriousness and mystery of the subject, and of the human responsibility they undertook, they so little questioned or doubted their own qualifications for this work.[31]

Agee saw the situation of documenting the tenant's lives for a distant public as, "curious, obscene, terrifying and unfathomably mysterious" in the sense that the lives of the people he and Evans "rashly undertook to investigate and record" were so full of "subtlety" and "importance" as to render intangible "the insights or revelations or oblique suggestions which under different circumstances could never have materialized."[32] Agee and Walker's insight is stunning because it recognizes the subtlety and "humanness" of the tenants, where the PARC report, for instance, seems not to make such a recognition (despite whatever best intentions PARC may have had) concerning the people of Appalachia.

Of further interest, extending from Agee, in the above cited PARC report passage is the notion of matching one's counterpart. Saying one has not matched her counterpart as a participant in economic development standardizes the notion of participation, prosperity, and success. And, the measure by which people are judged to be participants, who are prosperous and successful is rooted in a particular socioeconomic paradigm. For instance, to be successful, one must have a certain kind of job, make a certain amount of money, live in a certain kind of house, and eat a certain kind of food. These certainties emerge from an ideological apparatus that places particular groups in particular positions that play particular roles. As such, when the PARC stated that average Appalachians have not matched their counterparts in the rest of the United States, it should have come as no surprise. The people of Appalachia were not meant to match their counterparts.

In *Savage Inequalities*, Jonathan Kozol sheds some light on this apparatus, as it serves to structure inequalities in schooling.[33] His book documents, compellingly, differences between public inner-city schools and their counterparts in the more affluent suburbs. The disparity between what is afforded to some children and not to others is striking. Although Kozol, like Harrington, deals mainly with the problems of the urban poor, there are parallels to rural Appalachia. For instance, PARC describes the conditions in which Appalachians lived as "all too frequently deprived of the facilities and services of a modern society."[34] Kozol describes similar conditions of deprivation, in detail, in discussing the schools of East St. Louis where a flood backed up the sewage system such that raw sewage was flowing into a school's kitchen.[35]

There are clearly differences between urban and rural poor, but the "savagery" that separates the poor, of any locale, from their more affluent counterparts is common. The title of Kozol's book provides some insight here. With the word "savage," Kozol points to an interesting duality: savagery and civility. The line between savagery and civility has long been debated (both as to where it might be and whether or not there is such a thing) and I don't need to rehash that debate here. However, to say there are "savage inequalities" invokes what is perhaps the key to making the ideological apparatus that identifies some people (in our special case, focusing on the people of Appalachia) as poor visible. If we define savage as, "uncivilized; existing at the lowest stage of culture," then poor people could be labeled as savages; savage can also be defined as "remote from society, solitary."[36] Although the latter sense has become obsolete, the two cited senses of "savage" can be read together in order to realize a picture of Appalachia that has been painted for years: If people are at the "lowest stage of culture" then they are, in some ways, necessarily apart from the culture. Indeed, the title of the introduction to the PARC report is, "A Region Apart."

This apartness becomes manifest in the way that the people of the Appalachian region have been represented and, to some extent, the way they have represented themselves. Anthropologist Mary K. Anglin points out that though Appalachia has been portrayed for a long time as a land teaming with natural resources, the people have been cast as indigent at worst and colorful at best.[37] Anglin cites early twentieth-century economist J. Russell Smith saying, "[the residents of Southern Appalachia] only made a slum with a high death rate; a scattered slum of log hovels that would come into violent conflict with the sanitary regulations of a hundred municipalities."[38] Anglin credits Smith, as well as others, with wanting to "teach 'agricultural savages' better farming practices."[39]

Going forward from log hovels, the picture Smith paints is not just one of agricultural savagery but of a fundamental lack of humanity. If a hovel is a shed for sheltering animals, Smith, in a single stroke, dehumanizes Appalachians and places them in the subject position of chattel—as a utility, ripe for exploitation by people with enough power to use them to achieve whatever desired ends. This exploitation was particularly apparent in the Appalachian coal mines at the beginning of the twentieth century.

Miners were often forced to live in company towns that were owned and governed by coal companies. Further, miners were often paid only in company scrip (worth as little as sixty cents on the dollar), which they were often only to spend at the company store. What's more, miners were not compensated for their work but rather the amount of coal they extracted, and they often had to buy their own dynamite in order to do the extracting. To this end, many of the necessary operations that miners undertook in order to free coal from the earth was essentially unpaid for. These operations could, under certain circumstances, take most of the miner's time. It was not unheard of for miners to take their young sons into the mines with them in order to lend a hand in the operations—fetching needed tools or dynamite. Miners without the extra help of a son were known to run instead of walk to get a shovel or another needed implement.[40]

This treatment was not exclusive to the coal industry. Shirley Brice Heath points out similar oppressive treatments. In studying literacy learning and practices of people in the Piedmont area of South Carolina, Heath tells of how people from Appalachia who came to the Piedmont to work in the textile mills were regarded as white trash and were characterized as, "uninterested in schooling, willing to allow and even promote early marriages, and inclined to disrespect both cleanliness and godliness."[41] Heath discusses how mill owners, in order to reform the problems of these people, worked to make schooling compulsory such that the mill workers would learn manners and morals; Heath says schoolteachers "became preachers for the culture of the townspeople," and "they were charged to teach health and sanitation habits, grammar, self-control, neatness, and obedience."[42]

Where the oppression of Appalachian people in the coal industry seemed to have been primarily based in economic exploitation, Heath's story expands the oppression to culture. Where the coal operators needed muscle and sweat, the mill owners, in addition to labor, wanted the mind. Aiming to control the mind may well have been the right strategy. The history of the Appalachian coal fields was rife with violence as miners struggled to organize their labor against the coal operators. Though there was violence in the Piedmont in attempts to unionize, West Virginia saw martial law declared on numerous occasions. At one point, Billy Mitchell (credited as the founder of the Air Force) commanded a squadron in conjunction with National Guard troops in order to quell an uprising (The Battle of Blair Mountain) that stemmed from the famed Matewan Massacre.[43]

What is important in these accounts of oppression is understanding various aspects of culture in Appalachia were forcibly—through economic and physical violence and training—repressed and marginalized to the point where even the sound of one's speech was denigrated and reviled; this repression shows up in stereotypical representations of the Appalachian "hick" as a bumbling idiot, discussed previously. The question, then, is understanding the implications of this marginalization and potential strategies for overcoming it.

The primary implication is centered in the non-agency of Appalachian people. If even the sound of one's voice is ridiculed, then the chances of anyone actually listening to what that voice might say are significantly diminished. This diminution creates a buildup of pressure that must be released in some way or another and we see a mythical account of such a release in the Foxfire literature when Wigginton is discussing what caused him to start the project. Recall in the previously cited portion of the introduction to *The Foxfire Book* that the students were attempting to burn down their English classroom. Though Wigginton claims the act was literal, it provides a compelling metaphor for the tension these students were experiencing as they tried to negotiate the terms of their student and Appalachian identities. Wigginton writes of his role in this negotiation, and, as it turns out, the negotiation of his own teacherly identity:

> I had never been in a situation before where I was so completely confused by all that was going on around me. I wasn't panicked. Just confounded by the fact that the conventional logic I had learned to apply to times of crisis in college seemed

to have no place here. It was a through-the-looking-glass world where the friendlier I was in class . . . believing that would generate cooperation, the more liberties the students took and the harder it became to accomplish anything. . . . And so I would crack down, kicking students out of class for several days at a time, or using my grade book and my power to fail them as a retaliatory weapon . . . and the mood would turn sullen and resentful and no sharing or learning would take place. They would be captives, praying for the bell to ring.[44]

One of the biggest challenges facing a new teacher, Wigginton might say, is figuring out how to relate to students—and help them relate to teachers—in a way that balances authority with trust. On the one hand, if a teacher positions herself or himself as a tyrant, the students might see this position as a threat and the one in the position as a person who is unbending, insensitive to their needs, and ultimately not interested in helping them unless they fall into lockstep with the agenda of the institution, which the teacher represents. On the other hand, if a teacher is too friendly, she or he opens the possibility for ensuing chaos, of being run over by an alternative agenda that inhibits the type of learning that is supposed to happen in the classroom.

Interestingly, viewing such a situation as a challenge—or even as a situation—is indicative of a sort of meta-agenda that is inextricably tied to the ideological apparatus that serves to structure educational institutions in the form of teachers running classrooms that are bounded by walls that are bounded by campuses and so on. And, this institutional structure serves to perpetuate other structures that maintain common perceptions of what it means to be "successful" and what it means to be "poor" (read as unsuccessful) in a sort of Foucauldean notion of discipline and control.[45]

The "confusion" that Wigginton spoke of then is not necessarily wrapped up in balancing authority with trust; rather, it stems from the task of maintaining the authority of the institution (which operates as a component of the greater ideological apparatus) while producing useful citizens who will fill particular subject positions within the institution and later within the greater power structure. Any trust that is invoked is not trust in the teacher but in the institution and thus the system that sponsors the institution.

Wigginton's proverbial "throwing the book at them" served only to make the system, as he represented it, less trustworthy. Further, in the sort of mythos of Foxfire constructed by Wigginton in his introduction to the *The Foxfire Book*, we see this distrust becoming manifest in behavior (water pistols, paper airplanes, lighting the classroom on fire, and the particularly rural knives in the floor boards) that ultimately only serves to reify the Appalachian students' entrenchment in the deviant white trash subject position, a position in need of reform. Attempting such reformation could be seen as the perpetual role of teachers whose own positions depend upon the deviance of the students. In other words, because average Appalachians, as mentioned here, are not meant to match their counterparts in other parts of the country, the role of the Appalachian school is to train people, by whatever subversive design, to be subordinate. This type training plays out in many locations in addition to Appalachia: East St. Louis, as Kozol points out, and abroad.

At the RGNS (the school where Foxfire began), the Farm Family Program made education available to people who might not have had access to it otherwise and instilled a sense of self-reliance marked by Appalachians doing for themselves what others would not or could not do for them. However, though the Program seemed to be a remarkable way of helping people to better themselves, the fact that it recognized people as in need of help and betterment defers the possibility that the way people were living, on their own farms in the hollows and hills, validated itself, that such a life could be viewed as alternative rather than deviant or savage and thus subordinate.

Viewing the life of the hollows and hills as a valid alternative to the system that sponsors school flies in the face of the status quo; and interestingly, it accounts for the failure of Wigginton's conventional logic to adequately deal with a situation in which he had difficulty establishing a productive relationship with his students. Wigginton's terms were not suited to the subject matter he was attempting to engage. Viewing the life of the hollows and hills as a valid alternative to the status quo and conventional logic is precisely what Foxfire encourages. We must, however, keep in mind that Foxfire does not rupture or defeat the system. Rather, it invites its students to join the system in a different capacity by encouraging them to view the system in a different way; and, with this invitation, the system is altered somewhat as well.

This encouragement is a hegemonic process. In so many words, hegemony is a dominance of one group in a society achieved not through force but through consent.[46] Consent is an important notion; it implies a need for work. A hegemonic structure must be in a constant state of reconfiguration in order to maintain dominance, and such dominance is couched in maintaining a particular view of what is legitimate or natural. Further, as Dick Hebdige reminds us, "hegemony can only be maintained so long as the dominant classes succeed in framing all competing definitions [of legitimate and natural] within their range"; and (drawing from Gramsci), this state is a "moving equilibrium containing relations of forces less favourable to this or that tendency."[47]

How then is the notion of formal education maintained as legitimate and natural in light of conflicting terminologies that emphasize different values? I don't expect to answer this question at a global level. However, the question drives to the heart of the Foxfire project; this is a primary issue that Foxfire engages.

Consent requires some measure of identification. Even if consent were to be derived from force (whether implicit or explicit), there must be a connection between those who are acting and those who are being acted upon. For instance, Kenneth Burke defined identification, in part, as "a name for the function of sociality," and said that even violence can be construed as a social intercourse and thus a form of sociality.[48] In this sense, the task of constructing consent is essentially rhetorical if we define rhetoric as a process of negotiating the terms of identity.

In our present case, when RGNS instituted the Farm Family Program, it was garnering consent concerning the value of education. The plan made education available to the uneducated mountain people not through presuming that it was something they really wanted but by creating an environment that emphasized the relevance of formal education to their lives. Interestingly, the school's motto is, "Work, Study, Worship."[49] With these three terms, we see a collection of values that are not inherently connected. Where work and worship would likely have been things that mountain folk valued, "study" seems likely to have been the odd one out. However, by sandwiching "study" between the other two terms, the school emphasized the connection and thus relevance of schoolwork to established values. This emphasis, then, can be seen as part of a negotiation that worked toward identification between the school and the people it intended to serve.

Further, in the sense that the school emphasized the relevance of mountain culture (i.e., agriculture) to formal schooling, the face of mountain culture was changed. Introducing the civility of education to the hitherto savages of the mountains created a space where the collective identity of the mountain people could be reconstructed in terms that included citizen; but the agency from which this identity flowed was also a reconstruction in the sense that it had to change somewhat to allow for the inclusion of people who could not previously identify with the type of culture they were being asked (or in some senses forced) to join.

We can view the Farm Family Program as the first step in a civilizing process. The program got people, willingly, into the classroom. However, as Wigginton discovered when he arrived at Rabun Gap—after the demise of the program—getting the people into the classroom was not the same thing as getting the classroom into the people, so to speak. Wigginton's initial experience, at least the way he presents it, was with students who, for all intents and purposes, were retaliating against the system symbolized by the classroom. Wigginton's lament concerning the various strategies of irreverence deployed by the students invoked what he termed a need to start over, and the diegesis of this restart invites readers into the negotiation of identity in which Foxfire takes part.

The means by which Foxfire goes about negotiating is centered in an emphatic return to the value of mountain culture. Where negative representations of Appalachia were foremost in status quo definitions of the region, the work of Foxfire moves to unseat these representations. The narratives given in Foxfire tell a story of a "resilient and steadfast" people who can take care of themselves. This telling then functions as a call to action, an entreaty to view the stories as an inspirational model of who Appalachian people really are, as the authentic Appalachia.

The Foxfire books provide a good case in point. The first book reads as a sort of primer for a particular way of life that is based in an idea of the way things should be. The first two chapters of the book provide profiles of people who live/lived the way the rest of the book "tells you how to." The introduction discusses the inspiration for starting the Foxfire project. Students, again, were trying to burn down their English classroom because, as Wigginton professes, he had "bored them unmercifully" with material that seemed to be totally irrelevant to them.[50] Further into this introduction, Wigginton recalls his own high school experience: "Those who cannot remember the past not only relive it; they tend to impose it, mistakes and all, on others. My own high school—monumentally boring texts and lectures, all forgotten; punishments and regulations and slights that only filled a reservoir of bitterness."[51] With these words, Wigginton is acknowledging that he did not provide, in the material he presented, an image that worked toward making visible whatever invisible idea he was trying to teach, and was, by projecting onto his students his own "reservoir of bitterness," depriving students of the opportunity he thought they deserved.

In the introduction to the second volume, Wigginton connects such deprivation to a greater scheme of the way some young people are treated by their parents, other relatives, and teachers. In anecdotal form, he recounts a story of how a student was working on developing a print in the Foxfire darkroom. The work was challenging, and it caused the student to be late for his English class (one taught by different teacher). Though the print was later used on the cover of an edition of the magazine and was reprinted in the book, the student was chastised by his teacher and had to write, "I will not be late to English class any more" 500 times.

Of this English class, which the student was late for, Wigginton mentions, "The teacher read some poems aloud that nobody listened to, so she spent the whole hour reading to herself while kids hacked off—or slept."[52] An interesting tension develops within this story. The student's work in the darkroom led to something that was useful and gave the student a voice in a publication, but the immediate outcome of this work was punishment. The authority of the English teacher was maintained, even to the point where she used what she nominally owned—English or writing—as punishment. Making him write his punishment served to strip away any agency the student might have gained through his photograph, placing such agency back where it belonged: the teacher as symbolic of the institution. The student's place then was not in the darkroom, it was sitting quietly at his desk in the classroom—seen not heard—no matter whether he was paying attention.

The tension here is centered in a negotiation of identities. The student was attempting to deliver himself, via a photograph, to the institution as a person of importance. The English teacher was attempting to maintain authority. The outcome of the negotiation, as evidenced by the punishment, was in favor of the teacher. The status quo was maintained. What did not happen was learning anything about English—at least how we might imagine the English teacher defining it. This is not to say that learning did not take place. Without any intervention, the student would likely have learned to keep his mouth shut, to attend class, to be subordinate, to stay dumb. This is not the lesson Wigginton professes to have wanted to teach his students. Rather, the opposite: attend class and speak, loudly and clearly.

The scenario of this anecdote plays out all over—it is not particularly to Appalachia. However, the student's attempt to speak, through his photograph, of where he lived (i.e., "the mountains"), when coupled with the stigma of that place, made the punishment become a sort of penance, an enforced mortification that worked toward breaking any spirit maintained from the mountain and reified not only the authority of the teacher but the alterity of the Appalachian student. In *The Foxfire Book* we see an attempt to change this situation. Where the "penance" reified a particular kind of authority, one of dominance, held by the elders of the students, *The Foxfire Book* places the authority of older people in a different light by recasting the relationship between older and younger people in romantic terms.

Chapter 2 of the book consists in profiling "Aunt Arie" through two, student written, editorial introductions and a transcription of the conversations the Foxfire students had with her. Here is an excerpt of the first editorial introduction:

> Far back in the neighboring mountains, alone in a log cabin with no running water and only a single fireplace for heat, lives an elderly lady. She draws her water from a well; she raises her own vegetables in the spring. Even though her husband died several years ago, and one side of her body was later paralyzed due to a stroke, Aunt Arie refuses to leave. With her husband's clothes still hanging inside, washed and ready to wear, her home has become a sacred place over which she alone must now keep watch . . . talking to her was like talking to one's own grandmother. She told us stories of her past . . . and she also gave us some advice in her reflections about living in today's world.
>
> It is somehow reassuring to know that even now, in our time, there are Aunt Aries left from an age which has so much to teach us [empahasis added].[53]

Notice the "italics," these statements establish a remoteness, an elsewhere, that is geographical/physical, temporal, and spiritual; but there is a connection, a point of access, to this "elsewhere" insofar that talking to Aunt Arie is like talking to "one's own grandmother." What this passage does is set the stage for a journey into "an age which has so much to teach us." In other words, the passage creates a desire for immersion in this age in hopes of being taught—by someone who has been there.

The second editorial introduction picks up with the desire created in the first:

It wasn't until I had worked on Foxfire for five months that an inexplicable void between myself and the old people of our region disappeared. This void was mysterious, but it still existed. Maybe it was instilled hostilities toward older generations. Maybe it was the fact that I just couldn't see their importance or the relevance of what they had to say to the way I live today.

Then I met Aunt Arie. It was a cold day, and I can remember the jeep traveling far back into a remote area. I was apprehensive because I didn't know what to expect. Her log cabin was a time machine taking me back to the eighteen eighties. Everything she had—from stern-looking pictures of her grandparents to the fireplace that was her only source of heat—made me stop and look deeply for the first time.[54]

Here, the "elsewhere" projected in the first passage becomes more concrete. We are transported from abstract ideas of the past through the time machine of Aunt Arie's cabin into filling the mysterious void that prior to meeting Aunt Arie separated the speaker from the old people of his region with concrete images. Further, the last sentence of the passage encourages us to, along with the speaker, look deeply. The material of the rest of the chapter is a transcription of tape-recorded meetings with Aunt Arie, which constitute the "deep looking."

These passages are representative of the form of Foxfire articles in general. Most of the Foxfire stories, in one way or another, feature a sense of elsewhere that can be accessed through the memories of the informants. The form of the passages moves us from abstract ideas of the past into concrete images. This form, in this particular case, centralizes a self-reliant woman, standing watch over the sacred old ways, ready to teach people about the real Appalachia. The cabin is decidedly not a log hovel, which is certainly how some people might have viewed it. Aunt Arie is not chattel; rather, her position is one of great value: She is an emissary from simpler times when people were closer to nature, to the earth—an emissary of the authentic Appalachia.

Further, in the second passage, we see the speaker move to fill the void that separates him from the "old people" of the region. This movement speaks, in addition to discovering the real Appalachia, to more widespread issues of the time. As the material of *The Foxfire Book* was collected in the mid to late 1960s, and drawing from the authority of elders discussed above, "old people" takes on an interesting connotation (e.g., the sixtiess maxim, "Don't trust anybody over thirty"). Aunt Arie was in her eighties when the Foxfire students met with her, but where does one draw the line that separates young from old? If "old" fits within the sixties aphorism, then the speaker is talking about a much larger void than that which may have separated him from octogenarians. The time machine reference also works here as Aunt Arie's cabin takes people out of a time where old people are not to be trusted and repositions them, in a simpler time, as respectful auditors, or "deep lookers."

The mechanism that makes this repositioning possible is problematic. Time travel, for many reasons is not possible. The past cannot be marked without the contingency of the time from which it is examined. In this way the "time travel" of the cited passages creates a romantic representation that, even though it is presented as authentic, celebrates an imaginative Aunt Arie and, more importantly, creates a romantic relationship between young people and "old" people in general. Such a creation is interesting because it opens the door to a way of living that many were seeking in the 1960s.

Foxfire and the 1960s

Foxfire started in 1966, clearly a time of much political and social upheaval. It was in that year that Lester Maddox was elected governor of Georgia. Maddox was a notorious racist who ran for governor on a segregationist platform that played into a widespread dissatisfaction with desegregation. Maddox owned and operated a restaurant called the Pickrick Cafeteria in Atlanta, and, to promote the Pickrick, Maddox ran a series of weekly advertisements called "Pickrick Says." These advertisements turned out to be the launching pad for Maddox's political career as they did not just advertise the restaurant but also provided an outlet for Maddox's political views. This was especially the case after the 1954 school desegregation decision (Clifford Hodges Brewton Collection).[55] His outspoken defiance of the Civil Rights Act of 1964 thrust Maddox into the national spotlight and in 1965 he announced his intention to run for governor of Georgia in the 1966 election, which he won. Maddox was sworn in as governor on January 10, 1967.

In answer to the endemic racism represented by people like Maddox, was the 1966 adoption of the slogan (and guiding principle) "Black Power" by the Student Nonviolent Coordinating Committee and the establishment, by Huey P. Newton, of the "Black Panther Party." Nineteen sixty-six also saw the election of Edward Brooke as U.S. Senator from Massachusetts, the first to be elected by popular vote. Before serving as a senator, Brooke was the first African American state attorney general (also in Massachusetts), and in 2004, Brooke was awarded the Presidential Medal of Freedom by President George W. Bush.

In addition to the Civil Rights movement (and outcries against it), the time around Foxfire's founding saw other highly charged social and political movements. The National Organization for Women (NOW) was founded in 1966 and since then has become the largest feminist activist group in the United States with some 500,000 members working to "eliminate discrimination and harassment in the workplace, schools, the justice system, and all other sectors of society . . . end all forms of violence against women; eradicate racism, sexism and homophobia; and promote equality and justice in our society."[56]

Along with internal social and political upheaval the country was ramping up military operations in Vietnam. Following the Gulf of Tonkin attack (in which U.S. Navy ships were attacked while steaming in "international waters") of August 1964, President Lyndon Johnson asked Congress for a resolution against North Vietnam, which would grant him far reaching powers in escalating the use of military force in the region. The resolution was passed, after two days of debate, with only two dissenting votes, those of Senators Wayne Morse (Oregon) and Ernest Gruening (Alaska). Five months later, U.S. ground troops were widely deployed to Vietnam. President Johnson then offered North Vietnam aid in exchange for peace, but the offer was rejected. Shortly thereafter, open warfare involving U.S. troops began in Vietnam.

The war in Vietnam, in many ways, fed the burgeoning counter-culture of the 1960s and served as a major point of contention for activist groups in the sense that it provided evidence of a widespread feeling that the "establishment" (which we might read as "old people") abused its authority. This feeling was evident in the popular culture of the day, surfacing in music, art, and other outlets.

For instance, Bob Dylan's third album, *The Times They Are a-Changin'* (released in 1964), features a track with the ironic title "With God on Our Side." The song takes the listener through a series of historical events, including the slaughtering of Native Americans and World War I, and laments that Americans have been taught to accept the validity of these undertakings and not ask questions because "God is on the side" of America. From the song: "But now we got weapons/Of the chemical dust/If fire them we're forced to/Then fire them we must/One push of the button/And a shot the world wide/And you never ask questions/When God's on your side.[57]

The title track of *The Times They Are a-Changin'* also speaks clearly of the burgeoning feeling of a need for change: "The line it is drawn/The curse it is cast/The slow one now/Will later be fast/As the present now/Will later be past/The order is/Rapidly fadin'./And the first one now/Will later be last/For the times they are a-changin'.[58]

In any case, the time in which Foxfire came about was filled with radical sentiments, and Foxfire's progressive bent was timely. Indeed, Foxfire might not have been at all had it not been for the particular social climate of the mid-1960s, and the popularity of *The Foxfire Book* (the series as a whole has around nine million copies in print) can certainly be traced to its release in 1972. The ten-year period surrounding the release of *The Foxfire Book* was rich with publications that invoked similar material.

For instance, Stewart Brand's *The Whole Earth Catalogue,* first published in 1968, and its successor, *Whole Earth* magazine—started in 1974 as *Co-Evolution Quarterly*—published all sorts of counter-culture pieces that dealt with presenting types of knowledge similar to those given in Foxfire but with a more activist bent. Another magazine, *Mother Earth News*, started publishing similar material in 1970.

These publications fall in line with the so-called back-to-the-land movement. Helen and Scott Nearing's book on "simple living" (first published in 1954 and reprinted five times between then and 1970), can be seen, in part, as the beginning of the flurry of publications that speak to living in "harmony" with the environment, whether it be the physical, spiritual, or social.[59]

The popularity of publications like the ones above indicate that by the mid-1960s narratives that dealt with simple living had gained cogency, and the sentiment that underlies, the content of these narratives is nostalgia for simpler times.[60] It would be difficult—at best—to assign causality for the rise of such cogency. However, regardless of the cause, Foxfire came of age in a time when people were hungry for the types of things it had to say. This hunger boded well for the Foxfire students because it provided them access to a wide-ranging audience that really wanted to hear what they had to say and was willing to listen despite all of the mainstream baggage attached to Appalachian culture. Foxfire, we could say, provided a valuable part of the "counter" in counter-culture in its representation of authentic affairs of plain living.[61]

In this sense, the nostalgia for simpler times represented by Foxfire is not principally Appalachian nor is it adolescent as might be surmised given that the students in the project were teenagers or the fact that the counter-culture was driven largely by young people. Rather, the nostalgia of Foxfire was tied to a wide ranging feeling of disenfranchisement with the status quo. For instance, the experience documented in Helen and Scott Nearing's book resulted, they say, from their decision to leave the hustle and bustle of New York City and construct a homestead in rural Vermont. Although their move happened some twenty years before Foxfire came about, the stimulus that moved them remained well intact for many others even into the 1970s (evidenced by the numerous reprints of their book).

Perhaps one of the best known instances of a sort of mass migration, whether physically or emotionally, to the country occurred with the establishment of agricultural communes (i.e., "hippie" communes). For instance, The Farm, a well-established commune, started operating in 1971 near Summertown, Tennessee, with Stephen Gaskin as its spiritual guide. At its height, The Farm had a population of nearly 1,500 people engaged in communal agriculture and an alternative spirituality based largely in open-ended discussions stemming from Gaskin's invocation, "'let's talk about how we're gonna be'. Not 'how we're gonna stop the war' or 'how we're gonna make it fair', but 'how we're gonna be'."[62]

Interestingly, Stephen Gaskin initially started these discussions in 1966 when he was a teacher at San Francisco State College, the same year Foxfire started. The question, "How are we going to be?" sets the tone for Foxfire's exploration of Appalachian life-ways. As Wigginton set out to teach basic writing skills, he asked his students to get in touch with an accessible and, perhaps more importantly, acceptable version of their past. In "getting in touch" the students constructed, through the interviews they conducted, a vantage point from which they could become writers and in so doing "citizens" rather than "savages."

In this sense, nostalgia became a method of agency, a means by which Foxfire gained a voice. More specifically, by making itself the nostalgic voice of expertise in areas of interest in its time, Foxfire represented a sort of elder statesperson of simple living: you want to know how to live simply, off the land? Our people have been doing it for a long time, here's how. The tenor of this question and rejoinder comes through in the closing two paragraphs of the introduction to the "Building a Log Cabin" chapter in *The Foxfire Book*, which is germane to the so-called back-to-the-land movement:

> To those who would look on such a project as a farce, or a chore not worth the time, we have little to say. We speak instead to the individual who feels some loss in the realization that this age of miracles, miraculous though it is, has robbed us of the need to use our hands. We speak to the individual who feels that someday, somewhere the use of the instructions contained in these pages will be a source of tremendous satisfaction. And we speak, in a sense, to the child in man—that free spirit still building tree houses in the woods.
>
> To the enthusiastic, all-things-are-possible child spirit, and to the man who longs for the peace that independence and skilled self-sufficiency brings, we address ourselves in this chapter. And we wish him well. He's one of us.[63]

The "we speak to" statements are of particular interest as they first identify an audience and recognize the value of the knowledge the chapter conveys: those who value "the need to use our hands" and would gain "tremendous satisfaction" from such use. This identification of an audience leads to the identification with an audience that we see in the last sentence: "He's one of us." The identification of Foxfire with people who long for the peace of self-sufficiency taps into the feelings of disenfranchisement that the back-to-the-land movement worked to dispel. The first paragraph of the first chapter of the Nearing's book provides a clear example:

> Many a modern worker, dependant on wage or salary, lodged in city flat or closely built up suburb and held to the daily grind by family demands or other complicating circumstances, has watched for a chance to escape the cramping limitations of his surroundings, to take life into his own hands and live it in the country, in a decent, simple, kindly way.[64]

The notions of "escaping one's surroundings" and "taking one's life into her own hands" clearly speak to people who have feelings of loss tied to what Foxfire called "this age of miracles." The Nearings had a much more skeptical view of the age of miracles, as was stated, "After careful consideration of developments in Europe and Asia, as well as North America, we decided western civilization would be unable henceforth to provide an adequate, stable and secure life for those who attempted to follow its directives."[65] In a sense, although it was not explicitly acknowledged, the conditions that gave rise to Wigginton's lament and the start of Foxfire are directly related to the decision about social and economic conditions made by the Nearings. This relationship is evidenced by the instability of the interactions Wigginton initially had with his students despite (or because of) his attempt to follow the directives of the school.

In any case, addressing the rhetorical situation that gave rise to the-back-to-the-land movement and reading the situation in terms of nostalgia for simpler times helped create a wider agential space for Foxfire, and Foxfire filled this space by providing articles about the history, technology, and personality of people who were able to live off of the land. In this sense, Foxfire took part, in some fashion, in speaking to the 1960s counter-culture's nostalgia for "simpler times." Foxfire's role was in presenting as authentic a version of Appalachian culture derived from the tension between mainstream representations of Appalachia and an alternative to those representations that ostensibly provided a mechanism by which Appalachia could be validated and thus valued. In this sense, Foxfire was able to speak in an authentic voice to the back-to-the-land movement.

Notes

1. "Foxfire," *The Foxfire Fund*, http://www.foxfire.org.
2. "Georgia Population of Counties by Decennial Census: 1900 to 1990," http://www.census.gov/population/cencounts/ga190090.txt, *United States Census Bureau*.
3. James Branscome. "The Crisis of Appalachian Youth," in *Appalachia in the Sixties: Decade of Reawakening*, edited by David S. Walls and John B. Stephenson. (Lexington: University of Kentucky Press, 1972), 225.
4. Branscome, "The Crisis of Appalachian Youth."
5. There is vast literature concerning the emergence and meaning of stereotypes associated with the people of Appalachia. Some scholars have pointed to publication of the "local color stories" written by Mary Noailles Murfree in the late nineteenth century as contemporary with the emergence of the image of the Appalachian person as stupid, ignorant, lazy, barefoot, drunk on moonshine, etc. Further, popular culture is filled with such images—from *Lil' Abner* to the *Beverly Hillbillies* (though the "Clampetts" are technically from the Ozarks) in the mid-twentieth century to "Cletus the Slack Jawed Yokel" in *The Simpsons* today.

6. Cara Finnegan. "What's This a Picture Of? Some Thoughts on Images and Archives." *Rhetoric and Public Affairs* 9, no. 1 (2006): 116.
7. Finnegan, "What's This a Picture Of?"
8. Finnegan, "What's This a Picture Of?"
9. James Agee and Walker Evans, *Let Us Now Praise Famous Men* (New York: The Library of America, 2005).
10. Eliot Wigginton, *Sometimes a Shining Moment* (New York: Anchor, 1986), 11.
11. "School History," http://www.rabungap.org/our_school/history/index.html, *Rabun Gap-Nacoochee School.*
12. Wigginton, *Sometimes a Shining Moment,* 9.
13. John L. Puckett, *Foxfire Reconsidered: A Twenty-Year Experiment in Progressive Education,* (Urban: University of Illinois Press, 1989), 10.
14. "Hambidge Center for Creative Arts and Sciences," http:/www.georgia encyclopedia.org/nge/Article.jsp?id=h-2579, *New Georgia Encyclopedia.*
15. "Hambidge Center for Creative Arts and Sciences."
16. Wigginton, *Sometimes a Shining Moment,* 9.
17. "Hambidge Center for Creative Arts and Sciences."
18. Puckett, *Foxfire,* 11.
19. Eliot Wigginton and His Students, eds. *The Foxfire Book* (New York: Anchor, 1972), 9-10.
20. Wigginton, *The Foxfire Book,* 9-10
21. Wigginton, Eliot and His Students eds., *Foxfire 2* (New York: Anchor, 1973), 8.
22. Wigginton, *Foxfire 2,* 8-9.
23. Eliot Wigginton and His Students, eds., *The Foxfire Book, 15-16.*
24. John Dewey, *Experience and Education* (New York: Collier, 1963), 25.
25. Dewey, *Experience and Education.*
26. Wigginton, *Sometimes a Shining Moment,* 280.
27. For an in-depth discussion of Wigginton's and Foxfire's connection to Dewey, progressive and experiential education, see Puckett, Part Three "Issues and Effects Writ Large: Foxfire and the Global Contexts of American Education." See also the Association for Experiential Education.
28. Michael Herrington, *The Other America: Poverty in the United States* (Baltimore: Penguin, 1962), 9-10.
29. President's Appalachian Regional Commission, *Appalachia: A Report by the President's Appalachian Regional Commission, 1964,* http://www.arc.gov/index.do?nodeId=2255, xv.
30. James Agee and Walker Evans, *Praise.*
31. Agee, *Praise,* 24.
32. Agee, *Praise,* 24.
33. Jonathan Kozol, *Savage Inequalities: Children in America's Schools* (New York: Crown, 1991).
34. President's Appalachian Regional Commission, *Appalachia: A Report by the President's Appalachian Regional Commission, 1964,* 16.
35. Jonathan Kozol, *Savage Inequalities,* 23.
36. *Oxford English Dictionary,* online edition, "savage."

37. Mary K. Anglin, "Lessons from Appalachia in the 20th Century: Poverty, Power, and the Grass Roots," *American Anthropologist* 104, no. 2 (2002): 565-582.
38. Quoted in Mary K. Anglin, "Lessons from Appalachia," 565.
39. Mary K. Anglin, "Lessons from Appalachia," 565.
40. The first I heard of these stories about coal mining was from my grandfather who, along with his father, worked in the coal fields of Pennsylvania.
41. Shirley Brice Heath, *Ways with Words* (Cambridge: Cambridge University Press, 1983), 22.
42. Heath, *Ways with Words*, 23.
43. For an account of the Battle of Matewan from the perspective of organized miners, see "Matewan," http://www.umwa.org/history/matewan.shtml, *United Mine Workers of America*. For a journalistic account, see Robert Shogan, *The Battle of Blair Mountain: The Story of America's Largest Labor Uprising* (Boulder: Westview, 2004).
44. Wigginton, *Sometimes a Shining Moment*, 9.
45. See Michel Foucault, *Discipline and Punish* (New York: Vintage, 1977).
46. Antonio Gramsci, *Gramsci's Prison Letters: a Selection*, edited and translated by Quentin Hoare and Geoffrey Nowell Smith (London: Pluto Press, 1988), 213-214.
47. Dick Hebdidge, *Subculture: The Meaning of Style* (London: Routledge, 1979), 16.
48. Kenneth Burke, *Attitudes Toward History* (Berkeley: University of California Press, 1959), 266-277.
49. "School History," *Rabun Gap-Nacoochee School.*
50. Wigginton, *The Foxfire Book*, 10.
51. Wigginton, *The Foxfire Book*, 10.
52. Wigginton, *Foxfire 2*, 9.
53. Wigginton, *The Foxfire Book*, 17.
54. Wigginton, *The Foxfire Book*, 10.
55. Clifford Hodges Brewton Collection of Lester G. Maddox Speech/Press Records 1964-1976, http://www.libs.uga.edu/russell/collections/lmaddox.html.
56. "About," *National Organization for Women*, http://www.now.org/organization/info.html.
57. Bob Dylan, "With God on Our Side," *The Times They Are a-Changin'*, Columbia Records, 1964.
58. Bob Dylan, "The Times They are a-Changin'," *The Times They Are a-Changin'*, Columbia Records, 1964.
59. Helen Nearing and Scott Nearing, *Living the Good Life: How to Live Sanely and Simply in a Troubled World* (New York: Shocken, 1954).
60. For in depth discussions of "nostalgia," see Svetlana Boym, *The Future of Nostalgia* (New York: Basic Books, 2001). And Andreea Deciu Ritivoi, *Yesterday's Self: Nostalgia and Immigrant Identity* (New York: Rowman and Littlefield, 2002).
61. Wigginton, *The Foxfire Book*, frontispiece.
62. "The Farm," http://www.thefarm.org/lifestyle/miller.html.
63. Eliot Wigginton and His Students, eds. *The Foxfire Book*, 55.
64. Helen Nearing and Scott Nearing, *Living the Good Life*, 3.
65. Nearing, *Living the Good Life*, 4.

Chapter Eight
The Trivialization of Traditional Southern Religion in the Film
The Grass Harp
Michael P. Graves

Charles Matthau's artfully crafted motion picture taken from Truman Capote's short novel, *The Grass Harp*, is not only a film of rare and delicate beauty, but also an instance of cinematic art, which admirably captures much of the novel's original narrative, given the limits of film adaptation.[1] The film is a minor masterpiece from script to casting, from direction to cinematography, from choice of locations to editing. But my intent in this essay is not to praise the film except initially. Instead, I wish to interrogate the film with respect to its depiction of Southern religion. The film, like Capote's beautifully written novel, features the virtues of natural healing and a transcendental approach to nature—in essence, elevating and advocating a beguiling and haunting naturalistic and mystical religion. In itself, this focus is not troublesome, but the elevation of nature religion in the film is accomplished at the expense of the portrayal of traditional Southern religious practices. In other words, the film unnecessarily stereotypes and negatively depicts traditional Southern Protestant religion. This essay will illustrate how the film valorizes nature religion and trivializes two strains of Southern Protestant Christianity: (1) the traditional small town congregational culture and (2) the tent revival tradition. The essay will also raise initial questions about the differing capacities of written and filmic narrative to present religious expression fairly.

Film Synopsis

Initially, we must begin with a brief synopsis of the film. The narrative, which takes place in a 1940s small Alabama town, tells the story of Collin Fenwick, an eleven-year-old boy who has recently lost his mother through illness. Collin goes to live with his father's cousins, two sisters, Dolly and Verena Talbo. Verena, though younger than Dolly, is an entrepreneur who owns several businesses in town and wields power in the town's civic affairs. Dolly, a sprightly woman who rarely leaves the house, is an herbalist who brews a financially successful treatment for edema—her "dropsy cure"—from a formula taught to her in rhyme by gypsies. The story unfolds through the memory of an older Collin, who narrates the film. Significantly, Dolly tells Collin early on that the Indian grass that grows in the River Woods "knows the stories of all the people on the hill, of all the people who ever lived, and when we are dead it will tell ours, too."

The plot concerns Verena's attempt, with the aid of a sly Chicago man—Dr. Morris Ritz, supposedly a chemical engineer—to market Dolly's secret elixir, but they fail in their attempt to persuade Dolly to write out her secret formula. After a confrontation with her sister, Dolly, young Collin, now sixteen, and Dolly's friend, the outspoken housekeeper, Catherine Creek—an African American woman who nevertheless claims she is a full-blooded Indian—remove themselves from the Talbo house and take up residence in a tree house in the River Woods where the Indian grass grows high. Soon the rootless young rebel orphan, Riley Henderson, Collin's idol, joins them.

The plot thickens when Verena enlists the aid of Sheriff Candle, joined by Reverend Buster, his wife, and assorted townspeople, including Judge Cool, who attempt to roust the little group out of the treehouse. Judge Cool surprises the others and sides with the tree-dwellers, resisting their advance, but is brushed aside by the Sheriff. Sheriff Candle climbs the ladder, followed by the Judge, who attempts to stop him, and by Reverend Buster. In quick succession, Sheriff Candle, almost to the top of the ladder, grabs Collin by the trouser leg, but Dolly douses him with a bucket of water and they all fall to the ground in a heap. Dolly then drops the empty bucket on Mrs. Buster's head.

The Sheriff and company retreat and Judge Cool, stricken by Dolly's beauty and character, joins the community in the treehouse. Over the course of the evening and the next day, the Judge courts and proposes marriage to Dolly Talbo.

Meanwhile, Verena Talbo discovers that Morris Ritz has stolen $12,000 in negotiable securities and $700 in cash from her and skipped town. Additionally, a traveling evangelist, Sister Ida—and her fifteen illegitimate children—hit town and set up a tent revival, to the chagrin of Reverend Buster. Reverend and Mrs. Buster, Sheriff Candle and others interrupt the revival service, forcing the well-attended meeting to close down, and Reverend Buster confiscates the offering.

Eventually Sheriff Candle and his deputies arrest Catherine Creek, en route to the treehouse, and throw her into jail. The remaining treehouse company, now enlarged with the addition of Sister Ida and her children, prepare to fight off a second attempt by the Sheriff and company to scare them out of their roost. In the midst of the standoff, which proves Ida's children to be facile stone-throwers and good aims with sling shots, the sharp report of a firearm is heard and young Collin falls from the tree, wounded in the shoulder. The company vacates the treehouse and everyone, including Reverend Buster and the Sheriff, show concern for Collin.

As night falls, Dolly, who has grown into a stronger person during her stay in the treehouse, an energized person with an emerging sense of her own worth, stands up to her now humbled sister, yet chooses to move back into the house with Verena rather than leaving Verena alone and marrying Judge Cool.

Collin recovers from his wound and eventually makes plans to attend a Halloween party dressed as a skeleton. Dolly stitches his costume and, in celebration, dances enthusiastically with the costumed Collin, but collapses, having suffered a stroke that will shortly claim her life.

In the closing moments of the film, the viewer sees Collin, having decided to make his own way in the world, leaving the Talbo house forever to pursue a career as a writer. He is seen walking through the tall grass with Catherine, Judge Cool, and Verena listening for Dolly's voice in the "grass harp."

The Film's Depictions of Religious Experience

Mystical, Animistic Nature Religion

The brief narrative recounted here already hints the film paints a complementary image of a type of nature religion. The film is framed by opening and closing images of tall Indian grass. The initial shots of grass emphasize visually for the viewer that at least part of the film's title is to be taken literally.

Dolly, an herbalist, takes special notice of the grass in River Woods. Collin the narrator remarks: "About all natural things Dolly was sophisticated." She came by her formula because she was kind to three gypsy women whom she surprised one night in the barn. One of the women gave birth to a child, and because Dolly did not turn them out into the cold as her father surely would have done, one of the grateful women imparted the formula to Dolly in rhyme. But Dolly's knowledge of "natural things" does not end with the "dropsy formula." She is an ardent, yet childlike and innocent, observer of nature. For example, at the end of the film during her final and crucial confrontation with Verena, at the very moment when Dolly is choosing between a life of marriage to the judge and life with her sister, Dolly asks: "Have we had our lives?" The Judge replies: "We're not dead." But this answer does not satisfy Dolly, and she responds: "Some plants, though, they bloom just once, if at all, and nothing more happens to them. They live, but they've had their life."

Dolly's herbal knowledge is neither scientific nor technological. She refuses to reduce the oral, poetic dropsy formula to writing and she shares its secret with no one, not even Catherine, her best friend, nor Collin, whom she loves deeply. She will have no part in the marketing scheme hatched by Verena and Ritz. Dolly's approach to the formula, indeed to all of life, is mystical and childlike. She not only believes in the immanent and animistic theology of the grass harp—that all humans are wind and when we die, the grass collects us, and true believers can hear our voices in the grass—but she also testifies: "I've heard papa clear as day [in the grass]."

Dolly leaves the sanctity of the Talbo house only once a week, and then solely with the expressed purpose to gather herbs and roots for her dropsy formula. Only at the point of crisis with the Verena/Ritz duo does she decide to take up residence outside the Talbo house in the treehouse, which is located in the River Woods surrounded by the tall Indian grass. The treehouse is not so much a house as a raft, for it has no walls and is open to the sky. Dolly is completely at home in the treehouse, which, significantly, is perched above the earth and consequently nearer to heaven. During the first confrontation between the treehouse community and the Sheriff and company, Dolly responds to an accusation by the preacher's wife that she has ended up far from God, with these words: "Consider a moment, Mrs. Buster, that we are nearer God than you by several yards." Indeed, their brief life in the treehouse and its environs—the River Woods—is Edenic, except when troubled by the Sheriff and townspeople. It is there that the Judge courts Dolly.

The beginning of Judge Cool's courtship ritual is important because it offers us further evidence from the film itself that Dolly is meant to be seen as a spiritual figure. The Judge says: "All the years that I've seen you, never known you, not ever recognized, as I did today, what you are: a spirit, a pagan." Dolly responds quickly: "A pagan?" To which the judge replies: "At least, then, a spirit, someone not to be calculated by the eye alone. Spirits are accepters of life, they grant its differences—and consequently are always in trouble." The Judge seems to be saying that Dolly is like a priestess of a pagan religion, or perhaps a witch. The notion that Dolly is a witch is not made explicit in the film, although the allusions to secret knowledge, pacts with gypsies, and herbalism may lead the viewer toward that interpretation.

To bolster Dolly's connection to non-satanic "white" witchery, we have to turn directly to the Truman Capote novel, the language of which the film script attempts—for the most part—to follow closely. For example, though the film merely shows us everyone in the treehouse community sleeping peacefully at night, including Dolly and Judge Cool sleeping together side by side, Collin the narrator of the novel tells us these two "were asleep with their cheeks together" "like two children lost in a witch-ruled forest."[2] The word "witch" is also employed by Capote in a simile earlier in the novel, when Collin describes how the dropsy cure was brewed: "Dolly—Dolly, hovering over the tub dropping our grain-sack gatherings into boiling water and stirring, stirring with a sawed-off broomstick the brown as tobacco-spit brew. She did the mixing of the medicine alone while Catherine and I stood watching like apprentices to a witch."[3] Indeed, the novel indicates that Dolly possesses skills often attributed to witches. Regarding Dolly, Collin of the novel tells us: ". . . she had the subterranean intelligence of a bee that knows where to find the sweetest flower: she could tell you of a storm a day in advance, predict the fruit of the fig tree, lead you to mushrooms and wild honey, a hidden nest of guinea hen eggs. She looked around her, and felt what she saw."[4] Arguably, if Dolly had lived three centuries earlier in Salem, Massachusetts, she might have found herself before a Puritan court because of her adeptness at the art of curing, her secret knowledge, and her antisocial ways.

There is no hint of "dark" or evil knowledge in the novel or the filmic depiction of Dolly's nature religion. In fact, the film clearly reveals to the viewer—as does the novel to the reader—that her brand of mystical nature religion is the most tolerant, ethical, moral and real religion depicted in the entire narrative. Its reality is born out in the positive changes in the lives Dolly touches, especially those of Collin, Judge Cool, and most significantly, Verena, but her religion is also portrayed as real in a theologically specific sort of way. Dolly states her religion's universalistic, animistic eschatology unapologetically in the film: ". . . the wind is us—it gathers and remembers all our voices, then sends them talking and telling through the leaves and the fields."[5] In one of the film's final sequences after Dolly's stroke, we see Collin and Judge Cool in the parlor of the Talbo home, waiting for word from the doctor about Dolly's condition. Her lace shawl, which is draped over a hall tree mirror, begins to shudder in a sudden mild gust of wind. The Judge and Colin exchange glances. "She's left us," the Judge says. It is clear to the viewer that Dolly's religion "pans out." It is depicted as real through imagery. At the film's close, the final shot of grass with the sound of the wind reinforces for the viewer the ambiguous spirituality of the film's title: *The Grass Harp*. We now know the grass provides voice for departed human spirits. It is significant that Capote chose the word "harp," with its manifold connections to Christian lore about heaven, but Dolly's nature religion is not Christian.

Traditional Southern Protestant Religion

Traditional small town Protestant congregational culture is a filmic foil to Dolly's animistic and mystical theology. We first encounter this type of traditional Southern religion—the novel calls it "Baptist"—when the film cuts from the opening shots of grass and the treehouse (with narrative voiceover) to a depiction of selected events at Collin's mother's funeral, a scene that does not appear in the novel. The funeral sequence is significant because it sets up an ambiguous frame for traditional religion that will inform all subsequent references and depictions of this culturally significant Southern expression of Christianity.

The sequence begins with Dolly and Verena walking slowly toward the church and cuts to the ceremony, where Reverend Buster says:

> The Lord giveth and the Lord taketh away. He has returned unto Him our sister, Mary Fenwick, obedient wife, devoted mother, a woman of rare virtue.
>
> Let us turn to the Proverbs of Solomon, the Son of David, King of Israel. He asks: "Who can find a virtuous woman? for her price is far above rubies. Strength and honor are in her clothing. In her tongue is the law of kindness. She looks well to the ways of her household and eateth not the bread of idleness."

Then the congregation begins to sing the hymn, "Rock of Ages," which includes these words:

> Rock of Ages, cleft for me,
> Let me hide myself in Thee;
> Let the water and the blood,
> From Thy riven side which flowed,
> Be of sin the double cure,
> Cleans me from its guilt and power.
>
> While I draw this fleeting breath,
> When mine eyes shall close in death,
> When I soar to worlds unknown,
> See Thee on Thy judgment throne . . .

At this point, the mature Collin interrupts the scene as voiceover narrator, while we see Collin's father express his grief by taking off his tie and laying it on Mary's folded hands in her coffin.

The sequence is remarkable for its authentic portrayal of traditional Southern Protestant beliefs. The film affirms the Hand of Providence in all matters of life and death; the duties of espousal, motherhood, and virtue are reiterated, and the Scriptures are tacitly acknowledged as a source of wisdom and truth. Nothing is new here. Reverend Buster has spoken these words hundreds of times before and they are welcomed not because of their innovation, but because of their familiarity. The hymn, "Rock of Ages," echoes the themes of timelessness and the "cure" for sin, a thoroughly conservative approach to spirituality.

This scene appears nowhere in Capote's novel, but has been added by scriptwriter, Stirling Silliphant, principally in order to raise the question that helps pull the tale together thematically: the Scriptural query, "Who can find a virtuous woman?" The scene accomplishes this purpose admirably and also sets up the utter vulnerability of Collin's father, who later dies in a car accident, which Collin believes is a suicide. Curiously, however, the invented scene also begins subtly to anticipate and accelerate the negative and stereotypical portrayal of Southern Protestantism. Just as Reverend Buster is saying the words "In her tongue is the law of kindness," the camera completes a slow tilt upward from the white congregation in the main floor pews to view the loft in the back of the church building, a loft filled with African Americans. The juxtaposition of the phrase "law of kindness" with the blatant presence of racial segregation in the church raises initial doubts about Reverend Buster's sincerity and appears to presage his later unethical behavior. Thus, what might have been a positive portrayal of traditional Southern religion, one that acknowledges that good Southern people of the period had faith in an eternal God ruling over the lives of men and women, is undercut by a blatant and unnecessary reference to their racism, and not mentioned in the novel.

Additional sequences help advance my thesis that traditional Southern religion is questioned, trivialized and stereotyped in the film, but I do not have space to deal with all of them in detail. Instead, I will focus briefly on the depiction of traditional Southern religion in the first confrontation between the Sheriff (and Reverend Buster) and the treehouse community.

During the first confrontation mentioned in the recount of the film's plot, the Reverend Buster, his wife and Mrs. Macy Wheeler, representatives of the good church people, are depicted as pompous pawns of the powerful Verena Talbo. The Sheriff is cut short by Mrs. Buster, who reminds him they had agreed to let *Reverend Buster* begin the proceedings, which he does in a sonorous voice reminiscent of the funeral sequence: "Dolly Talbo, I speak to you on behalf of your sister, that good gracious woman. . . ." He is interrupted with the response: "That she is," voiced by his wife and Mrs. Wheeler. He continues: ". . . who has this day received a grievous shock." "That she has," reply the ladies. In the ensuing dialogue, Dolly is accused of being far from God as evidenced by her behaviors such as sitting in a tree and smoking cigarettes like a "floozy, while your sister lies in misery flat on her back." Catherine takes umbrage at the word "floozy" and, defending Dolly, threatens Mrs. Buster: "I'll come down there and slap you bowlegged." Mrs. Buster's response is to turn to Sheriff Candle and have him note the threat made by the *"Nigger."* Once again, the film's scriptwriter has gone out of his way to emphasize racism in the film when it is not as apparent or verbally overt in the novel. Capote does not put the word "Nigger" in Mrs. Buster's mouth, and the intent of the film appears to be to make these Southerners more odious to contemporary viewers than they actually are.

There follows an exchange between Mrs. Buster and Judge Cool over what can be accounted as "Christian" behavior, at which point Reverend Buster blurts out: "Answer me this, Judge. Why did you come with us if it wasn't to do the Lord's will in a spirit of mercy?" Judge Cool responds: "The Lord's will? You don't know what that is any more than I do. Perhaps the Lord told these people to go live in a tree."

At this point the Sheriff makes his attempt to dislodge the treedwellers. You will recall the struggle described previously, ending with a pile of bodies on the ground and Mrs. Buster with a bump on her head from the pail dropped by Dolly Talbo. Mrs. Buster and Mrs. Wheeler have the last words of the scene: "Never mind Sheriff. They've had their chance. [Turning to the people in the treehouse] You may imagine you are getting away with something. But let me tell you there will be a retribution—not in heaven, right here on earth." As Mrs. Wheeler echoes the judgment—"Right here on earth"—the entire party exits the scene in a haughty manner. Note the parody of the white version of African American "call response."

The viewer now understands, in the film's created reality, traditional Southern religion is not only captive to economic power, but places its true faith in worldly justice—right here on earth—rather than in the Providence of an Almighty Judge, which is a doctrine they proclaim only on Sunday. Other unflattering negative stereotypes of traditional Southern religion will emerge in the brief discussion of the tent revival which follows, but let me close this section with the observation that the viewer is set up by the end of the film to see the traditional route as corrupt and vacuous, void of ethics, morality and spiritual power. This conclusion is made clear to the viewer when Collin encounters Reverend and Mrs. Buster on the street as he leaves town at the end of the film. Buster warns him: "That city is an evil place. See that you don't fall victim to the ways of sin. God bless you, boy." But the warning and blessing fall on deaf ears because Collin now knows that Buster's words are empty. Any truth they contain is drowned out by the messenger. After all, what can this hypocritical, blustering sycophant know of eternal verities? The viewing audience, instructed by the film's carefully managed negative depiction of traditional Southern Protestantism, is encouraged to agree with Collin and choose something real and authentic—Dolly's nature religion.

The Tent Revival Tradition

Southern tent revival religion is depicted in the film in a bizarre manner by the appearance of Sister Ida and her "Soul Roundup," a rollicking combination of Amie Semple McPherson dramatics and implied hokum. The viewer's first hint that a revival is coming occurs in a scene in the town barbershop following the first confrontation at the treehouse. In the scene, Little Homer Honey, dressed as a cowboy, comes through the shop enthusiastically saying "Praise Jesus," as he hands out flyers for Sister Ida's Soul Roundup. Amos Legrand, the loquacious barber, opines: "It's not like we can't use a good revival. There hasn't exactly been a shortage of lost souls around here lately." His statement accurately reflects the traditional wide spread Southern affection for revival meetings that traces its roots back to the camp meeting movement of the nineteenth century.

However, Reverend Buster does not share the barber's enthusiasm, calling Sister Ida an "infamous trollop" and seeking legal restraints on the revival from the Sheriff, who initially rebuffs him. Reverend and Mrs. Buster decide to visit the tent meeting to gather evidence.

Although the revival is never directly depicted in the novel, the film viewer is treated to a scene in the tent featuring Sister Ida playing the accordion and singing "God's Clothesline" to a mixed race audience, a song that includes the line: "We come together in the sweet by and by." As she sings, several of her children hold strung out clotheslines down the rows so that people can pin their folding money on the line while Little Homer Honey displays his roping skills on the small raised platform. Sister Ida runs her hands over a man's face and sits in another's lap, but no one in the audience seems to care. They are obviously having a good time.

Sister Ida next launches into the Gospel classic, "Joshua Fit the Battle of Jericho," an apt lyric considering a battle is brewing, with Reverend and Mrs. Buster about to descend upon the tent and see its "wall come a-tumbling down." Presently, the two arrive and notice the clotheslines drooping with money. Reverend Buster intones: "Fleecing the flock," implying this is his "flock" and he doesn't appreciate seeing the money, which should rightly come to his church, wasted on this woman with loose morals. Reverend Buster phones Verena telling her that this hussy is calling Verena an "enemy of Jesus" in her meeting— obviously a bold-faced lie—and Verena, understandably alarmed, enlists Sheriff Candle's help to close down the tent revival, a demand the Sheriff apparently cannot refuse.

When the Sheriff and his deputies interrupt the meeting and give Sister Ida her walking papers, Reverend Buster makes a dash to the money clothesline, saying: "This is the Lord's money. I'm confiscating it in His behalf." To Sister Ida he shouts: "Whore of Babylon! Repent!" One of Ida's smallest children sidles up to Reverend Buster, grabs him around his knee and calls him "Daddy." Buster replies angrily: "I'm not your daddy! Get away from me!" However, Mrs. Buster seems not to be certain about the Reverend's quick and vociferous denial of paternity and begins to accuse him, but the standoff is interrupted by Sister Ida's plea: "That is *our* money!" and the Sheriff's reply: "Just call that money a fine."

The confrontation in the tent further questions the character of Reverend Buster by depicting him as condemnatory and judgmental and by exposing him as a liar and a greedy man. His sexual morality is also questioned, although there is ambiguity in the charge, since one could interpret the actions of the accusing child as having been taught her by her manipulative and apparently lascivious evangelist mother. Either way, the image of traditional Southern religion comes out the loser.

We see Sister Ida in subsequent scenes where, penniless and out of gas, she seeks out Dolly Talbo for help. At length, she encounters Dolly and recounts her strange life story, including her admission that she has a fondness for the feel of a man's touch. In these conversations, the scriptwriter emphasized the sensual details of Ida's journey at the expense of her spiritual struggle, which is revealed in much greater detail in the novel, where Capote includes a lengthy description of Sister Ida's call to the ministry. Ida shares that she had not been allowed to attend her father's funeral because the family was ashamed of her being pregnant out of wedlock. She continues:

> It happened this day, with them off at the burial and me alone in the house and a sandy wind blowing rough as an elephant, that I got in touch with God. I didn't by any means deserve to be Chosen: up till then mama'd had to coax me to learn my Bible verses; afterwards, I memorized over a thousand in less than three months. Well I was practicing a tune on the piano, and suddenly a window broke, the whole room turned topsy-turvy, then fell together again, and someone was with me, papa's spirit I thought; but the wind died down peaceful as spring—He was there, and standing as He made me, straight, I opened my arms to welcome Him. That was twenty-six years ago last February the third; I was sixteen, I'm forty-two now, and I've never wavered.[6]

One wonders why this poignant and authentic "testimony" does not appear in the film, which likewise glances over Sister Ida's relationship with the preacher, Mr. Honey, about which Ida shares in some detail with Dolly and her company in the novel:

> It wasn't until I met Mr. Honey that I saw why the Lord had chosen me and what my task was to be. Mr. Honey possessed the True Word of God; after I heard him preach that first time I went round to see him: we hadn't talked twenty minutes than he said I'm going to marry you provided you're not married a'ready. I said no I'm not married, but I've had some family; fact is there was five by then. Didn't faze him a bit. We got married a week later on Valentine's Day . . . when the Lord brought us together He knew certain what He was doing: we had Roy, then Pearl and Kate and Cleo and Little Homer—most of them born in that wagon you saw up there. We traveled all over the country carrying His Word to folks who'd never heard it before, not the way my man could tell it.[7]

Mr. Honey then disappeared in Cajun country. On his disappearance, Ida remarks in the novel: "I don't give a hoot what the police say; he wasn't the kind to run out on his family; no sir it was foul play."[8]

It is clear that the novel places Sister Ida's character on a higher plane than the film's reconstruction of Ida. Capote's novel presents the complex character of a female evangelist who is fully invested in the revival tent tradition—warts and all—but a woman who, nevertheless, claims a firsthand experience with God and is pursuing her "calling" for the long haul. Incidentally, Sister Ida's "calling" quoted above includes a reference to a divine wind that broke a window and spun the woman around the room, followed by an apparent encounter with God, which is probably a hint that her experience has a sense of authenticity and may be related to the wind that rustles through the tall grass, perhaps linking the tent revival religious experience to mystical animistic religion. Both appear to possess a level of authenticity in the novel. Instead of presenting us with the novel's complex depiction of Sister Ida, the film constructs a stereotypical "weird" character out of selected parts of Capote's picture of Ida. The result is the reduction and trivialization of the Southern revival tent heritage.

Conclusion

There are good reasons to argue that, whatever the virtues of the film *The Grass Harp*—and they are numerous—it presents an unfair and distorted image of traditional Southern religion in the 1940s, a negative image well beyond that presented in Truman Capote's novel from which the film is drawn. Capote's image of Southern religion is much more complex and ambiguous than the film's depiction, running a bit more truly along lines suggested by Richard M. Weaver, who wrote:

> Although the South was heavily Protestant, its attitude toward religion was essentially the attitude of orthodoxy: it was a simple acceptance of a body of belief, an innocence of protest and schism by which religion was left one of the unquestioned and unquestionable supports of the general settlement under which men live. One might press the matter further and say that it was a doctrinal innocence.... Religion was a matter for profession, and after one had professed, he became a member of a religious brotherhood.... Throughout the South and West there occurred the anomalous condition of an incredible flowering of sects together with the more primitive type of emotional response to religion. Travelers expressed a double amazement at the multiplicity of sects and at the lack of friction or ill will between them.[9]

Interestingly, Weaver's perspective appears to be inclusive of Dolly Talbo's mystical nature religion as expressed in both the film and the novel, but the inclusive and tolerant capacities Weaver saw as characterizing the "older religiousness" of the South is unrealized in both the film and the novel. However, the film falls much farther from Weaver's vision than the novel because of its trivialization of traditional religious expressions.

This study of three depictions of Southern religion in *The Grass Harp* also calls into question the capacity of film as a medium to present any historical and traditional Southern religious expression without automatically trivializing it through stereotype. For example, the tent revival tradition has always attracted and gathered together "strange" personalities and featured behaviors, which are considered quaint or bizarre when viewed by those outside its community. In an increasingly secular society of moviemakers and moviegoers, it may be the case that filmic portrayals of traditional Southern religious styles will be automatically created and responded to as odd, humorous, or hyperbolic "performances."

Notes

1. *The Grass Harp*. New Line Home Video, 1997. All subsequent references to the film are the same.
2. Truman Capote, *The Grass Harp, Including A Tree of Night and other stories* (New York: Vintage International, 1993), 47.
3. Capote, *The Grass Harp*, 17.
4. Capote, *The Grass Harp*, 14.
5. Capote, *The Grass Harp*, 9.
6. Capote, *The Grass Harp*, 75.
7. Capote, *The Grass Harp*, 75-76.
8. Capote, *The Grass Harp*, 75-76.
9. "The Older Religiousness in the South," in George M. Curtis, III and James J. Thompson, Jr., eds., *The Southern Essays of Richard M. Weaver* (Indianapolis, Ind.: Liberty Press, 1987), 135.

Chapter Nine
College Football Fanaticism and Online Communities: A Reflection of Football as a Religious Experience in the South
Dedria Givens-Carroll & Alison Slade

"*I can't be more blessed to be part of a whole team like this. God was with us.*"
—Auburn's Head Football Coach Gene Chizik on winning the 2010 BCS NCAA football championship[1]

"*A recent poll by the Mobile Register found 90 percent of the state's citizens describe themselves as football fans. Eighty-six percent of them pull for one of the two major football powers there, Alabama or Auburn. . . . To understand what an absolute minority nonfans are in Alabama, consider this: they are outnumbered there by atheists.*"[2]

Sports have played a vital role within American popular culture for centuries. In the United States, there are many sports from which sports fans can choose. The amount of media coverage devoted to sports is testament alone to its prominence within society. All in all, "sports coverage occupies 20 percent of all newspaper space and twenty-five percent of television's weekend and special event coverage . . . 19 percent of all newspaper reporters cover sports, as do 21 percent of all consumer magazines."[3] The surge in popularity of sports can be directly linked with the growth of newspaper circulations, specifically, the advent of the penny press in the 1830s bringing news and sports coverage to the working class. In the Southern United States, a strong argument can be made for recognizing the most popular sport as college athletics, most notably college football. As the fan bases of sports teams and readers of sports media have grown, both industries have been quickly adapting to the digital age of media, finding new and creative ways to reach out and connect to fans.

From thirty thousand to one hundred thousand National College Athletic Association (NCAA) football fans pack their stadiums during any given Saturday in the fall to root their teams to victory. The teams are divided by conferences, some claiming to be stronger than others: the Atlantic Coast Conference (ACC), the Big 12, the Big East, the Big Ten, the Pacific 10, the Southeastern Conference (SEC) and the independents, which belong to no conference (Army, Navy, Notre Dame and Western Kentucky). Some of the conferences have a play-off system, which names a season champion, while others do not. For now, the Bowl Championship Series (BCS) governs the way the college football awards the NCAA national champions. But, it is the fans of the SEC in the Southern United States and how they connect with their teams that will be the focus of this chapter.

The first intercollegiate football game played in the Deep South can be traced back to 1892 when Auburn beat Georgia 10-0 and evangelical leaders called the game a "theater of mud and blood."[4] The SEC was formed just two years later, in 1894, when seven Southern schools came together in Atlanta, Georgia for the Southeastern Intercollegiate Athletic Association (SIAA).[5] The current configuration of the SEC was finalized a century later, in 1992, and consists of twelve Southern schools (Auburn University, Louisiana State University, University of Alabama, University of Arkansas, University of Mississippi, Mississippi State University, University of Florida, University of Georgia, University of Kentucky, University of South Carolina, University of Tennessee, and Vanderbilt University). With the victory of the Auburn University Tigers in the 2010 BCS National Championship, the SEC has now won five national championships in a row (2010, Auburn University; 2009, University of Alabama; 2008, University of Florida; 2007, Louisiana State University; 2006, University of Florida). The SEC has the most all-time NCAA college football national championships of any conference with seventeen victories.

Although the victories accumulated by the SEC can arguably be attributed only to those team members battling on the field, there is some credit due to the devoted fan base of these teams in the Southern United States. For the twenty-seventh straight year (2007), the SEC led all major conferences in total attendance for college football as the league drew 6,687,342 fans to its eighty-nine games. SEC schools averaged 75,139 fans per game, which was also number one in the nation. SEC stadiums were filled to 97.69 percent of capacity for the 2007 season. Six of the nation's top ten schools in total attendance were from the SEC: Tennessee (4), Auburn (5), Georgia (6), LSU (7), Alabama (8) and Florida (9). Tennessee averaged 103,918 fans per game.[6] This year alone, more than six million people will witness an SEC game in person, tens of millions more will watch on CBS or ESPN.[7] So, how big is football in the SEC? According to Chad Gibbs in 2010, "the combined athletic budgets of the twelve schools exceed eight hundred million dollars. That's more money than the GDPs of twenty-four of the world's poorest countries."[8]

This chapter explores the unique relationship between college football and fans in the Southern United States and traces the literature comparing these relationships to religious experiences. These comparisons are rooted within the frameworks of cultural myths and rituals. According to Bain-Selbo, "the person who has the personality type of a 'passionate devotee' can be found in a stadium or in a church and, more often than not, in the former on Saturday and the latter on Sunday. Human beings can express their religiosity in the sporting world or in church or in both. In this sense, expressing one's religiosity predominantly in the context of one's college football team in the South is really no different from being a Methodist or a Baptist."[9]

Although there is ample literature denoting the college football experience as a religious ritual, the literature has not explored current trends in fan interactions and social media. This chapter argues the traditional methods of viewing or participating in the sport of college football has reached new heights with the advent of social media, as social media have become the new houses of worship and deification of the key figures in college football in the South. Specifically, this chapter seeks to answer the question does social media, specifically the social networking site Facebook, illustrate the religious experiences of being a football fan in the South.

Ritual, Cultural Myth and the Sports Fan

Rituals provide members of society with "affirmative personal identity within the boundaries of our culture."[10] The ritual of sport can be classified in a variety of categories, but specifically, this ritual of participation in fan communities involving sports can be considered a rite of spectacle. When considered at face value, these rituals may simply seem to be a form of diversion or entertainment, but in reality, the ritual of spectacle serves to reinforce deep-seated cultural belief and value systems. Before specifically considering the impact of the ritual of sport on the Southern United States, it is important to define the meaning of a fan.

Being a fan of a specific sports team comes with a set of predetermined cultural belief system and values. Scholars have focused on the pathological deviance or excessive participation of sports fans. Fiske defines fans as "subordinated formations of the people, particularly . . . those disempowered by any combination of gender, age, class and race."[11]

More specifically, in the Southern United States, this ritual is deification of college football heroes and gods battling on the gridiron.

Football Fanaticism in the South

Football in the South is on a different level than the rest of the country. Throughout history, football fans of all ages and in all locations will battle for the honor of their favorite team. But in the South, this philosophy takes on a whole new meaning. In 2008, fans of the University of Alabama and Louisiana State University got into a scuffle over the game, and as a result the shotguns were pulled out and two men lost their lives. Much like the defending the honor of mother or sister, the men were fighting for the love of their schools, their own personal deification of the sport itself manifesting in violence.

Football fans in the South are fanatics, according to noted football broadcaster Keith Jackson's foreword to *Southern Fried Football* when he called 2007 the "wildest, most unpredictable college football season in my thirty years as a sportswriter."[12] That was the year Alabama signed Head Coach Nick Saban to an eight-year, $32 million contract, Florida dominated Ohio State (41-14) to win the BCS national championship and on January 7, 2008 LSU "surprisingly made it to the national championship game because the BSC ranked number one and two teams lost the last game of regular season play— beat the Ohio Buckeyes, 38-24, in New Orleans to give the SEC its second national championship in 12 months."[13] Also in 2007, Georgia stormed the field after scoring its first touchdown against Florida in Jacksonville—a neutral rivalry site for the World's Largest Outdoor Cocktail Party held there annually since 1933— and the Bulldogs were penalized for unsportsmanlike conduct. However, the passion of that rivalry netted the most points ever scored by each team against each other. Auburn made history by beating Alabama in 2007 for the sixth straight season. Houston Nutt resigned as Arkansas' head coach and just four short hours later was coaching at Ole Miss. The BCS rankings in the SEC just didn't matter in 2007. "Auburn went 13-0 in 2004 and did not get a sniff at the national championship, a fact that still leaves Southerners seething. If Auburn had been given a chance, the SEC would be entering the 2008 season having won four of the last five national championships."[14]

Sociologists say college football has thrived in the South because the game pushes all the hot buttons of its people. The South was left behind in the economic expansion after World War II, but football was always a way for the agrarian South to prove its worth against the industrialized North. Southerners knew many Northerners looked down on them as uneducated hicks. Football was one area where the South could be superior. Further, there is a long held notion in the South of the importance of college football juxtaposed with the importance of being an upstanding Christian member of society: one who follows the game as closely as they follow the preacher on Sunday mornings.

Football Faith in the South

"Thou shalt have no other gods before me," the first of the Ten Commandments Moses brought down from Mt. Sinai, must not have included football as a god,[15] but Southerners, who claim to be predominately Christian, still seem to worship the pig skin. "In a nation that has historically considered itself Christian, the Southern states are by far the most Christian-y. A 2004 Gallup Poll that tracked religious affiliations state by state showed in eight of the nine SEC states, over eighty-six percent of participants considered themselves Christians."[16] When one attends a church in the South, most certainly other congregants will be talking football, especially during football season. The pastor of one Baptist church is Baton Rouge has said repeatedly the outcome of the LSU football game certainly has a direct effect on our Sunday morning worship services. If LSU wins we'll have upbeat services, if they don't win then we don't."[17] According to Gibbs:

> Worshipers will gather before the service and discuss in reverent tones what went right and wrong the day before. The pastor will usually reference Saturday's happenings by either praising a team's win or mourning its loss, while oftentimes taking a playful dig at the misfortunes of a rival school. Churches sometimes encourage this blending of faith and fanaticism with "wear your team's colors" day or by having viewing parties for big games—with halftime testimonies, naturally. Churches have to schedule around football. Apart from tailgates and viewing parties, a church event planned on Saturday in the fall is guaranteed to be a colossal failure. The people have chosen today what they will worship, and it looks like God is a two-and-a-half touchdown underdog to the Tigers, Bulldogs, and Gators.[18]

A survey conducted of Southern college football fans in the fall of 2005 and 2006, found that "out of a choice of seven options, college football ranked, on average, just behind family, friends, and just ahead of church."[19] In the American South, "God and football scrimmage daily for the people's hearts and minds."[20]

Southern College Football as a Civil Religion

At a 2009 LSU football game, one eighty-nine-year-old fan demonstrated her passion for her faith and football on a custom printed t-shirt that said "Jesus in my King, LSU is my team." Bain-Selbo notes "there is a compelling case to conclude that college football in the South is a form and expression of religious life . . . its myths, symbols, and rituals, as well as sacred time, objects, and places. College football in the South has become part of the civil religion of that region for many people."[21] "One example of the complex ties between 'official' religion and 'popular' religion is civil religion, the close relationship between nation and religion, or in this case, region and religion. It has been embodied in the official religion of the churches, but it has also been diffused through southern culture, appearing in such rituals as football games."[22] The region's civil religion is demonstrated as a "popular religion on Confederate battle flags with Elvis Presley's image in the middle and on special issue Coca-Cola bottles with Bear Bryant's image on them. Southerners have long believed God works directly through Southern history. A famous painting in Alabama shows Bear Bryant walking on water."[23]

"The modern, middle-class, urban and suburban South" find college football to be "a new kind of religion but one closely allied with traditional Evangelicalism."[24] "College football has long enjoyed enormous popularity among evangelical Protestants of the American South. Southern evangelicals gather together for college football on Saturday afternoons and for church on Sunday mornings with a similar spirit of respect for the traditions and values they associate with regional identity."[25] Ed McMinn, a retired pastor living in Georgia, has penned a series of books for almost every SEC football team that serves as daily devotionals for "die-hard fans" and combines "the great passion" of fans with "the great passion of the fan of Christ."[26] The stories, reflections and Biblical references are coupled with "legendary games, improbable victories, and historical events all told with a twist: They are all tied to God's story."[27]

As religion comes in all forms and varieties, we would be remiss to not include the world of black magic, superstition and even voodoo, all elements of a more atheistic and/or pagan view within religion. Above all, superstition, as an element existing in possibly any religion, is important to fan culture. Fans use ritualized behaviors to cope with certain elements of televised sports experiences.[28] For example, fans can wear specific game day clothing each Saturday or never eat with their right hand during the game. These experiences are extensions of the ritualized behaviors in the live arena, such as the players touching a specific sign before running onto the field.

Southern Ritual and Religion: Football as Myth

The ritual identification of fans with sporting events, teams and players includes a variety of mythic dimensions. Myths are closely associated with narratives, cultural parables and stories "woven into culture which dictates belief, defines ritual, and acts as a chart of the social order."[29] Myths imply a sense of order to chaos, and speak to us of traditions and norms, much like the ritualistic behaviors of the sporting events noted previously. Myths are also defined as "bedrock cultural beliefs, which provide the foundation of a mind-set."[30]

The cultural narratives born of the fans, rituals and myths surrounding each team are legendary in the South. "Not only is there myth, folklore, and legend in Southern college football, there is also symbols, rituals, and a sense of sacrality that permeate the religious experience that is Southern college football."[31] These narratives and myths are instilled into Southern football fans of all ages, passed down from generations to solidify membership into the cultural subgroups of fan nations. For example, take the storied historical glory of Punt Bama Punt, in which during the 1972 Auburn and Alabama rivalry game (the Iron Bowl) featured two blocked punts in the final minutes of the game to give the Alabama team its first defeat of the season. The Punt Bama Punt game is legendary, and listed as the eighth most painful football game outcome in history.[32] Another historical cultural narrative woven into the mythical fabric is the Earthquake Game. In 1988, Auburn was playing in LSU's stadium, referred to as Death Valley. When LSU scored a late touchdown to take the lead, the roar of the crowd was so great that the earth shook—confirmed by a seismograph reading in the in the university's geology department. The myth or legend is about the "loyalty and exuberance of the fans of LSU" and "nothing was more meaningful than the event—the ritual. The experience was a manifestation of the sacred: something powerfully meaningful and qualitatively different occurred."[33]

Football in the South, like religion, has a distinct group of worshippers where myths symbols and rituals facilitate the total experience . . . "the spirit of man, in sport and religion is an exercise of personal venture. The arenas and coliseums are little more than shrines for spiritual activity"[34] The sacred spaces where football games are tested in the South are stadiums, much akin to the churches where mass worship is performed. Any worship service in a Southern church would be incomplete without some form of music, just as marching bands are a strong component of the rituals of college football. The Golden Band from Tigerland, LSU's band, salutes the fans as they march down the hill from the Greek Theater to a slow cadence until it reaches the gates of Death Valley and the crescendo peaks as the band runs into the stadium. "The Pride of the Southland Band at Tennessee culminates its march through campus at an intersection near the stadium and at the foot of The Hill. The band delights the crowd with the Tennessee fight song and several renditions of Rocky Top."[35]

Another strong component of Southern worship services is "fellowship," where the congregants meet and greet each other, visiting before they gather. "The sacrality of a church service, for example may begin when the minster calls the congregants to prayer or when the choir leads them in the opening hymn—rituals to mark the beginning of a sacred time."[36]

At Southern football games, "fellowship" is practiced before and after games. Fans gather to "tailgate" on the backs of station wagons, or more likely pickup trucks, which are used as a table to hold food and visit with other fans prior to the games kick-off. "Perhaps no campus has perfected this ritual more than the fans of the University of Mississippi famous for 'the Grove,' an expanse of tree-lined property in the middle of the campus. This pregame ritual is what other SEC fans would call 'fancy' tailgating, where the tables are covered with linen, bottles of fine wine and finger sandwiches highlighted by bouquets of fresh flowers."[37]

At the end of most church services in the South, an invitation is offered where worshippers are invited to respond to the sermon or another presentation made during the service. The end of the sacred time is culminated with those who respond by walking the aisle to be converted, make a profession of faith, join the church's membership, or make another decision publicly. Auburn's after-game ritual is like no other, especially when their team wins. "Fans head to Toomer's Corner in the middle of town and stream toilet paper rolls through the trees and street lamps" until they look like snow. "After victories in Georgia, many fans, including a great number of children, line up to ring the Chapel Bell."[38] To the delight of fans after the games, the winning coaches and most outstanding players are often quoted on their successes. Cam Newton, Auburn's Heisman Trophy winner and outstanding player in the 2010 BCS National Championship game, described his journey after much adversity: "It's a God thing. I thank God every single day. I'm just his instrument. He's using me as a consistent basis daily to extend His Word. I'm a prime example of how God can turn something bad into something very great."[39]

"The Bear": Southern Football's Saint

Many of college football's players and coaches in the South are turned into demagogues, where they seem to be the religion's disciples and are a source of mythicization. Tim Tebow, the former Heisman Trophy winner, who led the Gators to a national championship, although wildly popular in the state of Florida was criticized for a controversial Focus on the Family television commercial which appeared during the 2009 BCS championship game. Tebow is also known for wearing scriptures from the Bible plastered on temporary tattoos underneath his eyes and leading his team in prayer just before a game. According to Doyle, "pregame invocations by ministers and postgame prayers by members of the Fellowship of Christian Athletes unite players and fans in a ritual of fealty to shared beliefs. Many southern coaches proudly contend that their work reinforces the Christian values that their players learn at home and in church."[40]

Perhaps the most mythological or legendary figure is the history of Southern college football is Alabama's former head coach Paul "Bear" Bryant. Born into abject poverty in a small Arkansas village in 1913, Bryant rose to become one of the greatest cultural icons of the South—perhaps second only to Elvis. His nickname came from accepting a challenge as an adolescent to wrestle a bear. Though the bear eventually got the better of him (it even drew blood by biting his ear), Bryant earned a nickname.[41]

Bryant coached at the University of Maryland, the University of Kentucky and Texas A&M University before finishing out the last twenty-five years of his coaching career at Alabama. George Blanda, a Kentucky quarterback, remarked upon seeing him, "This must be what God looks like." Another player on the Kentucky team, Harry Jones, said: "In those days, the coach was like God," adding that Bryant "was the most impressive human being I have ever been around. . . . He was everything you wanted to be."[42] Bryant was a symbol for any Southerner's aspiration to rise above the kind of poverty that typified much of the region. He was a symbol of what hard work and dedication could achieve. He was a symbol of victory.[43] His life became an archetype for future coaches to follow at Alabama and for many men and boys throughout the South. According to St. John, "one poll indicates that approximately a quarter of Crimson Tide fans "associated the Bear with 'godlike qualities.'"[44] These god-like, hero qualities have become a standard measure for the subsequent coaches at Alabama. In fact, only one coach since Bryant's departure in 1982 has not had a former connection with the Bear. Bill Curry, who led the Alabama Crimson Tide from 1987 to 1989, had no connection with the legend, and after losing to in- state rival Auburn three years in a row, Curry was forced out of the head coaching position.[45]

Another illustration of the power of Bryant's god-like status at Alabama and in the South is in his death.

> The Bryant funeral, in terms of sheer numbers, was probably unsurpassed in southern history. Both Christianity and the University of Alabama figured prominently in the service, which opened with the reading of a telegram from Billy Graham, the high priest of interdenominational evangelical religiosity. One of Bryant's former players and a devoted protégé, Steadman Shealy, gave the eulogy and told of Bryant kneeling after his last football victory to lead his team in prayer, thanking God for allowing such a long coaching career. Estimates were that fifteen hundred people attended the service, with ten thousand mourners in downtown Tuscaloosa, most lining the streets to watch the post-funeral procession to the cemetery.[46]

To this day, Bryant's grave in Tuscaloosa, Alabama remains a shrine, adorned much like the grave of Elvis Presley in Memphis. A sure way to lose the interest and ruffle the feathers of both Bryant and Elvis fans alike is to remind them their heroes are indeed, dead.

The Worship Service: Traditional or Contemporary?

Fans worship their teams differently, just as there are different kinds of worship services held at Christian churches throughout the south. Most worship services can be categorized as either traditional or contemporary, where the messages, the medium and the music are distinctly different. The traditional service for college football in the South would have been performed via radio or television. The broadcasting of college football to the masses is still relatively new, with radio broadcasts of football games beginning at the University of Pennsylvania in the 1920s and complete and total access across television channels becoming available in 1984.[47] "Television acts as a cultural forum, in which televisual communication is the process of ritualized negotiation of cultural reality."[48]

Watching televised sports serves to empower the fan, as the fan can manipulate the meanings within the televised texts to suit their own feelings and ritualized behaviors concerning their team of choice.[49] For example, fans can negotiate and renegotiate the particular impact of one referee's call over and over, whether on instant replay or through the replay of the play on DVR or TiVo. Further, the ability of the fan to feel connected to the event, albeit through televisual representations of the game, allows the fan to feel empowered and connected to their favorite player and team. The connection between fan and televised football can also be connected to the religious ritual, including the act of praying on the field prior to a game. The empowerment of the fan also incorporates the sense of belonging the fan has with other members of the mass group.[50] Fans will determine ritualized behaviors based on how they individually perceive themselves to fit into the group. Televised sports allow for this empowerment to a degree, but it's the new, contemporary means of worship on a Saturday that truly empowers fans today.

The Contemporary Service

Although most worship services are communal—and so are football bleachers packed to the gills with fans—the traditional media has taken a backseat to individual fans connecting to their teams via the social media. Southern religion bends toward evangelism and the personal experience of being "born again," while making an individual connection to Jesus Christ.[51] "One's salvation, for example, is one's own responsibility and is achieved, in a certain sense, alone. The individual is not dependent on an institution or ecclesiastical hierarchy or church doctrine to achieve the spiritual end."[52] Wilson notes "this emphasis on personal religious experience obviously has a parallel on game day. The passion and fervor and even ecstasy of the college football fan takes place in a communal setting, but it is the personal experience that feeds the psyche or (dare I say) soul."[53] In Southern college football not everyone can or wants to attend the mass gatherings that take place on any given fall Saturday in a mega-stadium.

With televised sports, "the fan at home is aided and abetted in interpreting the contest by the television camera, which focuses on action deemed important."[54] However, social media is changing fan interaction, and the guide to interpretation has become other fans and their perceptions. Social media, and in particular Facebook, has individualized the face of college athletics. Fans are able to connect immediately and receive instant gratification with news of their favorite teams, players and coaches. Social media will increasingly replace the more traditional outlets of viewing college football on television or in stadiums.

Additionally, social media have changed the way sports fans receive information.

In the past, news coverage was reported almost exclusively by seasoned journalists who served as the voice of record. . . . Some have used the term "reclinerporting" to describe the quality of the growing number of blogs that allow commentary with little to no direct contact to the individuals involved, and are written to an audience with a desire for bias toward their favorite teams.[55]

The 2004 Merriam-Webster Online (n.d.) word of 2004 was "blog," short for weblog, which was defined in their *Collegiate Dictionary Online* as "a website that contains an online personal journal with reflections, comments, and often hyperlinks provided by the writer." "Blogs, which date back to 1998, are now practically mainstream media in terms of numbers and influence."[56] According to Wilcox, "there were about 112 million blogs in 2007, with about 120,000 new ones being created every day. The vast majority do not have much readership, but others have gained a large following because their postings have gained a reputation for credibility and for breaking major stories, which are then picked up by traditional media."[57]

Blogs are the most dominant "manifestation" of social media and Facebook, a social networking site launched in 2004, has the highest number of users among college-focused sites, http://facebook.com.[58] According to Facebook's own website, they have about four hundred million active users, and state the mission of Facebook "is to give people the power to share and make the world more open and connected. Millions of people use Facebook every day to keep up with friends, upload an unlimited number of photos, share links and videos, and learn more about the people they meet."[59] The power of Facebook in achieving this mission is evidenced in their own statistics: more than 5 billion pieces of content (web links, news stories, blog posts, notes, photo albums, etc.) are shared each week, more than 3.5 million events created each month, more than 3 million active pages on Facebook, and more than 1.5 million local businesses have active pages on Facebook.[60]

Facebook is certainly considered to offer interpersonal relationships via the "friending" process, where the average user has 130 "friends" on the site, becomes a "fan" on an average of four pages per month and the average user spends about fifty-five minutes per day on the site.[61] Fan websites are increasingly making and breaking news in a way that is transforming the relationship between fans, athletes, coaches, and organizations.[62]

The knowledge stage of Facebook was prompted when the site was introduced in February 2004, with college students as the primary target. A major part of Facebook's growth, however, came in 2007 when registration was opened to all users.[63] Facebook claims that more than 20 million people become fans of pages each day and pages have created more than 5.3 billion fans.[64]

Facebook, therefore, acts as a social media blog, which provides an avenue on the Internet for sports fans to provide commentary. "Internet blogs have become an increasingly common technique for fans to further identify with their sport."[65] Michael Real argues that sports fans websites, or blogs, "have expanded the traditional watchdog function of the press by having eyes and ears everywhere."[66] Plus, he argues fan blogs can "make a fan feel local even when hundreds or thousands of miles away."[67]

Facebook fan pages have seen the development of both favorable and unfavorable attitude toward the innovation of social media in sport. For example, on April 20, 2009, on a popular college football site, fanblogs.com a post entitled "Recruiting Violations on Facebook?" focused on the NCAA taking action against a student who created a Facebook fan page dedicated to a potential football recruit. "The NCAA says that creating Facebook pages and groups during the recruiting season is out of bounds and a violation of recruiting rules. The NCAA believes that when fans create and post pages, they are acting as boosters in an attempt to influence the choice of a recruit." The blogger noted it was "time that the NCAA accepted the fact that Facebook is a real world environment. People are going to say things on Facebook. . . . You cannot police all speech, nor should a university be held liable for a Facebook fan page."

Another unfavorable attitude toward the innovation of Facebook and football fans encircled the BCS governance of awarding the NCAA national championship. The BCS committed "a major blunder" when it used its Facebook fan page to "simply present marketing information to fans" who responded with extreme criticism.[68] "The BCS learned quickly that if your product is hated, social media might not be the place for you."[69] Although the BCS claimed to have wanted a "two-way conversation" by turning to social media with the establishment of its Facebook page, the organization seemed to "haved close its eyes and jammed its fingers in its ears even as it goes on saying the same thing it's always said . . . saying the same thing over and over again expecting people to start believing."[70]

Critical Analysis

The Bleacher Report, which purports to publish the best college football newsletter on the Internet, listed "College Football's Fifteen Most Rabid Fan Bases." Of these fifteen teams, five are in the SEC (Alabama, LSU, Auburn, Florida, and Georgia). SEC football teams may have strong fan bases because of their winning records.

Therefore, this study focuses on the SEC. Although there are other conferences in Division I football with teams located in the South, this study only focused on the predominant football conference in the region. This research examined the question is social media simply an extension or outlet for the religious viewpoints to be embedded within fan interactions?

Qualitative content analysis was utilized to examine the themes found within fan interactions on official Facebook fan pages for the SEC. Qualitative content analysis allowed the researcher to analyze texts to discover and examine emerging themes and categories.[71] For this study, the themes were identified from the literature on ritual, myth, religion and college football in the South. We chose to examine fan interactions from the month of October, for a total of thirty days of fan interactions and over twenty five thousand posts. October is the middle of the college football season, and therefore, the beginning of the projections for success or failure of a team; specifically, October is the first month fans get a glimpse of the BCS picture through the first release of the computer rankings for NCAA teams. Qualitative content analysis allows the researcher to look at themes and categories in order to determine or understand the social reality in a subjective but scientific manner. A complete transcript of the entire month of October 2010 was printed with expanded comments as necessary. The average commentary on the Facebook fan posts was approximately eighty posts per comment.

To be clear, it is understood these fans may not reside within the Southern United States, however, the teams in the SEC are in the South, and therefore the fervent followings of these teams were examined, regardless of fan location. There was even one Facebook fan page entitled, "SEC: The Only Real Conference in College Football." The SEC Western Division had the largest Facebook fan base, LSU at the top with 405,390—the most in the entire SEC— followed by the Alabama Crimson Tide with 277,903; Auburn Football with 134,948; Arkansas Razorbacks with 60,657; Ole Miss Rebels with 35,527 and Mississippi State Bulldogs with 20,623. In the Eastern Division the Florida Gators Football fan page leads with 228,289; Tennessee Volunteers Athletics with 198,435 (a combined fan page for all sports, the university has no fan page specifically dedicated to football); South Carolina Gamecocks with 169,369; Georgia Bulldogs with 33,143; Kentucky Football with 2,352 and the Vanderbilt Commodores with just 293 football fans. Auburn, Alabama, Florida and LSU had the most interactive fans pages for the month of October.

Qualitative content analysis consists of purposively selected texts. This type of qualitative content analysis "pays attention to unique themes that illustrate the range of the meanings of the phenomenon rather than the statistical significance of the occurrence of particular texts or concepts."[72] The content analysis that we explored looked inductively at "latent meanings and themes . . . to explore the usage of the words/indicators" and immersed ourselves to "allow themes to emerge."[73] Also, when theme is used as the coding unit, the researcher is primarily looking for the expressions of an idea, and the sizes of the analyzed text can vary.[74] Therefore, when examining the fan interactions, the comments themselves were analyzed individually for the identified themes. The fan pages were examined for the following religious themes: God, faith, hope, believe, Jesus, pray(er), hell, peace, love, convert(sion) and bless(ings).

For example, in late October the Tiger match-up draws a big following on Facebook: when Auburn and LSU battle in the Western Division. Auburn's posts prior to the game focused on Cam Newton, their quarterback's, consideration for the Heisman Trophy and their aim to play in the BCS Championship game with the rallying cry "War Eagle." However one interesting post was a fan who took his young son to his first Auburn game. The response was that hopefully the son would become an Auburn "convert" for life. Another fan commented that LSU's lucky streak was over that Auburn was the "blessed team . . . and when we win, we give glory to God on national TV . . . blessings over luck by 20." There was lots of pregame "smack" about which team would actually win. However, as the game got underway on October 23, the posts from LSU changed to begging for a win.

The University of Alabama on October 9 was looking for a "miracle" according to their fan page administrator when they were trying to beat the South Carolina Gamecocks late in the fourth quarter when Carolina was ahead 35-21. Many of the posts mimicked the "miracle" term with even additional religious terms like "amen," "prayin for a miracle" and "we need help from the man upstairs." On October 12, a post on the LSU fan page remarked on the "faith and destiny" of the LSU team to win the national championship, directly asking the team to "keep the faith boys." After a large victory in the Florida stadium known as the Swamp, several LSU posts asked for some "amens."

"Hell" seemed to be one of the most popularly used religious words, although not always used in the context of the opposite of "heaven" as in a location where the damned burn forever in an eternal afterlife. The term "hell" was used in fan pages most often to represent strength as in "rammer jammer yellow hammer give 'em hell Alabama." The term was also used on a variety of pages to exclaim "this game is hell"; "I wish this game would end, I am in hell"; and "Get the hell off this page."

Prayers and references to God were rampant on a majority of the pages. Posts ran from commenting on the "love of God" to prayers to God for victory. The prayers to God were most often found within the time frame of a close game, but could also be seen on pages with teams who were struggling in the SEC for the 2010 season. For example, a post on the Kentucky page, which has a remarkably few number of fans, offered a prayer to God for a healthy team and a better season. Within the LSU and Florida pages, there were multiple references comparing the head coaches to God, but only after a thrilling victory had occurred. This is indicative once again of the power of the head coach in relation to the fan base, for after a close game against Tennessee, LSU fans were more focused on sending their head coach Les Miles to hell with the rest of the coaching staff. Miles' god-like qualities were in danger even after a close victory. Further, on both the Florida and LSU fan pages, discussion of salvation was also present, as some fans noted losing their current coaches would provide salvation to the team. Interestingly, on several of the fan pages commenters and administrator posts remarked on the ability of the fans to pull the teams through tough games. The fans take responsibility for the victories on the field, whether through their faith or prayer. Yet losses were blamed on the coaching and teams, with no fan accountability. Further, this research discovered minute-by-minute fan postings, game and score updates and interactions during the time frames of major games between SEC powerhouse teams. Though not illustrating religion, this does illustrate the ritualistic interaction social media provides for the football fan on game day. There were also a few references to the battlefield of glory on a variety of posts, conjuring images of good (God) and evil (Satan) fighting for victory in the Promised Land (the football gridiron).

Conclusion

Football in the South has long been regarded as a religion. In examining the research on football and faith in the American South, we can hold this statement to be truthful and justified. However, it is also important to acknowledge how social media is changing the face of traditional fan interactions and illustrates the religious communication and belief systems of these rabid fan bases in the South. This essay examined the correlation of religion and religious themes on the social media site Facebook. The limitations of this research, specifically analyzing only one month of the football season, shows only a brief glimpse into the religious rituals, myths and commentaries by the fans. Further critical analysis of not only additional time frames but also other social media sites could lend even more support for the findings of this study.

Notes

1. Gene Chizik, interview by Holly Rowe, *ESPN*, January 10, 2011.
2. Warren St. John, *Rammer Jammer YellowHammer: A Journey into the Heart of Fan Mania* (New York: Crown Publishers, 2004), 124.
3. Melvin L. DeFleur and Everette E. Dennis, *Understanding Media in the Digital Age* (Needham Heights, Mass.: Allyn and Bacon, 2010), 240.
4. Andrew Doyle, "Foolish and Useless Sport: The Southern Evangelical Crusade Against Intercollegiate Football," *Journal of Sport History*, 24, no.3 (1997): 317-340.
5. http://www.footballencyclopedia.com/sechome.htm Webpage, accessed January 14, 2011.

6. Tony Barnhart, *Southern Fried Football: The History, Passion and Glory of the Great Southern Game* (Chicago: Triumph Books, 2008), xv-xxxvi.
7. Chad Gibbs, *God and Football: Faith and Fanaticism in the SEC* (Grand Rapids, Mich.: Zondervan, 2010), 11-14.
8. Gibbs, *God and Football*, 11.
9. Eric Bain-Selbo, *Game Day and God: Football, Faith, and Politics in the American South* (Macon, Ga.: Mercer University Press, 2009).
10. Jack Nachbar and Kevin Lause, *Popular Culture: An Introductory Text* (Bowling Green, Oh.: Bowling Green State University Popular Press, 1992).
11. John Fiske, "The Cultural Economy of Fandom," in *Adoring Audience: Fan Culture and Popular Media*, ed. Lisa A. Lewis (New York: Routledge, 1992), 30-49.
12. Barnhart, *Southern Fried Football*, xv.
13. Barnhart, *Southern Fried Football*, xxx.
14. Barnhart, *Southern Fried Football*, xxxi.
15. Exodus 20:3 from the King James version of the *Bible*.
16. Gibbs, *God and Football*, 12.
17. Buck Hughes, interview by Dedria Givens-Carroll (May 1, 2010).
18. Gibbs, *God and Football*, 13.
19. Bain-Selbo, *Game Day and God*, 51.
20. Gibbs, *God and Football*, 13.
21. Bain-Selbo, *Game Day and God*, 213.
22. Charles Reagan Wilson, *Judgment and Grace in Dixie: Southern Faiths from Faulkner to Elvis* (Athens: University of Georgia Press, 2007), 144.
23. Wilson, *Judgment and Grace*, 143.
24. Wilson, *Judgment and Grace*, 142.
25. Doyle, *Foolish*, 317.
26. Ed McMinn, *Daily Devotions for Die-hard Fans: LSU Tigers* (Perry, Ga.: Extra Point Publishers, 2010), cover.
27. McMinn, *Daily Devotions*, 23.
28. Fiske, *Cultural Economy*, 32.
29. Myles Breen and Farrel Corcoran, "Myth in the Television Discourse," *Communication Monographs* 49, no. 2 (1982): 127-136.
30. Nachbar and Lause, *Popular Culture*, 85.
31. Bain-Selbo, *Game Day and God*, 213.
32. "Punt Bama Punt," *House of Pain: 50 Most Painful Outcomes in College Football History* 2010, http://espn.go.com/college-football/features/houseofpain/_/n/8 (accessed July 11, 2011).
33. Bain-Selbo, *Game Day and God*, 8-9.
34. Bain-Selbo, *Game Day and God*, 3.
35. Bain-Selbo, *Game Day and God*, 22.
36. Bain-Selbo, *Game Day and God*, 23.
37. Bain-Selbo, *Game Day and God*, 21.
38. Bain-Selbo, *Game Day and God*, 23.
39. Cam Newton, interview by Holly Rowe, *ESPN*, January 10, 2011.
40. Doyle, *Foolish*, 317.
41. Wilson, *Judgment and Grace*, xxv.
42. Keith Dunnavant, *Coach: The Life of Paul "Bear" Bryant* (New York: Thomas Dunne Books, 2005), 71-73.

43. Wilson, *Judgment and Grace*, 11.
44. St. John, *Rammer Jammer*, 124.
45. Jonathan Fravel, "Alabama Football: Stability and Excellence, A New Footprint for Coach Nick Saban," *The Bleacher Report* 2010, http://bleacherreport.com/articles/544101-alabama-football-stability-and-excellence-a-new-footprint-for-coach-nick-saban (accessed July 10, 2011).
46. Wilson, *Judgment and Grace*, 36-37.
47. Alison Miller and Dedria Givens-Carroll, "The History of Broadcasting College Football" (presented at the annual meeting of the Southern States Communication Association, Savannah, Georgia, April 2008).
48. Horace Newcomb and Paul Hirsch, "Television as a Cultural Forum," in *Television: The Critical View*, edited by Horace Newcomb (New York: Oxford University Press, 1987), 247.
49. Susan Tyler Eastman and Karen E. Riggs, "Televised Sports and Ritual: Fan Experiences," *Sociology of Sport Journal*, 11, (1994): 249-274.
50. Fiske, *Cultural Economy*, 35.
51. Bain-Selbo, *Game Day and God*, 316.
52. Bain-Selbo, *Game Day and God*, 316.
53. Wilson, *Judgment and Grace*, 7.
54. Lawrence A. Wenner, *Media, Sports and Society* (Newbury Park, Calif.: Sage Publications, 1989).
55. Paul D. Turman, Kevin A. Stein, and Matthew H. Barton, "Understanding the Voice of the Fan: Apologia, Antapologia and the 2006 World Cup Controversy," in *Sports Mania: Essays on Fandom and the Media in the 21st Century*, ed. Lawrence W. Hugenberg, Paul M. Haridakis, Adam Earnheardt (Jefferson, N. C.: McFarland, 2008), 86-100.
56. Dennis L. Wilcox and Glen Cameron, *Public Relations Writing and Media Techniques* (Boston: Pearson, 2009).
57. Wilcox and Cameron, *Public Relations*, 326.
58. Wilcox and Cameron, *Public Relations*, 323.
59. "Facebook About," Facebook, accessed April 6, 2010, http://facebook.com/facebook
60. "Facebook About."
61. "Facebook About."
62. Tim Layden, "Caught in the Net: Everyone's A Reporter in the World of Fan-Driven Rumor-mongering College Websites, Forcing Coaches and Players to Watch Their Every Step," *Sports Illustrated*, May 19, 2003, 98, 46-47.
63. Wilcox and Cameron, *Public Relations*, 333.
64. "Facebook About."
65. Lawrence W. Hugenberg, Paul M. Haridakis, and Adam Earnheardt, *Sports Mania: Essays on Fandom and the Media in the 21st Century* (Jefferson, N.C.: McFarland, 2008).
66. Michael Real, "Sports Online: The Newest Player in Mediasport," in *Handbook of Sports and Media*, ed. Arthur Raney and Jennings Bryant (New York: Lawrence Erlbaum Associates, 2006), 178-180.
67. Real, *Sports Online*, 179.
68. Rich Thomaselli, "If You're Wondering What Not to Do When it Comes to the BCS," *Advertising Age*, November, 30, 2009, 80(40).

69. Thomaselli, *If You're Wondering*, 80.
70. Ken Wheaton, "Social Media Alone Won't Change a Consumer's Mind," *Advertising Age*, November 20, 2009, 80 (40), 12.
71. Yan Zhang and Barbara M. Wildemuth, "Qualitative Analysis of Content," *Applications of Social Research Methods to Questions in Information and Library* 2009, http://ils.unc.edu/~yanz/Content_analysis.pdf (accessed December 5, 2010).
72. Zhang and Wildemuth, *Qualitative*, 2.
73. Zhang and Wildemuth, *Qualitative*, 2.
74. Victor Minichiello, Rosalie Aroni, Eric Tinewell, and Loris Alexander, *In-Depth Interviewing: Researching People* (Hong Kong: Longman Cheshire, 1990), 244-250.

Bibliography

"2008 Economic Forecast." *Mississippi Business Journal* 30, no. 2 (January 14, 2008), B62, in EBSCOHost database (accessed March 20, 2009).

Abelman, Robert. *Reaching a Critical Mass: A Critical Analysis of Television Entertainment.* Mahwah, N. J.: Lawrence Erlbaum Associates, 1988.

Agee, James, and Walker Evans. *Let Us Now Praise Famous Men.* New York: The Library of America, 2005.

Alridge, Derrick, and James Stewart. "Hip Hop in History: Past, Present and Future." *Journal of African American History* 90 (Summer 2005): 190-195.

Anglin, Mary K. "Lessons from Appalachia in the 20th Century: Poverty, Power, and the Grass Roots." *American Anthropologist* 104, no. 2 (2002): 565-582.

Applebome, Peter. *Dixie Rising.* New York: Harvest Books, 1997.

———. "A Sweetness Tempers South's Bitter Past." *New York Times,* July 31, 1994.

Archer, M. "Reality TV Seeks Modern-Day Scarlett O'Hara with a Twist." *The Daily Mississippian,* November 14, 2007.

Association for Experiential Education. http://www.aee.org/customer/pages.php?pageid=28 (accessed April 2007).

Ayers, Edward L. *The Promise of the New South.* New York: Oxford University Press, 1992.

Babin, Barry J., James S. Boles, and William R. Darden, "Salesperson Stereotypes, Consumer Emotions, and their Impact on Information Processing." *Journal of the Academy of Marketing Science* 23(1995): 94-105.

Bageant, Joe. *Deer Hunting with Jesus.* New York: Crown Publishers, 2007.

Bai, Matt. 2008. "The Way We Live Now: South Poll." *New York Times,* January 20. http://www.nytimes.com/ 2008/01/20/magazine/20wwln-ledet.html?r=1 (accessed October 15, 2009).

Bain-Selbo, Eric. *Game Day and God: Football, Faith, and Politics in the American South.* Macon, Ga.: Mercer University Press, 2009.

Barker, Chris. *Television, Globalization, and Cultural Identities.* Buckingham, England: Open University Press, 1999.
Barnhart, Tony. *Southern Fried Football: The History, Passion and Glory of the Great Southern Game.* Chicago: Triumph Books, 2008.
Barthes, Roland. *Mythologies.* London: Cape, 1972.
BAWI Bulletin, "Balance Agriculture with Industry," premiere issue, June 1945, 2. Mississippi State Department of Archives and History, Jackson, Mississippi.
BAWI Bulletin, September 1945, 1. Mississippi State Department of Archives and History, Jackson, Mississippi.
BAWI Bulletin, August 1945, 1. Mississippi State Department of Archives and History, Jackson, Mississippi.
BAWI Bulletin, February 1947, 3. Mississippi State Department of Archives and History, Jackson, Mississippi.
BAWI Bulletin, January 1947, 3. Mississippi State Department of Archives and History, Jackson, Mississippi.
BAWI Advertising Kit, "Mississippi: A Land of Industrial Opportunity" pamphlet, 1937, Mississippi State Department of Archives and History, Jackson, Mississippi.
BAWI Advertising kit, Mississippi Tourist Guide, 1937, Mississippi State Department of Archives and History, Jackson, Mississippi.
BAWI Pamphlet, "Mississippi, Heart of the Southland," January 1947, Mississippi State Department of Archives and History, Jackson, Mississippi.
Beck, John, et al. *Southern Culture: An Introduction.* Durham, N.C.: Carolina Academic Press, 2007.
Bennett, William J. *America: The Last Best Hope, Volume II.* New York: Thomas Nelson, 2007.
Berger, Arthur A. *Media and Society: A Critical Perspective.* Lanham, Md.: Rowman and Littlefield, 2003.
Bertelson, David. *The Lazy South.* New York: Oxford University Press, 1967.
Beyond Beats and Rhymes. Produced and Directed by Byron Hurt. Media Education Foundation 2006. Video recording.
Billings, Dwight B., Gurney Norman, and Katherine Ledford, eds. *Confronting Appalachian Stereotypes: Back Talk from an American Region.* Lexington: University Press of Kentucky, 1999.
Biographical Directory of the United States Congress, 1774-Present. 2009. http://bioguide.congress.gov/biosearch/biosearch.asp (accessed October 15, 2009).
Black, Earl, *Southern Governors and Civil Rights.* Cambridge, Mass.: Harvard University Press, 1976.
Black, Earl, and Merle Black. *Politics and Society in the South.* Cambridge, Mass.: Harvard University Press, 1987.
Black, Earl, and Merle Black. *The Rise of Southern Republicans.* Cambridge, Mass.: The Belknap Press, 2002.

Black, Earl, and Merle Black. *Divided America: The Ferocious Power Struggle in American Politics.* New York: Simon & Schuster, 2007.
Blake, Ted. "The Dukes of Hazard and Television's Simple South." xroads.virginia.edu. http://xraods.virginia.edu/~ug97/blake/part1.html (accessed March 28, 2008).
Blue Collar Comedians Bring in the Green. (June 25, 2007). *USA Today*, p. 3D.
Blue Collar Comedy Tour: One for the Road. DVD. Directed by C.B. Harding. Burbank, Calif.: Warner Bros. Entertainment, 2006.
Blue Collar Comedy Tour Rides Again. DVD. Directed by C.B. Harding. Burbank, Calif.: Warner Bros. Entertainment, 2004.
Blue Collar Comedy Tour: The Movie. DVD. Directed by C.B. Harding. Burbank, Calif.: Warner Bros. Entertainment, 2003.
Bolton, Charles C. *The Hardest Deal of All: The Battle Over School Integration in Mississippi, 1870-1980.* Jackson: University Press of Mississippi, 2005.
Boym, Svetlana. *The Future of Nostalgia.* New York: Basic Books, 2001.
Bretiman, George, ed. *Malcolm X: Selected Speeches and Statements.* New York: Pathfinder Press, 1965.
Branscome, James. "The Crisis of Appalachian Youth." In *Appalachia in the Sixties: Decade of Reawakening* edited by David S. Walls and John B. Stephenson. Lexington: University of Kentucky Press, 1972.
Breen, Myles, and Farrel Corcoran. "Myth in the Television Discourse." *Communication Monographs* (1982): 127-136.
Brinnin, John Malcolm. *Truman Capote: Dear Heart, Old Buddy.* New York: Delacorte Press/Seymour Lawrence, 1981.
Brown, Lester. *Encyclopedia of Television.* New York: Zoetrope, 1982.
Bryant, Jennings, and Dolf Zillmann. *Perspectives of Media Effects.* Hillsdale, N. J.: Lawrence Erlbaum Associates, 1986.
Bryan, Ferald J. *Henry Grady or Tom Watson? The Rhetorical Struggle for the New South, 1880-1890.* Macon, Ga.: Mercer University Press, 1994.
Bryan, Jerry. *Born in a Mighty Bad Land: The Violent Man in African American Folklore and Fiction.* Bloomington: University of Indiana Press, 2003.
Bullock, Charles, and Mark Rozell. *The New Politics of the Old South*, 3rd ed. New York: Rowman and Littlefield, 2007.
Burke, Kenneth. *Attitudes Toward History.* Berkeley: University of California Press, 1959.
Butler, Judith. *Gender Trouble: Feminism and the Subversion of Identity.* New York: Routledge, 1990.
Campbell, Edward D. C. Jr. *The Celluloid South: Hollywood and the Southern Myth.* Knoxville, Tenn.: University of Knoxville Press, 1981.
Capote, Truman. *The Grass Harp, Including A Tree of Night and other stories.* New York: Vintage International, 1993.
Carmines, Edward G., and James A. Stimso. *Issue Evolution: Race and the Transformation of American Politics.* Princeton, N.J.: Princeton University Press, 1989.

Carter, Dan T. *Scottsboro: A Tragedy of the American South*. Baton Rouge: Louisiana State University Press, 1979.
Cash, Wilbur J. *The Mind of the South*. New York: Alfred A. Knopf, 1941.
Chang, Jeff. *Can't Stop. Won't Stop: A History of the Hip Hop Generation*. New York: Picador Books/St. Martin's Press, 2005.
Chevalier, Jay. *Earl K. Long and Jay Chevalier: When the Music Stopped* Natchitoches, La.: Southern Legacies Press, 2003.
Chizik, Gene, interview by Holly Rowe. (January 10, 2011).
Cirlot Agency. "Fact Sheet." http://www.mississippibelieveit.com/faq/MBI08FactSheetNatl.pdf (accessed February 12, 2009).
———. "Frequently Asked Questions." http://mississippibelieveit.com/faq (accessed February 12, 2009).
———. "The Mississippi, Believe It! Campaign." http://www.mississippibelieveit. com/home/ (accessed February 12, 2009).
———. "Mississippi Campaign Shoots Down Negative Stereotypes." http://www. mississippibelieveit.com/faq/MBI08release.pdf (accessed February 12, 2009).
———. "Meet a Few of our New 'Good ole Boys'." 2006. http://www.mississippi believeit.com/ads/print_boys.html (accessed February 12, 2009).
———. "Mississippi. The First to Have a Change of Heart . . . and Lungs . . . and Kidneys." 2006. http://www.mississippibelieveit.com/ads/print_hearts. html (accessed February 12, 2009).
———. "No Black. No White. Just the Blues." 2006. http://www.mississippi believeit.com/ads/print_blues.html (accessed February 12, 2009).
———. "Yes, We Can Read. A Few of Us Can Even Write." 2006. http://www.mississippibelieveit.com/ads/print_read.html (accessed February 12, 2009).
———. "A State of Grace." 2008. http://www.mississippibelieveit.com/ads/print_ oseola.html (accessed February 12, 2009).
———. "Y'all May Think We Talk Funny, But the World Takes Our Music Seriously." 2008. http://www.mississippibelieveit.com/ads/print_ music.html (accessed February 12, 2009).
———. "Yes, Our Roads Are Paved . . . AND We Have the Best Student Drivers under the Sun." 2008. http://www.mississippibelieveit.com/ads/print_ solarcar.html (accessed February 12, 2009).
———. "Yes, We Have Running Water . . . Right Next to the World's Finest Appliances." 2008. http://www.mississippibelieveit.com/ads/print_ viking.html (accessed February 12, 2009).
———. "Yes, We Wear Shoes. A Few of Us Even. Wear Cleats." 2008. http://www.mississippibelieveit.com/ads/print_shoes.html (accessed

February 12, 2009).
Clark, Eric Charles. "Industrial Development and State Government Policy in Mississippi, 1890-1980." Ph.D. diss., Mississippi State University, 1989.
Clay, Martin. 1973. *Coozan Dudley Leblanc: From Huey Long to Hadacol.* Gretna, La.: Pelican Publishing Company, 1973.
Clifford, James. *The Predicament of Culture: Twentieth Century Ethnography, Literature, and Art.* Cambridge, Mass.: Harvard University Press, 1988.
Clifford Hodges Brewton Collection of Lester G. Maddox Speech/Press Records 1964-1976, http://www.libs.uga.edu/russell/collections/lmaddox.html (accessed July 2006).
Clinton, Bill. *My Life.* New York: Alfred A. Knopf, 2004.
Cloud, Dana. "Hegemony or Concordance? The Rhetoric of Tokenism in "Oprah" Winfrey's Rags-to-Riches Biography," *Critical Studies in Mass Communication* 13, no. 2 (1996):115-137.
Cobb, James. *Redefining Southern Culture: Mind & Identity in the Modern South.* Athens: University of Georgia Press, 1999.
———. *Away Down South: A History of Southern Identity.* New York: Oxford University Press, 2005.
Cochran, Augustus B. *Democracy Heading South: National Politics in the Shadow of Dixie.* Lawrence: University of Kansas, 2001.
Coles, Robert. *Farewell to the South.* Boston: An Atlantic Monthly Press Book, 1963.
Cooke, Jon. "Ted Turner Bans Speedy Gonzalez from Cartoon Network." Freerepublic.com. http://www.freerepublic.com/forum/a3a36c3ed264d.htm (accessed March 26, 2008).
Cosman, Bernard. *Five States for Goldwater: Continuity and Change in Southern Presidential Voting Patterns.* Tuscaloosa: University of Alabama Press, 1966.
Coward, John M. "Selling the Southwestern Indian: Ideology and Image in *Arizona Highways,* 1925-1940." *American Journalism,* 20 (Spring 2003): 13-31.
Cultural Criticism and Transformation. Produced and Directed by Sut Jhally. Media Education Foundation 1997. Video recording.
Curtis III, George M., and James J. Thompson, Jr., eds. *The Southern Essays of Richard M. Weaver.* Indianapolis, Ind.: Liberty Press, 1987.
Dailey, Jane, Glenda Gilmore, and Brent Simon. *Jumpin' Jim Crow: Southern Politics from Civil War to Civil Rights.* Princeton, N.J.: Princeton University Press, 2000.
Davis, Allison. *Deep South: A Social Anthropological Study of Caste and Class.* Chicago: University of Chicago Press, 1941.
D Davey, DJ. "Hip Hop's Bad Rap." *San Francisco Chronicle,* August 5, 2001.
DeFleur, Melvin L., and Everette E. Dennis. *Understanding Media in the Digital Age.* Needham Heights, Mass.: Allyn and Bacon, 2010.
Dent, Harry S. *The Prodigal South Returns to Power.* New York: John Wiley &

Sons, 1978.

De Klerk, Vivian, and Bosch, Barbara. "Linguistic Stereotypes: Nice Accent—Nice Person?" *International Journal of Sociology of Language* 116 (1995):17-37.

Dewey, John. *Experience and Education.* New York: Collier, 1963.

Dittmer, John. *Local People: The Struggle for Civil Rights in Mississippi.* Champaign: University of Illinois Press, 1995.

Doyle, Andrew. "Foolish and Useless Sport: The Southern Evangelical Crusade Against Intercollegiate Football." *Journal of Sport History* (1997): 317-340.

Duffy, Bernard K. and Martin Jacobi. *The Politics of Rhetoric: Richard M. Weaver and the Conservative Tradition.* Westport, Conn.: Greenwood Press, 1993.

Dunnavant, Keith. *Coach: The Life of Paul "Bear" Bryant.* New York: Thomas Dunne Books, 2005.

Durkheim, Emile. *The Elementary Forms of Religious Life.* Translated by Karen E. Fields. New York City: The Free Press, 1995.

Dylan, Bob. "The Times They Are a-Changin'." *The Times They Are a-Changin'.* Columbia Records, 1964.

———. "With God on Our Side." *The Times They Are a-Changin'.* Columbia Records, 1964.

Dyson, Michael Eric. "Hip Hop Is Alive and Well." *Ebony* 62 (June 2007): 60.

———. *The Michael Eric Dyson Reader.* New York: Basic Civitas, 2004.

Eastman, Susan Tyler, and Karen E. Riggs. "Televised Sports and Ritual: Fan Experiences." *Sociology of Sport Journal* (1994): 249-274.

Edsall, Thomas B. *Building Red America.* New York: Basic Books, 2006.

Edsall, Thomas B., and Brian Faler. 2002. "Lott Remarks on Thurmond Echoed 1980 Words." *Washington Post,* December 11. http://www.washingtonpost.com/ac2/wp-dyn/A37288-2002Dec10?language=printer (accessed October 15, 2009).

Edsall, Thomas B., and Mary D. Edsall. *Chain Reaction: The Impact of Race, Rights, and Taxes on American Politics.* New York: W.W. Norton Company, 1992.

Elvin, John. "Redneck Television Scores Low Rating from Critics." *Insight on the News.* http://findarticles.com/p/articles/mi_m1571/is_37_18/ai_92589569/ (accessed December 29, 2010).

Engels, Frederick. "Letter to Mehring," (1893), www.marxist.org.

Engvall, Bill. *Here's Your Sign.* Nashville, Tenn.: Thomas Nelson, 2005.

Epp, Jennifer, and Steven Burns, "Cultural (Mis-)Appropriation: A Reply to James O. Young." *Dalhousie Review* 80, no. 3 (2000): 317-319.

Eyerman, Ron. "False Consciousness and Ideology in Marxist Theory." *Acta Sociologica* 24, no. 1 (1981): 43-56.

Facebook About. 2011. http://facebook.com/facebook (accessed April 6, 2010).

"The Farm." http://www.thefarm.org/ lifestyle/miller.html (accessed March 2007).

Feinberg, Joel. *The Moral Limits of Criminal Law, Volume 1: Harm to Others.* New York: Oxford University Press, 1985.

———. *The Moral Limits of Criminal Law, Volume 2: Offense to Others.* New York: Oxford University Press, 1985.

Finnegan, Cara. "What's This a Picture Of? Some Thoughts on Images and Archives." Rhetoric and Public Affairs 9, no 1 (2006): 116-123.

Foucault, Michel. *Discipline and Punish: The Birth of the Prison.* New York: Vintage, 1977.

Fiske, John. "The Cultural Economy of Fandom." In *Adoring Audience: Fan Culture and Popular Media*, by Lisa A. Lewis, 30-49. New York: Routledge, 1992.

Foxfire Fund Inc., http://www.foxfire.org (accessed January 2006).

Foxworthy, Jeff. *You Might Be a Redneck If...* Athens, Ga.: Longstreet Press, 1989.

Franklin, Jimmie. "Black Southerners Shared Experience and Place: A Reflection." *Journal of Southern History* 59 (February 1994): 3-18.

Fravel, Jonathan. "Alabama Football: Stability and Excellence, A New Footprint for Coach Nick Saban." *The Bleacher Report.* 2010, http://bleacherreport.com/articles/544101 - alabama - football- stability -and-excellence-a-new-footprint-for-coach-nick-saban (accessed July 10, 2011).

Frederick, Jeff. *Stand Up for Alabama.* Tuscaloosa: University of Alabama, 2007).

Frederickson, Kari. *The Dixiecrat Revolt and the End of the Solid South: 1932-68.* Chapel Hill: University of North Carolina Press, 2001.

Fridland, Valerie, and Bartlett, Kathryn. "Correctness, Pleasantness, and Degree of Difference Ratings Across Regions." *American Speech* 81(2006): 358-386.

Friend, Tad. "Blue-Collar Gold: Comedy between the Coasts." *The New Yorker,* July 10, 2006, www.lexisnexis.com.

Gates, Henry Louis. *Thirteen Ways of Looking at a Black Man.* New York: Vintage Books, 1997.

Gerster, Patrick, and Nicholas Cords. "The Northern Origins of Southern Mythology," *Journal of Southern History* 43, no. 4 (1977): 568.

Getty Images. 2009. "Civil Rights Leaders Meet with John F. Kennedy." http://www.gettyimages.com/detail/ 3333637/hulton-archive (accessed October, 15, 2009).

Gibbs, Chad. *God and Football: Faith and Fanaticism in the SEC.* Grand Rapids, Mich.: Zondervan, 2010.

Gilmore, Glenda E. *Defying Dixie: The Radical Roots of Civil Rights, 1919-1950.* New York: W.W. Norton, 2008.

Glazer, James. *The Hand of the Past in Southern Politics.* New Haven, Conn.: Yale University, 2005.

Goldberg, Jonah. 2002. "Congressional Black Raucus: The Lott Affair." *National Review,* December 11. http://www.nationalreview.com/

articles/205358/congressional-black-raucus/jonah-goldberg (accessed October 15, 2009).
Goodman, Brenda. "Heard the One About Mississippi? It's Fighting Back." *New York Times*, November 8, 2006, Lexis-Nexis (accessed February 12, 2009).
Gordon, Lois, and Alan Gordon. *American Chronicles: Six Decades in American Life, 1920-1980*. New York: Atheneum, 1987.
Governor White's Introduction letter from the BAWI advertising kit sent to each member of the 1937 Mississippi legislature. Mississippi State Department of Archives and History, Jackson, Mississippi.
Graber, Doris. *Mass Media and American Politics*. Washington, D.C.: Congressional Quarterly Press, 1980.
Grady, Henry W. *The New South: Writings and Speeches of Henry Grady*. Savannah, Ga.: Beehive Press, 1971.
Gramsci, Antonio, *Gramsci's Prison Letters: a Selection*, edited and translated by Quentin Hoare and Geoffrey Nowell Smith, London: Pluto Press, 1988.
Grantham, Dewey. *The South in Modern America: A Region at Odds*. New York: Harper Collins, 1994.
―――. *The Life and Death of the Solid South: A Political History*. Lexington: University Press of Kentucky, 1988.
The Grass Harp. New Line Home Video. 1997.
Green, Lloyd M. 2007. "Clinton as Atwater." Modified March 23. http://politicalmavens.com/index.php/2007/03/23/clinton - as - atwater/ (accessed October 30, 2011).
Grem, Darren. "The South Got Something to Say: Atlanta's Dirty South and the Southernization of Hip Hop." *Southern Cultures*, 12 (Winter 2006): 55-73.
Griffin, Larry J. "Southern Distinctiveness, Yet Again, or, Why America Still Needs the South." *Southern Cultures* 6 (2000). Gale Cengage Literature Resource Center (accessed February 23, 2009).
―――. "The American South and the Self." *Southern Cultures* 12, no. 3 (2006): 6-28.
Guimond, James. *American Photography and the American Dream*. Chapel Hill: University of North Carolina Press, 1991.
Hair, William Ivy. *The Kingfish and His Realm*. Baton Rouge: Louisiana State University Press, 1991.
Hambidge Center. "Mission." http://www.hambidge.org/mission/index.shtml. (accessed September 2006).
Haralovich, Mary Beth and Michael W. Trosset. "Expect the Unexpected: Narrative Pleasure and Uncertainty Due to Chance in Survivor. In *Reality TV: Remaking Television Culture*, edited by Susan Murray and Laurie Oulette. New York: University Press, 2004.
Harold, Christine, and Kevin M. DeLuca. "Behold the Corpse: Violent Images and the Case of Emmett Till." *Rhetoric & Public Affairs* 8 (2005): 263-

286.
Heath, Shirley Brice. *Ways with Words*. Cambridge, Mass.: Cambridge University Press, 1983.
Hebdidge, Dick. *Subculture: The Meaning of Style*. London: Routledge, 1979.
Herrington, Michael. *The Other America: Poverty in the United States*. Baltimore: Penguin, 1962.
Heyd, Thomas. "Rock Art Aesthetics and Cultural Appropriation." *The Journal of Aesthetics and Art Criticism* 61, no. 1 (2003): 37-46.
Himmelstein, Hal. *Television Myth and the American Mind*. London: Sage Publications, 1994.
Hines, Darlene Clark and Earnestine Jenkins, eds. *A Question of Manhood: A Reader in United States Black Men's History and Masculinity, Vol 1*. Bloomington: University of Indiana Press, 1999.
Hooks, Bell. *We Real Cool: Black Men and Masculinity*. New York: Routledge, 2004.
"House of Pain: 50 Most Painful Outcomes in College Football." *ESPN*. 2010. http://espn.go.com/college-football/features/houseofpain/_/n/8 (accessed July 11, 2011).
Howard Baker Center. 2009. "Senator Baker." http.://bakercenter.utk.edu/main/howardbaker.php (accessed October 15, 2009).
Hugenberg, Lawrence W., Paul M. Haridakis, and Adam Earnheardt. *Sports Mania: Essays on Fandom and the Media in the 21st Century*. Jefferson, N.C.: McFarland, 2008.
Hughes, Buck, interview by Dedria Givens-Carroll. (May 1, 2010).
Hustle & Flow. Produced by John Singleton. Directed by Craig Brewer. Paramount Classic MTV Films, 2005. Motion picture.
The Internet Movie Database. "Business Data for Grass Harp, The (1995)." http://us.imdb.com/Business?0113211 (accessed October 30, 2011).
Jarding, Steve, and Dave "Mudcat" Saunders. *Foxes in the Henhouse*. New York: Simon & Schuster, 2006.
Jeter, Ida. "Jezebel and the Emergence of the Hollywood Tradition of a Decadent South," in *The South and Film*, ed. Warren French. Jackson: University of Mississippi Press, 1981.
Jhally, Sut, Susan Ericsson, Sanjay Talreja, Jackson Katz, and Jeremy Earp. 1999. *Tough Guise Violence, Media, and the Crisis in Masculinity*. Northampton, Mass.: Media Education Foundation.
Johnson, Donald B., and Kirk H. Porter. *National Party Platforms, 1840-1972*. Champaign: University of Illinois Press, 1973.
Johnson, Lyndon B. *The Vantage Point: Perspectives of the Presidency, 1963-1969*. New York: Holt, Rinehart and Winston, 1971.
Jones, Katharine M. *The Plantation South*. Indianapolis, Ind.: Bobbs-Merrill Company, 1957.
Kaminsky, Stuart. *American Television Genres*. Chicago: Nelson-Hall, 1985.
Kellner, Douglas. "TV, Ideology, and Emancipatory Popular Culture," in *Television: The Critical View*, ed. Horace Newcomb. New York:

Oxford University Press, 1987.
Keveney, Bill. "Engvall's Sign Says It's His Show." *USA Today*, July 13, 2007, www.lexisnexis.com.
Key, V.O. *Southern Politics*. New York: Vintage Books, 1949.
Klein, Rick. 2009. "Cantor Emerges as GOP Voice." *ABC News*, February 26. http://abcnews.go.com/Politics/story? id=6959092&page=1 (accessed October 15, 2009).
Kitwana, Bakari. *The Hip Hop Generation: Young Blacks and the Crisis in African American Culture*. New York: Basic Civitas Press, 2002.
Koesten, Joy, and Robert C. Rowland. "The Rhetoric of Atonement," *Communication Studies* 55 (2004): 68-87.
Kozol, Jonathan. *Savage Inequalities: Children in America's Schools*. New York: Crown, 1991.
Lamis, Alexander P. *The Two-Party South*. New York: Oxford University Press, 1984.
Laws, Judith, L. "The Psychology of Tokenism." *Sex Roles* 1, no. 1 (1975): 51-67.
Layden, Tim. "Caught in the Net: Everyone's A Reporter in the World of Fan-Driven, Rumor-mongering College Websites, Forcing Coaches and Players to Watch Their Every Step." *Sports Illustrated*, May 19, 2003: 46-47.
Leff, Leonard. "David Selznick's *Gone with the Wind*: The Negro Problem." *The Georgia Review*, 38 (1984):146-149.
Legislative Public Relations Packet from the Mississippi Advertising Commission to members of the 1937 state legislature. Mississippi State Department of Archives and History, Jackson, Mississippi.
Leuchtenburg, William E. *The White House Looks South*. Baton Rouge: Louisiana State University Press, 2005.
Lichter, S. Robert, Linda S. Lichter, and Stanley Rothman. *Primetime: How Television Portrays American Culture*. Washington, D.C.: Regnery, 1994.
Lippmann, Walter. *Public Opinion*. New York: The Free Press, 1922.
Long Legacy Project. 2009. http://www.hueylong.com/index.php (accessed October 15, 2009)
Maginnis, John. *The Last Hayride*. Baton Rouge: Darkhorse Press, 1984.
———. *Cross to Bear: America's Most Dangerous Politics*. Baton Rouge, La.: Darkhorse Press, 1994.
Magoc, Chris J. "The Machine in the Wasteland." *Journal of Popular Film and Television* 19 (1991): 25-35.
Malveaux, Julianne. "Mississippi: Much to Admire, Warts and All." *USA Today*, December 15, 2006, Lexis-Nexis (accessed October 29, 2008).
McAdam, Doug. *Freedom Summer*. New York: Oxford University Press, 1988.
McBride, James. "Hip Hop Planet: The Roots of the Music That Can't Be Ignored." *National Geographic* (April 2007).
McCain, Robert S. "Legends of Mississippi: Nation's Poorest State Spreads

Richness of Character." *Washington Times*, December 5, 2006, Lexis-Nexis (accessed October 29, 2008).
McGill, Ralph. *The South and the Southerner*. Athens: University of Georgia Press, 1992.
McGee, Marsha G. "Prime Time Dixie: Television's View of a 'Simple' South," *Journal of American Culture* 6 (1983): 100-109.
McMillen, Neil R. *Dark Journey: Black Mississippians in the Age of Jim Crow* Urbana: University of Illinois Press, 1990.
McMinn, Ed. *Daily Devotions for Die-hard Fans: LSU Tigers*. Perry, Ga.: Extra Point Publishers, 2010.
Mencken, H. L. "Darrow's Eloquent Appeal Wasted on Ears that Heed only Bryan." *Baltimore Evening Sun*: July 14, 1925. http://www.positiveatheism.org/hist/menck03.htm (accessed October 15, 2009).
Miller, Alison, and Dedria Givens-Carroll. "The History of Broadcasting College Football." *Southern States Communication Association*. Savannah, 2008.
Minichiello, Victor, Rosalie Aroni, Eric Tinewell, and Loris Alexander. *In-Depth Interviewing: Researching People*. Hong Kong: Longman Cheshire, 1990.
Minow, Newton N. "Television and the Public Interest," address to the National Association of Broadcasters, Washington, D.C., May 9, 1961.
Mississippi: A Land of Industrial Opportunity, pamphlet included in the BAWI advertising kit, 1937. Mississippi State Department of Archives and History, Jackson, Mississippi.
Mississippi Department of Education. "Mississippi Department of Education Announces Graduation, Dropout Rates for Class of 2007." June 11, 2008. http://www.mde.k12.ms.us/Extrel/news/2008/08GradDropout Rates.html (accessed April 15, 2009).
Mississippi Institutions of Higher Learning. "Institutional Research: Degrees, Five Year Trend Data, by Ethnicity and Gender." 2008. http://www.ihl.state.ms.us/research/stats.html (accessed April 15, 2009).
Mississippi Magic, July 1948. Mississippi State Department of Archives and History, Jackson, Mississippi.
Mississippi Magic, August 1948. Mississippi State Department of Archives and History, Jackson, Mississippi.
Mississippi Magic, October 1948. Mississippi State Department of Archives and History, Jackson, Mississippi.
Mississippi Magic, February 1949. Mississippi State Department of Archives and History, Jackson, Mississippi.
Mississippi Magic, February 1949. Mississippi State Department of Archives and History, Jackson, Mississippi.
Mississippi Magic, March 1949. Mississippi State Department of Archives and History, Jackson, Mississippi.

Mississippi Magic, June 1949. Mississippi State Department of Archives and History, Jackson, Mississippi.
Mississippi Magic, September 1949. Mississippi State Department of Archives and History, Jackson, Mississippi.
Mississippi Magic, February 1950. Mississippi Magic, November 1950, 8. Mississippi State Department of Archives and History, Jackson, Mississippi.
Mississippi Magic, July 1950. Mississippi State Department of Archives and History, Jackson, Mississippi.
Mississippi Magic, July 1950, special insert. Mississippi State Department of Archives and History, Jackson, Mississippi.
Mississippi Magic, November 1950. Mississippi State Department of Archives and History, Jackson, Mississippi.
Mississippi Magic, March 1952. Mississippi State Department of Archives and History, Jackson, Mississippi.
Mississippi Magic, December 1952. Mississippi State Department of Archives and History, Jackson, Mississippi.
Mississippi Magic, December 1952. Mississippi State Department of Archives and History, Jackson, Mississippi.
Mississippi Magic, December 1955. Mississippi State Department of Archives and History, Jackson, Mississippi.
Mississippi Tourist Guide, Mississippi State Board of Development, Advertising and Industrial Division, 1941. Mississippi State Department of Archives and History, Jackson, Mississippi.
"Mississippi Turning; State Promotion." *The Economist.* January 6, 2007. Lexis-Nexis (accessed October 29, 2008).
Moraru, Christian. "'Dancing to the typewriter': Rewriting cultural Appropriation in 'Flight to Canada.'" *Critique: Studies in Contemporary Fiction* 41, no. 2 (2000): 99-113.
Morris, Dick. 2008. "In Contrast to Obama, Hillary Plays the Race Card." Modified January 16, 2008. http://thehill.com/opinion/columnists/dick-morris/4790-in-contrast-to-obama-hillary-plays-the-race-card (accessed October 30, 2011).
Mumford, Laura Stempel. *Love and Ideology in the Afternoon: Soap Opera, Women, and Television Genre.* Bloomington: Indiana University Press, 1995.
Murphy, John M. "Domesticating Dissent: The Kennedys and the Freedom Rides." *Communication Monographs* 59 (1992): 61-78.
Nachbar, Jack. and Kevin Lause. *Popular Culture: An Introductory Text.* Bowling Green, Oh.: Bowling Green State University Popular Press, 1992.
Nagoruney, Adam. 2009. "In Gingrich Mold, a New Voice for Solid Republican Resistance." *The New York Times,* February 15. http://www.nytimes.com/2009/02/15/world/americas/15iht-15cantor.20195088.html (accessed October 15, 2009).

Naipaul, V. S. *A Turn in the South* (New York: Alfred A. Knopf, 1989).
Nast, Thomas. 1864. "Compromise with the South." *Harper's Weekly*, September 3. http://www.sonofthesouth. net/ Thomas_Nast.htm (accessed October 15, 2009).
National Organization for Women. "About." http://www.now.org/organization/info.html (accessed July 2006).
Nearing, Helen, and Scott Nearing. *Living the Good Life: How to Live Sanely and Simply in a Troubled World*. New York: Shocken, 1954.
Newcomb, Horace, and Paul Hirsch. "Television as a Cultural Forum." In *Television: The Critical View*, by Horace Newcomb, 222-247. New York: Oxford University Press, 1987.
New Georgia Encyclopedia. http:/www.georgiaencyclopedia.org/nge/Article.jsp?id=h-2579 (accessed September 2006).
Newton, Cam, interview by Holly Rowe (January 10, 2011).
Nichols, David A. *A Matter of Justice: Eisenhower and the Beginning of the Civil Rights Revolution*. New York: Simon & Shuster, 2007.
Ogbar, Jeffery O. G., Review *of Nuthin' but a "G" Thang: The Culture and Commerce of Gangsta Rap*, by Eithne Quinn. *Journal of American History* 92 no. 3 (December 2005).
Oklahoma Department of Libraries. 2009. "100 Years of Oklahoma Governors." http://www.odl.state.ok.us/oar/governors/walton.htm (accessed October 15, 2009).
Oklahoma Historical Society. 2007. "Governor Walton Declares Statewide Martial Law, 1923." Modified September 16, 2007. http://www.okhistory.org/okjourneys/martiallaw.html (accessed October 30, 2011).
Ono, Kent A., and Derek T. Buescher. "Deciphering Pocahontas: Unpackaging the Commodification of a Native American Woman." *Critical Studies in Media Communication* 18, no. 1 (2001): 23-43.
Pascoe, Craig, Karen Leathem, and Andy Ambrose. 2005. *The American South in the Twentieth Century*. Athens: University of Georgia Press, 2005.
PBS. 2002. "The Monkey Trial," *American Experience*. Boston: WGBH Productions.
Penazola, Lisa. "Commodification of the American West: Marketers' Production of Cultural Meanings at the Trade Show." *Journal of Marketing* 64, no. 4 (2000): 82-109.
Perkins, John. "State Finally Reaches Economic Landmark," *Jackson Daily News*, May 4, 1965, Sections 1, 2.
Portwood-Stacer, Laura. "Consuming 'Thrash': Representations of Poor Whites in U.S. Popular Culture." Paper presented at the annual meeting of the International Communication Association, May 24-28, 2007, in San Francisco, California.
Powell, Kevin. "Hip Hop Culture Has Been Murdered." *Ebony* 62 (June 2007): 61.
President's Appalachian Regional Commission. *Appalachia: A Report by the*

President's Appalachian Regional Commission, 1964. http://www.arc.gov/index.do?nodeId=2255 (accessed August 2006).

Puckett, John L. *Foxfire Reconsidered: A Twenty-Year Experiment in Progressive Education* (Urban: University of Illinois Press, 1989).

Rabun Gap-Nacoochee School. "School History." http://www.rabungap.org/our_ school/history/index.html (accessed August 2006).

Ransdell, Hollace. 1931. "Report on the Scottsboro, Alabama Case." American Civil Liberties Union. http://www.law.umkc.edu/faculty/projects/ftrials/scottsboro/SB_HRrep.html#REPORT%20ON%20THE%20SCOTTSBORO,%20ALA (accessed October 15, 2009).

Real, Michael R, and Robert A. Mechikoff. "Deep Fan: Mythic Identification, Technology, and Advertising in Spectator Sports." *Sociology of Sport, Journal*, 1992: 323-339.

———. "Sports Online: The Newest Player in Mediasport." In *Handbook of Sports and Media*, by Arthur Raney and Bryant, Jennings Bryant, 178-180. New York: Lawrence Erlbaum Associates, 2006.

Reeves, Miriam G. *The Governors of Louisiana.* Gretna, La.: Pelican Publishing Company, 1962.

Reston, James. 1983. "Washington: Baker's Turning Point." *New York Times*, January 12. http://www.nytimes.com/1983/01/12/opinion/ washington-baker-s-turning-point.html (accessed October 15, 2009).

Rice, Ronald, and Charles Atkin. *Public Communication Campaigns*, 2nd ed. Newbury Park: Sage Publications, 1989.

Ritivoi, Andreea Deciu. *Yesterday's Self: Nostalgia and Immigrant Identity.* New York: Rowman and Littlefield, 2002.

Roland, Charles P. *The Improbable Era: The South since World War II.* Lexington: University Press of Kentucky, 1975.

Roosevelt, Theodore. *The Strenuous Life.* Digireads Book Edition. Stillwell, Kan.: Digiread Books, 2008.

Rozell, Mark, and Clyde Wilcox. *The Christian Right in American Politics* Washington, D.C.: Georgetown University Press, 2003.

Rusher, William A. *The Rise of the Right.* New York: William Morrow, 1984.

Sanjay Talreja. Directed by Sut Jhally. Media Education Foundation 1991. Video Recording.

Sarig, Roni. *Third Coast: Outkast, Timbaland and How Hip Hop Became a Southern Thing.* New York: Da Capo Press, 2007.

Scammon, Richard M. *America Votes.* Washington D.C.: Congressional Quarterly, 1973.

Schaeffer, Michael D. "Heartland Humor: Nice-guy Comic Bill Engvall Found His Niche on the Blue Collar Comedy Tour." *Philadelphia Inquirer*, July 17, 2004, www.lexisnexis.com.

Schaller, Thomas. *Whistling Past Dixie.* New York: Simon & Schuster, 2006.

Schnitzer, Martin Colby. "The Use of Inducements By States and Communities in the Promotion of Industrial Development, with Special Reference to Mississippi," Ph.D. diss., University of Florida, 1960.
Schudson, Michael. 1982. "The Politics of Narrative Form: The Emergence of American Political Issues." *Daedalus* 111: 97-112.
Shafer, Byron, and Richard Johnston. *The End of Southern Exceptionalism.* Cambridge, Mass.: Harvard University Press, 2005.
Shenton, James P. 1960. "Fascism and Father Coughlin." *The Wisconsin Magazine of History* 44: 6-11.
Shimp, Terence A., Tracy H. Dunn, and Jill G. Klein. "Remnants of the U.S. Civil War and Modern Consumer Behavior." *Psychology & Marketing* 21(2004): 75-91.
Shogan, Robert. *The Battle of Blair Mountain: The History of America's Largest Labor Uprising.* Boulder: Westview, 2004.
Sindler, Allan P. *Huey Long's Louisiana: State Politics, 1920-52.* Baltimore: Johns Hopkins Press, 1956.
The Shootist. Produced by M. J. Frankovich and William Self. Directed by David Siegel. Paramount Pictures 1976. Motion Picture.
Shulman, Arthur and Youman, Roger. *How Sweet It Was: Television a Pictorial Commentary.* New York: Bonanza Books, 1966.
Slotkin, Richard. *Gunfighter Nation: The Myth of the Frontier in 20th Century America.* New York: HarperPerennial, 1993.
Smith, Stephen A. *Myth, Media and the Southern Mind.* Fayetteville: University of Arkansas Press, 1985.
Sommer, Doris. "Resistant Texts and Incompetent Readers." *Poetics Today* 15, no. 4 (1994): 524.
Sponsler, Claire. "In Transit: Theorizing Cultural Appropriation in Medieval Europe." *Journal of Medieval and Early Modern Studies* 32, no. 1 (2002): 17-39.
St. John, Warren. *Rammer Jammer Yellow Hammer: A Journey into the Heart of Fan Mania.* New York City: Crown Publishers, 2004.
State of Tennessee. 1925. "Tennessee Evolution Statutes." http://www.law.umkc.edu/faculty/projects/ftrials/scopes/ tennstat.htm (accessed October 15, 2009).
Steeves, H. Leslie. "Commodifying Africa on U.S. Network Reality Television," *Communication, Culture, and Critique* 1, no. 4 (2008): 416-446.
Stewart, Janice. "Cultural Appropriations and Identificatory Practices in Emily Carr's 'Indian Stories.'" *Frontiers: A Journal of Women Studies* 26, no. 2 (2005): 59-72.
Stone, I. F. *The Haunted Fifties.* New York: Vintage Books, 1963.
Stroupe, Phil. "Mississippi Closes 1953 with Biggest Industrial Growth in History," *Jackson Daily News*, January 3, 1953, Sections 1, 12.

Stuckey, Mary E., and Richard Morris. "Pocahontas and Beyond: Commodification and Cultural Hegemony," *World Communication* 28, no. 2 (1999): 45-77.
Swing, Raymond G. *Forerunners of American Fascism*. New York: J. Messner, 1935.
Thomaselli, Rich. "If You're Wondering What Not to Do When It Comes to the BCS." *Advertising Age*, November 30, 2009, 80.
Thomson, Craig and Kelly Tian. "Marketing the South: Commercial Mythmaking and Reshaping of Popular Memories." *Journal of Consumer Research* 34, no. 5 (2008).
Thompson, Edgar T. *Plantation Societies, Race Relations and the South* Durham, N.C.: Duke University Press, 1975.
Trujillo, Nick. "Hegemonic Masculinity on the Mound: Media Representations of Nolan Ryan and American Sports Culture." *Critical Studies in Mass Communication* 7, no. 3 (1991): 231-248.
Tucker, Neely. "Potbelly Laughs for the Cable Guy: Blue Collar Comic Smacks Suburbia on the Funny Bone." *Washington Post*, March 17, 2006, www.lexisnexis.com.
———. "Now in Mississippi: Four S's, Four I's, and a Dollop of P.R." *Washington Post*, December 3, 2006, Lexis-Nexis (accessed October 29, 2008).
Turman, Paul D., A. Stein Kevin, and Matthew H. Barton. "Understanding the Voice of the Fan: Apologia, Antapologia and the 2006 World Cup Controversy," in *Sports Mania: Essays on Fandom and the Media in the 21st Century*, by Lawrence W. Hugenberg, Paul M. Haridakis and Adam Earnheardt, 86-100. Jefferson, N.C.: McFarland, 2008.
"Turner South to Launch Friday, October 1, to Nearly One Million Subscribers." *Timerwarner.com*. September 29, 1999. http://www.timewarner.com/ newsroom/press-releases/ (accessed October 31, 2011).
UMKC School of Law. (1925). "Tennessee Anti-Evolution Statutes, Public Acts of the State of Tennessee Passed by the Sixty-Fourth General Assembly." http://law2.umkc.edu/ faculty/ projects/ ftrials/ scopes/ tennstat.htm (accessed October 30, 2011).
United Mine Workers of America. "Matewan." http://www.umwa.org/history/ matewan.shtml (accessed May 2007).
United States Census Bureau. *The Black Population*. United States Census Bureau Publication, 2000. Washington, D.C.: Government Publication Office, 2001.
———. *The American Community—Blacks*. United States Census Bureau Publication. Washington, D.C.: Government Publication Office, 2004.
———. "Georgia Population of Counties by Decennial Census: 1900 to 1990." 27 March 1995. http://www.census.gov/population/cencounts/ ga190090.txt (accessed August 2006).
USA Today. "Blue Collar Comedians Bring in the Green." June 25, 2007, www.lexisnexis.com.

Vaughan, Don Rodney. "Why *The Andy Griffith Show* Is Important to Popular Culture Studies." *The Journal of Popular Culture* 38(2004): 397-423.
Vidrine, Clyde C. *Louisiana Political Hijinks*. Baton Rouge: Claitor's Publishing Division, 1985.
Wakefiled, Dan. 1955. "Respectable Racism: Dixie's Citizens Councils" *Nation*, October 22.
Warren, Robert P. *All the King's Men*. New York: Harcourt, Brace & Company, 1946.
Weaver, Richard M. "The Older Religiousness in the South," In *The Southern Essays of Richard M. Weaver*, edited by George M. Curtis, III and James J. Thompson, Jr., 134-146. Indianapolis, Ind.: Liberty Press, 1987.
———. *The Southern Tradition at Bay: A History of Postbellum Thought*. Edited by George Core and M. E. Bradford, New Rochelle, N.Y.: Arlington House, 1968.
Weill, Gus. *You Are My Sunshine: The Jimmie Davis Story*. Waco, Tex.: Word Books, 1977.
Wenner, Lawrence A. *Media, Sports and Society*. Newbury Park, Calif.: Sage Publications, 1989.
Wheaton, Ken. "Social Media Alone Won't Change a Consumer's Mind." *Advertising Age*, November 30, 2009, 12.
White, Hugh L. "Mississippi Bids for Industry." *Review of Reviews* 93, no. 6 (Winter 1936): 30.
White, Walter. *A Man Called White: An Autobiography of Walter White*. New York: Arno Press, 1967.
Whitehead, Jack L., and Leslie M. Miller. "Correspondence Between Evaluations of Children's Speech and Speech Anticipated upon the Basis of Stereotype." *Southern Speech Communication Journal* 37(1972): 375-386.
Who Moves? Who Stays? Where's Home? Pew Social and Demographic Trends. Washington, D.C.: Pew Research Center, 2008. Online database at http://pewsocialtrends.org (accessed October 30, 2011).
Wigginton, Eliot and His Students, eds. *The Foxfire Book*. New York: Anchor, 1972.
———. *Foxfire 2*. New York: Anchor, 1973.
———. *Foxfire 3*. New York: Anchor, 1975.
Wigginton, Eliot. *Sometimes a Shining Moment*. New York: Anchor, 1986.
Wilcox, Dennis L., and Glen P. Cameron. *Public Relations Writing and Media Techniques*. Boston: Pearson, 2009.
Williams, G. Croft. *A Social Interpretation of South Carolina*. Columbia: University of South Carolina Press, 1946.
Williams, T. Harry. *Huey Long*. New York: Vintage Books, 1981.
Wills, Garry. *John Wayne's America: The Politics of Celebrity*. New York: Touchstone, 1997.

Wilson, Charles Reagan. *Judgement and Grace in Dixie: Southern Faiths from Faulkner to Elvis.* Athens: University of Georgia Press, 1995.

Wilson, Thomas C. "Cohort and Prejudice: Whites' Attitudes toward Blacks, Hispanics, Jews, and Asians." *Public Opinion Quarterly* 60(1996): 253-274.

Wood, Pamela. *You and Aunt Arie: A Guide to Cultural Journalism Based on Foxfire and Its Descendants.* Washington, D.C.: IDEAS, 1976.

Yancey, Kitty B. "Ads Throw Cold Water on Mississippi Stereotypes." *USA Today*, December 1, 2006, Lexis-Nexis (accessed October 29, 2009).

Young, James O. "Profound Offense and Cultural Appropriation." *The Journal of Aesthetics and Art Criticism* 63, no. 2 (2005): 136-145.

———. "The Ethics of Cultural Appropriation." *Dalhousie Review* 80, no. 3 (2000): 301-316.

———. "Cultural Appropriation Revisited: A Rejoinder to Epp and Burns." *Dalhousie Review* 80, no. 3 (2000): 320-322.

Zhang, Yan, and Barbara M. Wildemuth. "Qualitative Analysis of Content." n.d.

Index

ACC. *See* Atlantic Coast Conference
accent, 8, 10
Agee, James, 124, 130–131
Agricultural Adjustment Act of 1933, 65
American Idol, 15
The Andy Griffith Show, 10–12
Animation, 14
Appalachia, 123–144
Arizona Highways, 91
Armey, Dick, 76, 79–80
Atlantic Coast Conference (ACC), 160
Atwater, Lee, 75–76, 78–79, 81

Balance Agriculture with Industry, 89–102
Banner, David, 50–51
Barkley, Charles, 8
BCS. *See* Bowl Championship Series
The Beverly Hillbillies, 6, 10, 11, 15, 49
Birth of a Nation, 57, 64, 66
Black Panthers, 44, 46, 144
Blaxploitation films, 44, 46
Blue Collar Comedy, 14, 21–40
Boomerang, 15
Bowl Championship Series, 159–160, 162, 166, 170–172
Brock, Bill, 75–76
Brown v Board of Education of Topeka, Kansas, 66–68

Bryant, Paul "Bear," 164, 166–167
Bush, George H.W., 76, 79
Bush, George W., 81, 83
Bushwick Bill, 50
Byrd, Robert, 68, 74–75

cable, 13–17
Carter, Jimmy, 73–74, 79, 81
Carville, James, 78–79, 81
Christian Coalition, 77
Christian Right, 76–77
The Chronic, 49
Chuck D., 47–48
Civil Rights Act of 1957, 68
Civil Rights Act of 1964, 70–71, 140
Civil Rights Bill of 1968, 71
Clinton, Bill, 73, 76–81, 83
Combs, Sean "Puffy," 48
comedy, 10, 13–14, 21–40
Comedy Central, 14
commodification, 21–40
Connick, Harry Jr., 7
Cross, David, 24
crunk, 51
cultural appropriation, 21–22, 24–25, 27–28, 35, 36–38

Dallas, 10
Deen, Paula, 47
Delay, Tom, 76, 79–80
Deliverance, 14
Democracy in America, 57
Designing Women, 10
Dewey, John, 128–129

Dirty South Rap, 48–49, 51–52
Dukakis, Michael, 76, 78
Dukes of Hazard, 10, 12, 14

Eisenhower, Dwight, 68–70
Engvall, Bill, 14, 23–24, 27–28, 30–31
Evans, Walker, 130–131
Evers, Medgar, 69, 110
Evolution Act, 59

Facebook, 161, 169–173
Family Guy, 14
Favre, Brett, 8
Federline, 8
The Fighting Temptations, 43
Flinn, Dunbar, 16
Foghorn Leghorn, 15
The Foxfire Magazine, 123–144
Foxworthy, Jeff, 14, 21, 23–24, 26–27, 29-32, 34
Freedom of Expression, 36
Freedom of Speech, 36
freedom riders, 110

gangsta rap, def., 45, 48–52
Geto Boys, 49–50
ghetto aesthetic, def., 46
Gingrich, Newt, 76–77, 79–80, 82
Grady, Henry, 107–119
Great Depression, 89, 92, 124
Green Acres, 10–11

Harper's Weekly, 57
Hilton, Paris, 16
Hip Hop, def., 43
Hofsetter, Steve, 24
Huckelberry Hound, 15
Hustle & Flow, 49

ideology, 6–7, 10–11, 17
Inherit the Wind, 60

Jay-Z, 48
Johnson, Lyndon B., 69–71, 81

KDKA, 58
Kennedy assassination, 11
Kennedy, John F., 110
King, Martin Luther, 69–71
King of the Hill, 14
Knotts, Don, 12
KRS-One, 43
Ku Klux Klan, 59, 74

language, 8
Larry the Cable Guy, 14, 23–24, 27–28, 30–33
Lewinsky, Monica, 78–79
Long, Huey P., 60–65, 84
Looney Tunes, 15
Lott, Trent, 80–81
Ludacris, 51

Malcolm X, 53
masculinity, 44–47, 51–54
Mayberry RFD, 10–11, 17
McConaughey, Matthew, 7
Minow, Newton, 10
Mississippi Advertising Commission, 90, 94–95, 101
Mississippi Agricultural and Industrial Board, 89–102
Mississippi Believe It Campaign, 107–119
"Mississippi Magic," 89–102
Monitor South, 5
Moral Majority, 76–77

MTV, 16
muscularity, 45
My Big Redneck Wedding, 15
My Name Is Earl, 13, 16
myth narrative, 6–7, 11–13, 16
myths, 6, 161–166, 171, 173

O'Neal, Shaquille, 8

Passion Fish, 43
Peay, Austin, 59–60
Perry, Tyler, 43
Petticoat Junction, 10
Petty Pablo, 50
Plessy v Ferguson, 67
President's Appalachian Regional Commission, 130
profound offense, def., 30
Public Enemy, 47–48
Public Opinion, 6

racism, 9, 14, 30, 33–35, 153
Rainbow Coalition, 78
rap, def., 43
Reagan, Ronald, 74–76, 79
The Real Beverly Hillbillies, 15
reality television, 15–17
The Real McCoy, 10
The Real World, 16
Reba, 13, 16
religion, 147–158, 163–173
The Rick and Bubba Show, 17
Ritchie, Nicole, 16
Rolling Stone, 48
Roosevelt, Franklin Delano, 61
Roosevelt, Theodore, 53

Scarface, 50
Scopes Monkey Trial, 59–61
Scorcese, Martin, 49

Scottsboro Boys, 61–62
Seacrest, Ryan, 16
SEC. *See* Southeastern Conference
sexism, 30, 37–38
Share the Wealth Program, 63
Simple Life, 16
The Simpsons, 14
situation comedy, 10, 13
social media, 161, 168–173
Southeastern Conference, 160, 162–166, 170–173
Southern Living, 47
Sparxx, Bubba, 50
Spears, Britney, 8
Stanhope, Doug, 24
stereotypes, 5–17, 151, 157–158, 162
Survivor, 15
Sweet Home Alabama, 43

T.I., 51
Timbaland, 50
True Life, 16
Truman, Harry S., 65-67
Tulsa Race Riots, 59
Turner South, 16
Turner, Ted, 15–16

USMC, 10

Vibe, 48
Vietnam, 11, 24, 73

Wallace, George, 62, 66, 69, 71–73, 76, 84
Walton, John C. "Jack," 59
Warner Brothers, 15
Wayne, John, 53

White, Ron, 23–24, 26–27, 31–35
Wickard v Filburn, 65
Wiggington, Elliot, 123–144
Willie D, 50
Winfrey, Oprah, 7
Witherspoon, Reese, 7
Wright, Jim, 74–75, 79

About the Contributors

Wendy Atkins-Sayre (PhD, University of Georgia) is an assistant professor of communication studies and director of the Speaking Center at The University of Southern Mississippi. Her research interests center on issues of identity as constructed through discourse. Her research has appeared in the *Western Journal of Communication, Women and Language*, as well as two recently published scholarly volumes (*Arguments about Animals*, Greg Goodale and Jason Edward Black, Eds., and *Gender and Political Communication in America*, Janis L. Edwards, Ed.). Her reviews have appeared in *Women's Studies in Communication, Southern Communication Journal*, and *Quarterly Journal of Speech*.

Burt Buchanan (PhD, The University of Southern Mississippi) is an assistant professor of mass communication at Auburn University at Montgomery. Before entering his current academic position, he had a successful career in television production and public relations with both private and governmental organizations. He has worked as a news photographer, television news reporter, editor, director, and producer. He has taught full time at the university level 2003. His research interests include media portrayals and media history.

Franklin Forts is an associate professor of American history at Allegheny College in Meadville, Pennsylvania. He is working on his doctoral dissertation, *Cool Posing in John Wayne's America: African American Masculinity since the Civil Rights Movement*. He is a native of Atlanta, Georgia, and completed his doctoral coursework at the University of Georgia in Athens.

Dedria Givens-Carroll (PhD, The University of Southern Mississippi) is an assistant professor of communication at the University of Louisiana at Lafayette (ULL), where she teaches primarily public relations. She taught at Southern University in Baton Rouge, Louisiana and has thirty years of professional public relations practice, primarily in the southern United States. She earned a doctorate at the University of Southern Mississippi in Hattiesburg. Her roots run deep in Louisiana where she considers home to be "God's country in the Bible belt of the Deep South."

Mark Glantz (PhD, University of Missouri) is an assistant professor of communication at Coker College in Hartsville, South Carolina. His research interests are political rhetoric and critical media studies. He earned his master's degree at The College at Brockport (SUNY) and his bachelor's degree at SUNY College at Oneonta.

Michael P. Graves (PhD, University of Southern California), not the architect and teapot designer, has taught a wide variety of courses ranging from film, visual rhetoric, and the rhetoric of popular music for nearly four decades (he began teaching at the age of twelve). Humor serves him well as department and division chair, and associate dean at previous institutions. He was awarded four NEH Summer Seminar fellowships and is a past president of the Religious Communication Association, three times miraculously winning their best essay award (1985, 2001, and 2008). His scholarly work includes studies of Quaker preaching, writing and publishing, studies of visual rhetoric, and explorations into the rhetorical features of popular music. More than fifty of his essays and reviews are published in edited books and journals, which include *Quarterly Journal of Speech, Studies in Popular Culture, Review of Religious Research, Rhetoric and Public Affairs, Journal of Communication and Religion,* and *Quaker Studies.* He and David Fillingim co-edited and contributed to a volume of critical essays on Southern Gospel Music, *More than "Precious Memories": The Rhetoric of Southern Gospel Music* (Mercer University Press, 2004), which received the 2005 Ray and Pat Brown Award from the Popular Culture Association for the best edited book in Popular Culture Studies. Graves's latest writing project, *Preaching the Inward Light,* the product of nearly four decades of research and writing on early Quaker impromptu preaching, was published in 2009 by Baylor University Press. Michael directed twenty-eight doctoral dissertations and seventeen MA theses. He is also a published poet. In 2004 he and his spouse, Darlene, joined the Liberty University faculty to help launch a new MA program in communication studies. The Graves duo lives in Forest, Virginia, just a stone's throw from Thomas Jefferson's summer retreat, "Poplar Forest."

Amber J. Narro (PhD, The University of Southern Mississippi) is an assistant professor of communication and obtained her doctorate of mass communication from the University of Southern Mississippi. She specializes in multi-platform journalism and researches political news coverage, journalism trends, and communication for non-profit organizations. With professional experience in both journalism and public relations, she has practical knowledge to add to her courses in journalism, public relations, and public communication. Dr. Narro is the coordinator for the England study abroad program at Southeastern, and she has published articles in national and international journals. She has a bachelor's degree in mass communication and journalism and a master's degree in organizational communication, both of which she obtained from Southeastern Louisiana University.

Alison F. Slade (PhD, The University of Southern Mississippi) is an assistant professor of mass communication. Her research interests include reality television, social media, and fan culture. She is also the host of a nationally syndicated radio program, *The Alison Slade Show*, which focuses on politics and media.

Joshua Stockley (PhD, University of Oklahoma) is an assistant professor of political science at the University of Louisiana at Monroe. Stockley's teaching and research cover American government, state and local politics, campaigns and elections, political parties, Congress, presidency, Southern politics, culture and politics, public policy, and public administration. His works have appeared in the journal *Race, Class, and Gender* and edited volumes such as *The Roads to Congress*. Stockley has published several book reviews, presented numerous papers at professional conferences around the nation, and edited manuscripts for publishers and journals. He has worked on numerous grants at the local, state, and national level. Stockley writes a regular column for the Monroe *News-Star*, co-hosts a weekly radio show entitled *Inside Politics* on Fox 92.7 FM, and is quoted frequently by newspapers and other media outlets.

John Sutherlin (PhD, University of New Orleans), before coming to the University of Louisiana at Monroe (ULM), taught for seven years at Tulane University where he was nominated for the John H. Stibbs Award for Faculty. He was a finalist for the position of Secretary of the Department of Environmental Quality for the State of Louisiana under Governor Blanco in 2004. At ULM, Dr. Sutherlin was elected to the Faculty Senate, and received the 2007 and 2008 Award for Excellence for the entire university. He is the author of four books, producer and director of twenty-four documentary films and has two patented inventions. He is the Senior Consultant and Owner of The CAID Group, a consulting firm specializing in solving political, regulatory, environmental, and business problems in a cost-effective manner.

Kevin Unter (PhD, University of New Orleans) graduated from Colorado State University with a bachelor's in political science in 1990. He returned to Colorado State University for his master's in political science, graduating in 1992. Between 1998 and 2006, he served as a senior associate and director of research for a national consulting firm specializing in crime reduction strategies, working with police departments and criminal justice organizations in the following cities: New Orleans, Louisiana, Jackson, Mississippi, Baltimore, Maryland, Atlanta, Georgia, Los Angeles, California, and Cincinnati, Ohio. Unter began his career at the University of Louisiana, Monroe in 2007, and he is currently an assistant professor of political science and head of the department of gerontology, sociology, and political science. His book, *Melding Police and Policy to Dramatically Reduce Crime in the City of New Orleans: A Study of the New Orleans Police Department*, was published in 2009 by Mellen Press of New York City.

Jason Waite (PhD) is an assistant professor of English at Western Oregon University. His interests include urban influences on rural cultures, rhetorics of music subcultures, visual rhetoric, and riding skateboards.